# THE ACCIDENTAL AMBASSADOR

# THE ACCIDENTAL AMBASSADOR

From Parliament to Patagonia

TONY LEON

Picador Africa

First published in 2013 by Picador Africa
an imprint of Pan Macmillan South Africa
Private Bag x19, Northlands
Johannesburg, 2116
www.panmacmillan.co.za

ISBN 978-1-77010-241-5

eISBN 978-1-77010-275-0



Editing by Sally Hines
Proofreading by Sean Fraser
Indexing by Christopher Merrett
Design and typesetting by Triple M Design, Johannesburg
Cover design by K4
Cover photograph of Tony Leon © Marko Vomberger
Cover photograph of Buenos Aires © Miro Schaap
Printed and bound by Ultra Litho(Pty)Limited

*This book is dedicated with loving gratitude to my father, Ray, and to the imperishable memory of my late mother, Sheila.*

# CONTENTS

PREFACE

# 'IF YOU WANT TO APPRECIATE YOUR OWN COUNTRY, GO AND LIVE IN ANOTHER'

The guide book, for once, did not exaggerate: 'The City of San Salvador de Jujuy is often overlooked by tourists,' my *Footprint Travel Guide* cautioned readers. As I sat, towards midnight, in my hotel room, in early May 2010, in this far-northern outpost of the sprawling Republic of Argentina, I had already discerned the reason for this oversight: I had noticed nothing of charm or interest to detain the visitor here. And if, indeed, there were some hidden attractions, then this slightly seedy provincial hostelry was not among them.

But I was not here for sightseeing. I was accompanying the Argentine minister of mines (or *secretario* in local lingo) in my role as 'Ambassador Extraordinary and Plenipotentiary of the Republic of South Africa', to quote my official job description as inscribed in the 'Letters of Credence' that I had presented some months before, in separate ceremonies, to the presidents of my countries of accreditation – Argentina, Uruguay and Paraguay.

I was some 1 500 kilometres away from the comforts of my new official residence in Buenos Aires and, literally, an ocean away from my real home in Cape Town. I seemed to be a million miles removed from the clashing drama of South African politics, a stage on which I had, until fairly recently, played something of a leading role for over twenty years.

Of more immediate relevance, I was hungry and, therefore, irritated:

it had been about ten hours since lunch and I had left my trade officer downstairs to send word of arrival of the first course, since the pre-dinner cocktails had not ended, even as the Cinderella hour loomed. The trade officer and the food had yet to appear.

I began to wonder, not for the first time since my arrival in the Southern Cone of South America the previous September, how my presence here would do anything to advance or diminish my mission of 'strengthening still further the cordial relations and good understanding which so happily subsist between our countries'. This flowery and formulaic boilerplate had also accompanied the Letters that I had presented and bore the signature of my appointing authority, President Jacob Zuma.

As a newcomer to the diplomatic corps, I still took all this rather seriously. I was to wise up over time, but back then I had felt it imperative to the bilateral relationship to accept the invitation to be present that evening for National Mining Day in the utterly unremarkable, somewhat charmless, city of Jujuy (pronounced 'khoo-khooi').

The event, predictably, did nothing to advance or retard the relations between the two countries by one jot – but it, and countless others in the succeeding three or so years, did steepen my learning curve.

Everything about that endless evening provided a window into the world of diplomacy – with its high protocols and often low stakes – in which I was back then something of an apprentice. It also provided me with some useful insights into Argentina and the Argentines.

My summons to attend had been delivered a few days before, telephonically, by the minister of mines himself. He spoke a broken English and I a variant of Spanglish (a combination of stock phrases I had memorised – and kept forgetting – and some key words, which by then I understood and could utter in a very Anglo accent). We had, thus, a perfect understanding.

I guessed from the conversation that he deemed it essential that I, as the representative of a 'leading mining nation', accompany him to Jujuy for this stellar event. He threw into the invitation the promise of a chartered jet to whisk us there and the enticement of a splendid banquet and a networking occasion with the panjandrums of the local mining industry. Like politicians everywhere, the minister over-promised and under-delivered.

Now, it was 1 a.m., on the night in question, and we were finally seated: the splendid banquet had become a gruesome ordeal. As I hungrily wolfed down the over-tired salmon starter, I realised with dread that there were still three speeches and as many courses to go.

The conversation around me was delivered by self-assured Argentines in rapid-fire Castellano (as the local version of Spanish is called). I felt like a spectator at a foreign language movie in which the subtitles had been switched off. My minder, a rather charming and svelte young local (or *chica* as young women are universally termed here, in the most macho of societies, without heed to the vagaries of political correctness), then thoughtfully mentioned that we would leave the hotel around 7.30 a.m. the next morning. A full programme awaited us: a ceremony at the governor's house and further speeches, by the same speakers about to address us at the banquet. This would be followed by some or other 'protocol ceremony', and we would then attend more speeches and ceremonials at the local school of mines. 'Great', I thought to myself – perhaps four hours of sleep, then additional hours of ceremony and speechifying and no doubt a much-delayed return to Buenos Aires. By the time the obligatory, football-sized steak arrived at around 2 a.m., I had lost my appetite.

I thought back to several hours before, to the late departing plane from Ezeiza Airport that had transported us here. On it I was seated next to the ambassador of another 'leading mining nation'. 'You were right to accept this invitation,' he confided, with the confidence of a grizzled veteran. 'But just wait and see,' he continued, 'we diplomats are here simply as stage props for the minister. He will refer to us in his speeches and so boost his standing with the community. But you won't learn much from this outing, and when the events end, you will discover that the best thing about Jujuy is the road to the airport.'

Late the next day, after endless speeches and countless ceremonies, when I sighted the welcoming urban sprawl of Buenos Aires from the window of our (inevitably late) returning aircraft, I realised there was much truth in the warning of my diplomatic colleague. But I had, contrary to his assertion, learnt a few things, none of which I had necessarily anticipated.

I realised that anyone who complains about 'African time' has obviously never lived in South America. I had also learnt that the South African bureaucracy was Swiss-like in comparison to Argentina's, and that our political posturing and self-importance were almost British in their understatement when ranged against the local equivalent. But I had not answered the existential questions that were starting to buzz around my now over-tired brain: 'How on earth did I land up here? And is this going to be my life for the next few years?'

The answers to these questions unfolded over the next two and a half years. They form the basis of this book and their detail surprised, delighted, infuriated, enthralled, unnerved, energised and exhausted me. I was indeed 'The Accidental Ambassador'. Along the way, I learnt a great deal, forgot some old prejudices and acquired some new ones. I did not quite learn a new language, but I did discover some revealing truths about myself and some broad perspectives about a new country and its people, and revised many viewpoints about my own country and its rainbow nation.

My journey to these interesting discoveries in a strange and intriguing land began, however, in a decidedly familiar setting back in Cape Town in May 2009.

# ABBREVIATIONS

| | |
|---|---|
| ANC | African National Congress |
| BRIC | Brazil, Russia, India and China |
| DA | Democratic Alliance |
| DIRCO | Department of International Relations and Co-operation |
| ESMA | Escuela de Mecánica de la Armada (Naval Mechanical School) |
| GDP | gross domestic product |
| I&J | Irvin & Johnson |
| MP | member of parliament |
| US | United States |
| YPF | Yacimientos Petroliferos Fiscales |

CHAPTER 1

# AND NOW WHAT?

*It is a necessary fact of political biology that we never know when our time is up. Long after it is obvious that we are goners, we continue to believe it is 'our duty' to hang on, with cuticle-wrenching tenacity to the privileges of our post. We kid ourselves that we must stay because we 'would be letting people down' or that 'there is a job to be finished'. In reality we are just terrified of the come down. All politicians are masters of procrastination, but there is no day they find easier to postpone than the day of their own resignation.*
— Boris Johnson[1]

Jacob G. Zuma fixed me with his Mona Lisa-esque smile as he pushed his glasses up the bridge of his nose. The calm serenity and imposing order of the president's office in Tuynhuys, Cape Town, was in marked contrast to the messy and improbable journey Zuma had navigated to reach the presidential seat.

Tuynhuys – refurbished by apartheid strongman and erstwhile president, P.W. Botha – sits flush alongside the parliament of South Africa, in the Company Gardens – both symbols of the 'colonialism of a special type' in African National Congress (ANC)-speak that Zuma's party had vowed to supplant.

The legislature had also been my place of work, and centre of my life, for nearly twenty years. My recent, and voluntary, exit from its precincts had occurred a few weeks before, on the eve of the April 2009 general election.

Perhaps as improbable as Zuma's Houdini-like escape from the coils of criminal prosecution for corruption, and before that his acquittal on charges of rape, to his inauguration as South Africa's fourth democratic president, was my presence in the presidential midst.

I probably should have paid more attention to that smile. I later read that Zuma's middle name 'Gedleyihlekisa' means, according to him, 'someone who laughs while actually endangering you', or – even less reassuringly – according to a Zulu prince, 'a person who eats you up while he's smiling at you'.[2]

I suppose the best description for my presence in the presidential office on that autumnal Cape afternoon was for a job interview. I concealed my irritation that, without explanation or apology, he was over an hour late for the appointment. I cooled my heels in the vast waiting room and contrasted his dilatoriness with the studious punctuality of Nelson Mandela with whom I had often met in the very same office.

I reminded myself, however, that the South African president with whom I should have had the closest, formal and informal, contact during my seven years as leader of the opposition in parliament, Thabo Mbeki, had never once requested a meeting with me. Nor, to be perfectly fair, with one exception, had I ever sought to meet with him. His icy disdain for opposition, both of the external and internal sort, had hardly encouraged any encounters other than barbs across the parliamentary podium and the occasional, furious written correspondence.

Here the paradoxes truly abounded, or as my Harvard friend, and world-renowned historian, Niall Ferguson, would say, 'the wheel of politics is turned by the god of irony'. By the time of my encounter with Zuma, Mbeki was broodily sulking in the political wilderness, or setting up a leadership institute, something for which I thought his conspicuous lack of the essential attributes rather disqualified him. But it was Mbeki's fateful decision to 'release' Zuma from the deputy presidency in June 2005 that had led me to a rare, and public, act of enthusiastic support for his action. Just ten days before Mbeki announced his decision to a packed and subdued parliament, Zuma had been severely implicated in a Durban High Court judgment against his 'financial adviser' Schabir Shaik, who was found guilty of and subsequently imprisoned for multiple charges of corruption and fraud (although most of his very short spell in jail was spent in the comfort of a private hospital).

But the flames that then appeared to incinerate Zuma's further political ascent in fact later immolated Mbeki, whose leadership of the ANC was ignominiously terminated by a coalition of the disgruntled and disaffected at the seminal party conference in Polokwane in December 2007.

Appropriately, Zuma gave Mbeki the benefit of a full-frontal smile on that occasion. He had become the unlikely lightning rod for all the walking wounded of the Mbeki era, who, alongside a grab bag of trade unionists, Youth League arrivistes and political fortune-hunters, had prevented Mbeki from securing more than four votes out of every ten cast in that leadership election.

Mbeki's humiliation and hounding from public life was further compounded a few months later when he was 'recalled' by the ANC from the country's presidency. Fortune had not only returned Zuma's smile, but had also beamed on his friend Shaik, who in 2009 was released on 'medical parole' from his imprisonment, allegedly for a terminal illness (which, at the time of writing some three years later, he appears, Lazarus-like, to have shrugged off).

But Mbeki hardly stood alone as a casualty of Zuma's political resurrection: South Africa's high-profile and often effective corruption-busting unit, the Scorpions, had been defanged by a pliant parliament, while Vusi Pikoli, the national director of public prosecutions (who had incurred the wrath of Mbeki for arresting his hand-picked and serially corrupt police commissioner, Jackie Selebi) had been replaced by a more tractable successor.

Much constitutional and institutional wreckage littered the path of Mbeki's vertiginous descent and Zuma's improbable rise. However, in the court that really matters to politicians – public opinion and votes – Zuma's '100% Zuluboy' credentials (to quote his supporters' T-shirts) and that winning and enigmatic smile (alongside traditional dancing and singing) had ensured a convincing election victory and sealed his new presidency with the hope that the apparent detachment and denialism (on everything from AIDS to Zimbabwe) of the Mbeki years would yield to something more inclusive, human and hopeful.

## NAVIGATING THE WILDERNESS

My journey between stepping down as leader of the Democratic Alliance – South Africa's second-largest party – and as leader of the official opposition in parliament in May 2007 and the meeting with Zuma, had been, ironically, both busy and unfulfilling. At my final party congress, with no doubt an admixture of sincerity and hyperbole, my successor Helen Zille told the party faithful and the wider audience outside, that 'no one other than Mandela has done more to establish democracy in South Africa than Tony Leon'. Yet, as carefully as I had thought about the timing and manner of my leaving the party leadership after thirteen eventful and deeply exhausting years at the helm, I had been remarkably casual in answering the essential and existential question, 'And now what?'

In Charles Dickens' famous novel *David Copperfield*, Mr Micawber memorably asserted his faith that 'something will turn up'. I had a rather similar approach to the future. This was impelled perhaps by the burn-out of my moth-to-flame political ambition, which had drawn me towards the bright light of politics from an absurdly young age. In fact, my impatient desire to involve myself at every level of South African politics – fuelled by the high octane of South Africa's burning crises and no shortage of personal ambition – had more or less determined my personal and professional trajectory since leaving school in 1974.

Compulsory military service and six full years at the University of the Witwatersrand, where I obtained BA and LLB degrees, had been more backdrop than centre-stage to an ever-increasing political involvement, first in student politics and then in the labyrinths of the Progressive Federal Party – precursor to the Democratic Party. After qualifying as an attorney and a political apprenticeship in the Johannesburg City Council, coupled with my day job as a university law lecturer, I found myself one of the last seats, as the new member of parliament (MP) for Houghton, on the tricameral bus to parliament at the ripe age of 32 in 1989.

I will save the reader an account of the following twenty years, having fully canvassed this momentous and, at times, hair-raising period of South Africa's interregnum ('the old is not yet dead, the new is not yet born') from apartheid to democracy, in my 2008 autobiography, *On The Contrary: Leading the Opposition in a Democratic South Africa*.

In fact, it was writing the book, which eventually weighed in at a rather massive 770-plus pages, which was my primary occupation, and increasing obsession, after standing down as party leader. My full-time work as an ordinary MP hardly proved onerous, and led me to wonder how most of parliament's 490 MPs actually occupied their days.

The proportional representation system removed representatives from direct accountability to constituents and my new designation as 'Official Opposition Spokesman on Foreign Affairs' was a rather grand moniker for an essentially vacuous position. Wherever foreign policy was determined, it was clear that under Thabo Mbeki – then still clinging on to his presidency – the parliamentary Committee on Foreign Affairs had little role, and no power, in the formulation of South Africa's external affairs.

It was, indeed, something of a shock to return to a parliamentary committee after thirteen years of absence as party leader. The intervening years had, to put it at its kindest, hardly seen the rise of empowered and inquiring legislators. Christopher Hitchens's arch phrase, 'the mafia of the mediocre' seemed a good working description of my new committee, and its supine posture before the country's haughty minister of foreign affairs, Nkosazana Dlamini-Zuma.

If return to ordinary parliamentary life was numbing, then attendance at weekly parliamentary caucus meetings was positively anaesthetising. Even when leading the caucus, I found this ritual an endurance: a relic from the British constitutional system, the Thursday morning gathering had once, in its misty origins, been the cockpit of political party decision-making. But, with the modernisation of politics and the party machine, the truth was that individual MPs had little say, or power, over the direction of the party. During my years at the helm, I needed to keep focused on our performance in parliament and to provide a weekly lead to my flock. However, under Mbeki's centralising tendencies and the ruthless implementation of 'cadre redeployment', it was the governing party and its headquarters 1 500 kilometres away in downtown Johannesburg, rather than parliament in Cape Town, that was the true locus of power.

To some extent, the same pertained to the Democratic Alliance, where decision-making was largely determined in my office and among some key executives (Douglas Gibson as chief whip and close confidant; Ryan Coetzee as chief executive officer and indispensable strategist; Russel Crystal as his deputy; James Selfe as executive chairperson; and Mike Ellis, both as deputy chief whip and especially as good friend). However, the fact that I both led the party in parliament and in the country meant that the nation's legislature still loomed large in our strategy and in importance.

All this changed under Helen Zille. During Zille's long, public indecision on whether or not to stand for my position, after my announcement in November 2006 that I would not seek re-election, I had warned her that there was a danger in seeking to combine the position of national leader of the party with the post she then held as mayor of Cape Town. I reminded her of the peril (ascribed to a critic of Neville Chamberlain's transition from lord mayor of Birmingham to eventual prime minister of Great Britain) 'of seeing everything through the wrong end of a municipal drainpipe'. I had no doubt about Zille's stern fealty to principle, nor of her wide popularity in both the party and the media. But I thought that her decision (enthusiastically endorsed by the party congress in May 2007) to be leader-mayor would lead to a diminution of parliament and its focus in the fortunes of the movement I had led from there for so many years.

And so it proved: Zille's election as leader meant the caucus had to choose another person for the other position I had vacated, that of leader of the opposition in parliament (since, as mayor of Cape Town, she was ineligible for membership of the national assembly). The contest pitted my friend Sandra Botha, a liberal party stalwart from the Free State, against Tertius Delport. He had lived up to the famous political maxim, 'no good deed goes unpunished', by repaying my recruitment of him into a senior position in our party ranks from the National Party in 1998 (midst a howl of outrage from liberal purists) by actively undermining my leadership less than a decade later. During the contest, Zille had communicated an ambivalence, no doubt because, on the one hand, she felt obligated to Delport for his fervent support of her leadership bid, while, on the other hand, my former advisers who had now accommodated themselves in her leadership slipstream, disparaged

Delport and were frankly horrified at the prospect of him taking over the reins of our parliamentary leadership.

In the event, Botha won, but the leadership marriage, or more accurately split, between her and Zille was far from happy, and in any event Zille's appearances at our weekly caucus meetings were usually cut short by one or another call from the city of Cape Town that required her urgent attention.

The distractions at the top table of the party mirrored my discomfort in its lower reaches where I now found myself for the first time since 1993. I had determined to leave parliament at the next election in 2009, but found the following two years hard going. Fortunately, a successful nomination to Harvard University to assume a fellowship in the fall of 2007 at the Institute of Politics in the John F. Kennedy School of Government provided a marvellous antidote to the inevitable let down of relinquishing the leadership.

CHAPTER 2

# AMERICAN ODYSSEYS

My four months in the high-octane intellectual atmosphere of Harvard, the world's premier institution of higher learning, proved to be one of my most invigorating and intellectually revitalising life experiences.

Harvard, with an endowment of over 30 billion dollars, uses its prestige and great financial clout for fine public purposes, from subsidising student fees to paying top dollar to recruit and retain the best and the brightest academic minds in the world. A thoughtful by-product of the university's largesse was the provision of spanking new and well-appointed apartments for the five other superannuated politicians and public officials and me who constituted our fellowship. The apartment plus a reasonable stipend were in exchange for the rather modest demand of hosting a weekly seminar series on a theme of your choice, plus obligatory face time with the super-achieving (and curiously eager-to-please and authority-deferring) students. My Harvard experiences – which were also and amply enjoyed by my wife, Michal – ranged from the sublime and the stellar to the prosaic and the practical, but were never less than intense and absorbing.

In the former category was the chance to attend (or 'audit' in university parlance) any class of my choice. Choosing which of the several hundred tempting courses on offer that fall led to an early onset of the disease labelled by the students as 'FOMO' (or 'fear of missing out'). In the end, I chose Niall Ferguson's 'Financial History of the World' (which in his academically entrepreneurial way soon became the blockbuster book *The Ascent of Money* and a TV series of the same title); Ricardo Hausmann's lecture series on 'product space', or why countries' development economics propel them towards either wealth or poverty; and Samantha Power's fascinating and harrowing discourses on 'the history of genocide', aptly summarised in her major work on which the lectures were based, *A Problem from Hell*.

Flame-haired Power became precisely such a problem for Barack Obama, to whom she was very close, when during his contest with Hillary Clinton, she incautiously described the former first lady as a 'monster' and had to resign from his campaign staff. But becoming personally acquainted and socialising with my lecturers was another happy offshoot of the auditing process – which struck me, in the absence of having either to prepare papers or sit for exams, as the difference once delineated between parenting and grandparenting, 'pleasure without responsibility'.

Outside the lecture theatres, controversial, high-profile Harvard law professor Alan Dershowitz (who had achieved much American and international fame as a defence lawyer for a number of celebrity clients, including Claus von Bulow and O.J. Simpson, and as outspoken defender of Israel and scourge of its critics) provided abundant hospitality, as did many new and old friends, including ex-South African Doreen Beinart, whose marriage to eminent Harvard and American dramatist Bob Brustein had located her in a prime home close to the Harvard Yard where we enjoyed their congenial sociability and introductions to some eminent stars in the local firmament.

Dershowitz, whose role as a leading defence attorney was captured on celluloid in the movie *Reversal of Fortune*, was on a future visit to South Africa to become embroiled in a war of words over Zionism with another friend, Cape Town judge Dennis Davis. Before then, however, back at Harvard, when I invited his wife and him to join us for dinner at the rather grand Harvard Club, he offered an interesting example of his supreme and unselfconscious Judaism.

The club was an enclave of the WASP (white Protestant of Anglo-Saxon ancestry) establishment, and it was not that long ago, in its otherwise esteemed history, that the university had operated an explicit quota to restrict the number of Jewish students (and other minorities) admitted through its hallowed gates. Perhaps to make a very public point, before we settled down to order our dinners, Alan whipped out a small portable menorah (a Jewish candelabra), and proceeded to lead our group in singing Chanukah songs – the dinner having coincided with the commencement of the Jewish Festival of Lights.

I was amazed, perhaps even a little embarrassed, but beyond perhaps a raised eyebrow or two, the other diners seemed to regard this outsized demonstration of religious affirmation as perfectly normal. To my somewhat more understated sense of religious identity, the incident seemed entirely emblematic of the title of Dershowitz's autobiography, *Chutzpah*.

We also played host to a colony of South African students, pre-eminent among them my former speech-writer Joel Pollak and his girlfriend (now wife) Julia Bertelsmann; the daughter of my fiery Cape Town friend and political ally, Rhoda Kadalie; and my former head of office, David Maynier, today a rising MP in the Democratic Alliance fold. I dubbed the group, for whom Michal prepared on the day itself a fully stuffed, appropriately American, i.e., super-sized, Thanksgiving turkey, 'my government in exile'. However, my memory of that occasion is somewhat blurred due to my over-indulgence of the vastly overpriced South African wines I had patriotically purchased at the local liquor store.

My presence in America also coincided with the intense pre-primary phase of the battle for presidential nominations of the Republican Party and the Democratic Party, all the more intense since the unpopularity of retiring President George W. Bush portended a possible Democratic win. At that stage of the contest, Senator Clinton was the odds-on favourite for the party nomination. However, three years before I had been present – also in Boston – as an international guest of the Democratic Party at the nominating convention of Senator John F. Kerry, whose ill-starred bid to unseat Bush was, perhaps appropriately in view of what was to follow, overshadowed on that occasion by one of the most electrifying speeches I have ever witnessed. It was delivered by the largely unknown Illinois senate candidate, Barack Obama. His recounting of his personal story embedded in an eloquent take on the quest for unity across the gaping divide of American politics nurtured even my somewhat cynical political soul.

Before my Harvard sojourn, Obama had transmogrified into a United States (US) senator. Now he had a long-shot chance of wresting the party nomination for president from Clinton. On a balmy autumnal evening, I stood with some 10 000 others on the Boston Common once more to hear Obama. Again an address of rare conviction and hopeful promise was delivered. Later on, I was a little disconcerted when I recounted my breathless admiration for Obama's power of persuasion and promise of hope to Harvard grandee Michael Gergen (whose professorship at the Kennedy School of Government had been preceded by years as White House counsel to Presidents Reagan and Clinton). He somewhat curtly dismissed my enthusiastic report with the sharp put-down, 'So you think the ability to make a great speech means he will be a successful president?' Indeed, Obama had a mixed first term as president, and the consensus appeared to be that his governing never quite matched his soaring rhetoric. Still, he handily won re-election four years later and notched up some impressive acheivements, especially in the realm of health care provison and rescuing the US economy. However, the difficult political and treacherous fiscal waters he had to navigate suggested that it was not Gergen but former New York governor Mario Cuomo who got it right. He once famously observed, 'You campaign in poetry, you govern in prose.'

On the responsibility-practicality side, I set about preparing for my seminar series with rigour, since there was some competition among the fellows and our gimlet-eyed student assistants (or 'liaisons' as they were misleadingly named) to ensure maximum attendance. I need not have worried: I was the only foreigner among our number, and my rather grandiose seminar title 'Development and Democracy: A View from Africa' proved an exotic allure to the many internationally minded members of the student body.

Once again, Harvard's largesse kicked in: under the rules of engagement at the Institute of Politics, a fellow could invite a guest speaker from anywhere in the US or Canada (and the Institute would foot the bill) and, in addition, would fly in an international speaker of your choice. My network of Africa hands in the US – ranging from the scribe of Zimbabwe's immiseration, Peter Godwin, to *Economist* journalist and author of *The Shackled Continent*, Robert Guest, ensured full houses every week. As my international drawcard, I prevailed upon the former South African president, F.W. de Klerk, to address a packed seminar, followed by a public appearance of us both in conversation at an equally jammed, but much larger, public forum. The latter was somewhat marred by the immoderate behaviour of the so-called moderator Robert I. Rotberg, who spoke longer (and largely about his own, and hitherto unrecorded role in South Africa's democratisation) than De Klerk!

At its most prosaic but perhaps most useful, Harvard provided a compulsory correction to my hitherto technophobic ways. Incredibly, and perhaps shamefaced as it is now to record, until I set foot in the red-brick office building in John F. Kennedy Avenue, in Cambridge, Massachusetts, which housed the Institute of Politics, I had never sent an e-mail or effectively operated a computer. The age of the Internet, and more latterly Facebook (appropriately, conjured up in one of Harvard's dorms) had passed me by or, more accurately, had occurred during my long leadership years where, among myriad minor and major kindnesses, my faithful secretary, Sandy Slack, had provided a firewall against my acquisition of computing needs or skills. Her effortless shorthand and unerring ability to decipher my hieroglyphic handwriting had kept me captive to pre-Gothenburg (never mind pre-Zuckerberg) ways.

My new office at Harvard, sans secretary but with an imposing computer sitting menacingly on my otherwise unadorned desk, was to force-feed me into the eventually liberating ecosystem of cyberspace. There was no alternative, and aided by Michal's exasperated tuition and my visiting stepson Etai's more benign instruction, I started my navigation around the wondrous world of the web.

All too soon, the black ice encrusted on our lawn and chill winds that knifed through the winter mornings signalled the end of term and the return for me to normalcy in South Africa. But, of course, nothing was normal back then in South Africa. As we prepared to depart the shores of the US, Michal and I took a short vacation with family and friends in northern California. At the precise moment in December 2007 when Mbeki lost his political head at Polokwane, we had by pure chance stumbled into lunch at the Sonoma Valley vineyard of Hollywood producer (of *Godfather* fame), Francis Ford Coppola. As we were quaffing his rather expensive but (to my untrained nose, at least) ordinary wines, news filtered through my brother's BlackBerry that Thabo was a goner.

My descent from the rarefied atmosphere of Harvard Yard to the more routine domesticity of Cape Town coincided with a happy, slightly fraught, period of intense activity. This largely centred on the editing of my autobiography and panel-beating it (with some expert assistance) into book form and launch-readiness for August 2008.

Escapism has always been hard-wired into my DNA: at university, I always found the books *not* on the reading list far more alluring than the prescribed works. The same syndrome now seemed to infect my planning for a post-parliamentary career. Ever the voice of practical, if occasionally unwelcome, advice, my father intoned telephonically from Durban, 'What precisely are you going to do next year, Tony? You know at 52, you will be far too young to retire.'

When I responded that the crystal ball on my future appeared somewhat occluded, and that I had already achieved, largely, what I had set out to do, he said, 'You sound like Alexander at the doors of Constantinople: "I have no more empires to conquer."' If somewhat pompously, he had made an essential point.

No sooner was the book on the shelves (and, happily, moving off them) than my further career planning was again interrupted by another tempting invitation from the US. My former parliamentary counsellor and friend, Gareth Morgan, had found in Marian Tupy at the Cato Institute in the US a true believer in the cause of my party and, usefully for my immediate purposes, someone who thought my leadership of the Democratic Alliance to have been – in his words – 'heroic'. Such herograms translated into an invitation to spend the latter period of 2008 as a resident visiting fellow at the Cato Institute in the Rome of the new world order – downtown Washington, D.C.

My arrival in a rather desultory back office at the Cato Institute – high citadel of American libertarianism – coincided with the near collapse, and cardiac arrest, of the financial economies of America and the world. This was triggered by the twenty-first-century Visigoths and Vandals of US capitalism – subprime housing loans and securitised debt obligations, the very 'weapons of mass destruction' (as Warren Buffet accurately called them), which the light-touch regulatory regime and the so-called 'self-correcting powers of capitalism' ardently championed by my hosts at Cato had helped to bring about.

However gloomy the outlook appeared for the conservative wing of American politics, I delighted in Obama's continuing rise in the polls (he had by now bested Clinton to win the Democratic nomination and was surging ahead of Republican Senator John McCain in the looming national election). I was an eyewitness to history-in-the-making: 'present at the creation' of an apparently new political and economic order.

Indeed, the arrangement I had made with the *Business Day* editor, Peter Bruce, to pen a weekly 'Letter from Washington' for the sadly short-lived *Weekender* newspaper in Johannesburg, proved far more agreeable than the somewhat more dreary and essential task of churning out a lengthy research paper to pay my dues to Cato.

The subject I chose to address was not without merit or close personal and political interest: 'The State of Liberal Democracy in Africa: Resurgence or Recession?' But after having so recently completed my own lengthy political autobiography, I found the exigencies of writing a paper, the conclusion of which I had already discerned, hard going (I summed up to Michal the answer to the question posed by the rather portentous title of my paper as 'more than you would expect, less than I had hoped for').

While generous enough, and respectful of my different political perspective, the Cato Institute proved to be a far less comfortable ideological fit than Harvard had been only the year before, and the somewhat solitary existence of being a think tank wonk was ill-suited to my somewhat expansive and gregarious temperament. However, by a process of negative reinforcement, it at least helped rule out one possible future career path. This impression was fortified one morning at the Cato water fountain, when I asked an intern who was passing by, pushing a trolley containing a mountain of old publications published by scholars and fellows of the Institute, where he was headed: 'To the shredder', was his nonchalant, but disconcerting, answer.

As always, the out-of-office experiences at such a change-evoking moment in Washington proved heady stuff: from trampling around the

Virginia estate of founding father Thomas Jefferson to being reacquainted with distinguished diplomats such as Chester Crocker and Princeton Lyman (respectively, former US assistant secretary of state for Africa and a previous US ambassador to South Africa) and simply enjoying the vibrancy of our pulsating neighbourhood in Dupont Circle, made my second sojourn in America deeply agreeable.

During the election, Obama frequently invoked the observation of four decades before by Martin Luther King – on whose shoulders his campaign effectively stood – that 'the arc of the moral universe is long but it bends towards justice'. We celebrated election night in early November, with a party in the attic (home of our landlord's mega-size TV) of our brownstone rental for a group of visiting South Africans and a few locals.

Watching the drama unfold on the TV screen, it seemed less like political spectator sport, and rather more like a shimmering event of historical redemption. Fortified with the obligatory take-away pizzas and beers, we were all glued to the TV at that around-midnight moment when Obama passed the magic number of 270 electoral votes needed to clinch the presidency, and the networks proclaimed him the winner.

I turned away, almost choking on the historic significance of the fact that the next occupant of the White House – just a few blocks down the road – was part East African, and that he would soon inhabit a residence built two centuries before by slaves of West African origin, 'who had no last names or carried the names of their masters'.[3] I noticed that there were few dry eyes in our TV den as we observed the conjoining of a moment of American uniqueness with a reminder of its more shameful past.

CHAPTER 3

# JEWS SAY GOODBYE AND NEVER LEAVE

By the time the wheels of our plane from the US touched the tarmac in Johannesburg, in late January 2009, I was counting down the clock to a still unknown post-parliamentary life. I finally realised that the remaining legislative and political chores – from the official opening of parliament, to my speech in the president's state of the nation debate, and the election itself – would be my last. In each of these predictable pageants in our democratic tapestry I would be now more bit player than major star.

In my parliamentary office, surrounded by Stuttafords packing cases, Sandy Slack and I filled the cartons with the multiple scrapbooks she had meticulously collated and annotated with every press cutting in which I had featured for more than two decades. I reflected now, with some wry amusement, how hard I had so often striven for public notice and attention. By that measure, the many volumes reflected success of a sort; yet, now they were destined for a sort of elephant's graveyard or, more accurately, the political archive at the University of the Free State. And they seemed to me now of far less significance than the importance I had once attached to them, or to some of the events they described. I also could not help but reflect on a recent conversation with Helen Zille, when she commented that 'while other – perhaps more normal – people count their money and their share portfolios, we count our press clippings'.

In my final speech to parliament, I commenced with a joke e-mailed to me by Joel Pollak from America, which wittily encapsulated the fact that this was indeed the final farewell – having previously delivered a final speech as leader of the opposition, and after that, one to the Democratic Alliance congress, as party leader. Now in saying goodbye as an MP, I noted: 'The difference between Gentiles and Jews is that Gentiles leave without saying goodbye, while Jews say goodbye and never leave.'

In my speech I touched on the momentous events I had witnessed as an MP, since my first major day in parliament on 2 February 1990, when President F.W. de Klerk turned his back on the convictions of a lifetime and inaugurated the epoch of negotiations and democracy, and the advent of Nelson Mandela's rainbow presidency. I noted how the wheel of history, which I had been privileged in some small measure to help turn, had seen South Africa move from pariah of the world to one of the more admired members of the community of nations. But, as was my characteristic wont, I wrapped my admiration for our accomplishment with a warning of the need for future action: 'I celebrate the fact of South Africa's exceptionalism: we are today the only large, ethnically diverse and resource-rich African country to be rated a free democracy. We should acknowledge this achievement, not in the glow of self-congratulation, but with an urgent determination to repair the breaches in our democratic path.'

## BE CAREFUL WHAT YOU WISH FOR

As a freshly re-minted ordinary citizen of South Africa, I was not entirely reassured by my new surrounds, or by the uncertain joys of liberation from the fetters of public office for which I had so often hungered. Navigating the world without Sandy (not to mention a battery of other highly motivated staffers who had populated my office with cheerful efficiency) was the deepest, most painful, adjustment to my new normalcy. Perhaps discovering how well the party I had founded seemed to be managing its election campaign without my presence as leading drawcard at every event, was another. When dismissing pleas, a few years before, from fervent supporters for me to remain at the party helm, I had glibly reassured them all with the wise mantra of my first political boss, J.F. Oberholzer, of the Johannesburg city council, that 'West Park

Cemetery is filled with indispensible people'. Did I, subconsciously perhaps, hope to be the mortal exception to this iron rule?

After all the exhausting battles of politics past – which at one level I had longed to leave behind – I now seemed to inhabit a sort of nebulous zone, between being 'the ex-leader' and a future who-knows-what? Previously, my idea of heaven would have been an undisturbed weekend at home with family and friends, walking the dogs in Newlands Forest, without the interruption of a political, often petty, urgency.

'Be careful what you wish for,' the wise Chinese once intoned. I now began to think that unbridled, unstructured domesticity might be the toughest battle of all. Never much of a fan of the great British playwright, I found my new life's Pinteresque pauses and silences – so different from the background clatter and chatter of my political years – bewildering.

Before my inner broodings and outward adjustments could collide, two seemingly unrelated events occurred, which were to provide – in the jargon of the Hegelian dialectic I had vaguely studied as an undergraduate – a 'synthesis' for a new career.

First off, Peter Bruce at *Business Day*, clearly pleased with my scribblings from Washington the year before, commissioned me to write a series of colour-pieces for his newspaper focusing on the campaigns of the key political leaders – the Inkatha warhorse, Mangosuthu Buthelezi, my successor, Helen Zille, and the ANC leader, and inevitable next state president, Jacob Zuma. The success of such a venture was, of course, contingent on access to them, which given the longevity of my relationship with each, gave me a unique advantage. In fact, of the three, it was Zuma I knew the least well. We had been on affable, but essentially distant, terms in parliament when he served as deputy president. More recently, during my Cato fellowship we had enjoyed a non-drink drink (he quaffed nothing stronger than rooibos tea) at the sumptuous Four Seasons Hotel where he was sequestered during a visit to Washington to reassure nervous investors that he was not a hostage to the anti-market left, which had propelled him to the party leadership. But I could hardly claim to know him at all.

Was he a case – in Texan argot – of 'all hat and no cattle', that is, charm without substance? Or did he have hidden depths my amateur journalism could plumb? I hoped that my new assignment for *Business Day* might provide an answer or two.

But as I awaited Zuma for a preliminary interview on a March morning at his home in Forest Town, Johannesburg – disconcertingly, according to reports, purchased by one of his many mystery financial backers – I took some comfort from the equally American habit of misdiagnosing predictions of future presidential performance based on objective qualification.

I recalled how Ronald Reagan had once, prior to his election in 1980, been dismissed with the put-down, 'If you tread into his inner thoughts you won't get your ankles wet.' Yet he went on to be acclaimed as one of the most consequential and successful presidents of the twentieth century; while the man he beat, Jimmy Carter, who apparently entered the White House with one of the highest IQs ever recorded by a holder of that office, was later evaluated as one of its least successful incumbents.

My meeting with Zuma that morning did not unlock the mystery any further for either me or my future readers. He was his usual affable and somewhat enigmatic self, seeking refuge behind the collective views of his movement. That morning he salted very few clues, and a lot of generalities, as to his likely performance in office, post-election. However, as I was more concerned with securing his agreement for accompanying him, close-up, on a forthcoming campaign swing through the township of Langa in Cape Town, my short-term journalistic needs were of more importance than my concerns as a citizen, soon to be subject to his governance.

In the back and forth of our discussion, Zuma politely enquired about my post-parliamentary plans. Since I had nothing concrete to disclose, I mumbled out some formula along the lines of 'looking forward to serving South Africa in a non-partisan fashion.' He suggested we discuss something more definite after the election.

The second event was in far more familiar company, albeit a continent or two away. My good friend and long-time political ally, Douglas Gibson, had been appointed South African ambassador to Thailand in 2008.

He was following a precedent I had helped engineer when, in the aftermath of the 1994 elections, I had sought and received from Nelson

Mandela an ambassadorship (to the Netherlands) for my predecessor as leader of the Democratic Party, Zach de Beer. Our truly dismal performance in those elections under his baton had necessitated his resignation. But I felt that his long and distinguished service to the liberal cause in South Africa deserved some high recognition from the first democratic president, and Mandela was (after endless bureaucratic delays) happy to oblige. When I later visited Zach in his rather stately, if crumbling, official residence at The Hague, he told me he found the job 'largely boring; a bit like being the lord mayor'. I put this down to his post-election depression, but I thought there was probably some merit in the observation. De Beer stayed just two years at his post, and died quite suddenly on the eve of the next election, in June 1999.

Gibson (who was shortly followed into diplomatic service by the unhappy parliamentary leader Sandra Botha and then by another party colleague and friend, Sheila Camerer) was cut from a different and far more cheerful cloth than De Beer. I used to call Gibson 'Pollyanna', given his relentless optimism in even the direst political and personal circumstances. Perhaps that is why I always found his company and counsel so deeply agreeable; it was a necessary counterpoint to my often more gloomy mood as we wrestled with making our initial two-bit (or rather seven-MP) party into a more formidable enterprise.

So when, just before the April election, an e-mail from a thriving Gibson suggested Michal and I join him and his wife Pam for an Easter vacation in Bangkok and surrounds, with a side visit to Cambodia, it was an easy sell. Helen Zille and the new leadership had exceptionally modest requirements of me on the campaign trail (I was asked to address only two political rallies) and my journalistic task had been squared away. Thailand beckoned!

'The Land of Smiles', as the Thai tourist authorities brand their South East Asian kingdom, was anything but when we arrived there in April 2009. Endemic and violent clashes between political factions – dubbed the 'red shirts' and the 'yellow shirts' – had, shortly before, rocked the country and its capital. Predictably, however, Gibson's disposition was as sunny as ever.

It was during this trip that I had a light-bulb moment, a sort of future career epiphany. I realised that even discounting Gibson's relentless optimism, there was merit and worth in the job he was doing. He was actually running the equivalent of a small business, with motivated staff. His goals (boosting trade and tourism, and performing myriad acts of public diplomacy) were peculiarly, perhaps almost uniquely, aligned to the skills set that he had acquired during a long career in politics. And, now that I thought about it, this applied to me as well. I was, truth to tell, also not entirely unaffected by the staff who tended to our every need at his and Pam's handsome official residence, to which we were ferried in a chauffeur-driven car.

After our return home and a series of interventions too boring to recount here, my summons eventually arrived for a post-election appointment with the newly enthroned President Zuma at Tuynhuys. He did, indeed, as he had vaguely suggested a few months before, have a post-parliamentary, non-partisan role in mind for me. 'I would like you to serve on the Human Rights Commission,' the president said.

I remembered the unhappy period both Helen Suzman and Rhoda Kadalie had spent on that notionally important and independent, but in reality ANC-dominated, body. I countered with my own question: 'Would you make me the chairman?', thinking this extremely improbable but, in the unlikely event, would enable me to make the commission a true protector of our constitutional settlement, rather than a poodle for the politically powerful.

Zuma became vague and said, 'Well, we could see about that over time.' I immediately sensed my suggestion was the political equivalent of 'a bridge too far', and the conversation moved around to other options. Flush with my recent and happy idyll in Thailand, a job in international diplomacy seemed the right stuff. The president fixed me with a final half-smile and suggested an ambassadorship would be 'no problem'.

'Just make sure it is to somewhere significant!' I cheerily advised the president of South Africa before departing his office.

CHAPTER 4

# 'NOT ARGENTINA?'

'Argentina? You must be completely mad!' exclaimed Michal. One of the many virtues, and occasional irritations, of being married to my plain-speaking Israeli partner is that she never hesitates to share her thinking with me on topics, great or small. Where in the world President Zuma proposed to send us to for the next few years clearly fell into the former category.

Dr Ayanda Ntsaluba was the director general of the newly renamed Department of International Relations and Co-operation. Apparently its previous and plainer moniker 'Foreign Affairs' was deemed insufficient to convey our 'Ubuntu' credentials to the world at large. Shortened to the acronym DIRCO, a wag at head office soon re-christened this mouthful as the 'Department of International Rumours and non-Co-operation'. I was to learn, over time, the validity behind this levity.

It was to Dr Ntsaluba that the task fell of finding me a 'mission', as embassies are termed in the trade. He advised me, during various telephonic discussions, that only Argentina was immediately vacant. If I preferred, he said, I could wait a few months for Portugal to become available.

However, the director general stressed that Argentina was a G-20 country (i.e., in the club of the leading twenty economies of the world) and was a key partner in South Africa's 'South-South' diplomacy. 'Besides,' he added, no doubt intending to seduce, 'the ambassador's official residence in Buenos Aires is one of our most impressive properties abroad.'

I remained deeply uncertain and asked for a few days to respond. I had actually visited Argentina on holiday, with family and friends, in 2006 to celebrate my 50th birthday. I had been suitably charmed by the faded grandeur (although I was later to learn that as a resident the adjective trumped the noun) of its Parisian belle époque architecture and its wide boulevards. We had been duly impressed by the compulsory tango show at the futuristic Philippe Starck-designed Faena Hotel and much enjoyed its fine steaks and its marquee Malbec wines.

The country – or my very brief encounter with it – seemed to represent an interesting intersection between high-end living and baleful reminders of its conflicted and fairly recent authoritarian past. On the one hand, we shopped in edgy and upscale Palermo Soho; on the other hand, we witnessed the weekly parade of the Madres de Plaza de Mayo, whose children and relatives had 'disappeared' during the murderous regime of the military junta.

It was as though the boutiques of Sandton Square and the horrors exposed by the Truth Commission existed in the same realm, which of course they did back in South Africa. A more hedonistic memory takeaway was of the impossibly perfect figures of the *porteño* (as residents of Buenos Aires are called) women who apparently enjoyed the services of plastic surgeons and psychotherapists in equal measure.

Beyond a nodding acquaintance with Argentina's Virgil, Jorge Luis Borges, and a much closer appreciation of the more middlebrow musical *Evita*, I knew little of its history and even less of its present and likely future trajectory, other than the standout fact that it had collapsed economically in 2001. Back then it posted the largest sovereign debt default in world economic history (Greece was very much in the future at that stage). But its high energy levels and the conspicuous consumption in the shopping malls suggested a strong recovery was well on track by the time of our visit.

I would have done well to have remembered the observation of my Harvard friend, Robert Lawrence, who once cautioned that high-end tourists and conference junketeers live, in their brief visits to new countries, in a bubble he called 'five star': it often matters little for these charmed inhabitants whether you are in Bangalore, Belgrade or Buenos Aires. You glide through good restaurants and swanky hotels and tourist enclaves and you experience local eccentricities as charming or quaint. You might scratch the gilded surface, but you certainly do not plumb often-murkier depths. Living in such a place, however, is to inhabit a parallel universe.

Beyond my quite fond remembrance of that sultry Christmas in the 'Paris of South America', as Argentines somewhat optimistically dub their capital, another consideration propelled me towards acceptance.

When an ambassadorship was first mooted, I decided that I would not advance policies or diplomatic stratagems that conflicted with my principles. Never mind having my cake and eating it (although I never understood the meaning of that cliché), I believed it would be perfectly possible, even appropriate, to advance South Africa's interests without becoming a mealy-mouthed sell-out of everything I had stood for during my political career. This would certainly rule out accepting ambassadorship in a major European Union or North American country. In those places I would doubtless, on key issues from press freedom in South Africa to democracy in Zimbabwe, find myself more in agreement with my host country than with my diplomatic principals. The old diplomatic adage (much harnessed by South Africa's anti-National Party diplomats during the apartheid years) that you serve your government 'with equal measures of loyalty and contempt' held little appeal.

It became clear, in any event, that the diplomatic posts where such loyalty would conflict with principles were off the table. Only the elect (i.e., ANC insiders) would be offered these positions – and in good conscience, probably only they could serve in the chanceries of London, Washington or Brussels.

Of the second-string nations, Argentina – whose gross domestic product (GDP) I quickly Googled, approximated South Africa's – seemed a reasonable fit.

None of this, what I thought to be impeccable logic held much sway with my dear wife. She thought the entire project and the place selected for its execution to be bizarre. And, as always, she was frank enough to share her feelings.

'You know, T,' as she calls me in moments of exasperation or endearment (i.e., most of the time), 'I have spent ten years adjusting to becoming a South African. Now you want us to up sticks, relocate far away from the children [then progressing through universities] and be even further away from the family in Israel.'

She then reeled off a list of secondary objections – ranging from language and culture and ended with the admonition, 'Anyway, Argentina is way below your pay grade.' On the latter point, I countered with my no-conflict-of-conscience argument. She remained unmoved.

By then, however, I had got the bit between my teeth. I deployed on her, in a more measured way, the tactic I had so often used against my political opponents, external and internal: I wore her down. She relented. A few days later, I placed the fateful call to the director general, informing him that I accepted the offer of Buenos Aires.

## THE REACTION

When word got out (leaked from the presidency, I was to discover) of my new assignment, reactions were, predictably, varied. When, for example, I phoned Helen Zille to inform her, I thought I detected a note of relief in her voice, doubtless pleased I would be so far away from her leadership project. Douglas Gibson – whose own ambassadorial lifestyle I had found so agreeable – assured me that I would hate the bureaucracy and the technicalities of the job. However, he did add that my late mother Sheila (of whom he was a firm favourite), 'would have been immensely proud of you but would have regarded this as no less than your due'. The old Progressive Party warhorse, and one of my predecessors as leader of the opposition, Colin Eglin, was encouraging. 'You and Michal really do belong with the international set,' he enthused. 'You should find Buenos Aires very cosmopolitan.'

*Business Day* published a very positive piece and *The Citizen* splashed the news on its front page. From other quarters, however, a sourer note sounded. One of my particular bêtes noires, Richard Calland, harrumphed in his column in the *Mail & Guardian* that he could not believe that 'Tony Leon's strident and negative form of opposition' had been rewarded with such a plum post. But in a life and career that had so often encountered, perhaps invited, critical reaction, I was pleasantly surprised by the overall positive, even enthusiastic, response to my middle-age career move.

Of all the messages that reached me at that time, I set the greatest store by an effusive communication that I received from Jorge Heine. Jorge was an old friend – but of more immediate relevance, he had been Chile's ambassador to Pretoria during the Mandela presidency when I led the Democratic Party. It was an extraordinary fact that at a time when every diplomat of any country of consequence fought for a posting to the world's most acclaimed democratic success story (as South Africa was back then), an emissary from Chile should have been the standout ambassador of that golden age. But such was Jorge's magnetic presence (ably assisted by his ultra-charming wife Norma) that he was, for many, the most attractive and respected member of the diplomatic community. Now pursuing an academic career in Canada, Jorge wrote – doubtless with a touch of Latino extravagance – that 'you will be as brilliant a diplomat as you were a political leader'.

CHAPTER 5

# HOW TO BECOME AN AMBASSADOR IN THREE AND A HALF WEEKS

In a memorable line in *The Hollow Men*, T.S. Eliot, a favourite poet of mine, wrote: 'between the idea and the reality falls the shadow'. This seemed an excellent working definition of the world I had now entered.

Having spent all of my political life in opposition politics, I was utterly unfamiliar with the ways and wiles of government. My first brushes with it did little to improve my hitherto jaundiced view of its workings. Several weeks elapsed between agreeing to my new job and posting and actually commencing training for it at DIRCO headquarters in Pretoria.

A veritable Eliotesque 'shadowland' seemed to descend on matters both major (arranging for the *agrément* with my receiving country – a necessary prerequisite to a formal announcement) and minor (finding out where I was to stay in Pretoria and obtaining an air ticket to get there). On all these matters, the bureaucracy appeared to be akin to a black hole – into which objects (or, in my case, requests) disappeared, never to return.

While I awaited word from my new masters and mistresses, I busied myself – doubtless far too late in the day – with finding out what exactly 'Heads of Mission' – or ambassadors – did with themselves. The initial results were decidedly undermining. The classical statesman Demosthenes described it all rather gloomily: 'Ambassadors have no battleships at their command or heavy infantry, or fortresses; their weapons are words and opportunity. In important transactions opportunities are fleeting; once they are missed they cannot be recovered.'

Wondering how much it had actually changed in the 2 300 years – give or take – since he uttered this bleak description, I decided to reread the appropriately entitled *Diplomacy for the Next Century* penned in 1998 by the Israeli statesman Abba Eban. He rose to fame as the Jewish state's most eloquent spokesman both in the earliest years of its existence and in its battles for survival until 1973. Interestingly enough, I flipped through its pages in Cape Town, which I discovered was his birthplace.

His update, however, was also less than reassuring: 'The period since World War Two has seen a vast increase in the number of officials in the world exercising a diplomatic function. Yet this has been accompanied by a sharp decline in prestige and influence. The professional ambassador is the loser on all fronts,' he noted. 'His masters do much of the negotiations and usurp some of his symbolic function in celebrating and dramatising international friendships.'[4]

I wondered whether Eban's description of the modern decline and fall of ambassadorial importance applied to the special diplomatic animal I was categorised as: the so-called political appointee? As I pondered and researched whether or not there was any distinction between these two breeds, the professional and the political, it had simultaneously been leaked that two veteran – and recently retired – ANC cabinet ministers had also been named as 'Heads of Mission Designates': Dr Zola Skweyiya and Ngconde Balfour – to London and Gaborone, respectively.

I was to join my new colleagues in a specially convened class of three to receive instruction in the practice of diplomacy at head office in Pretoria. Michal waspishly advised that I would no doubt be taught 'how to hold a knife and fork properly'.

Awaiting the by now wearyingly unresponsive administration to provide the details of this exercise, I was less than reassured to be told during one telephone conversation that the entire exercise was to be shoehorned into just three and a half weeks. Douglas Gibson had assured me that normal diplomatic training lasted approximately four months.

## 'DISGUISED UNEMPLOYMENT'

As I eventually winged my way to Pretoria in early August, I took with me another volume. One of my favourite 'public intellectuals' was the liberal economist John Kenneth Galbraith. He, too, had been picked by his president (admittedly in his case, in the mighty form of John F. Kennedy) to serve as America's ambassador to India in the early 1960s. Self-described 'a transient member of the diplomatic community' (an exact fit for me, I thought), his biography was pretty crushing on the distribution of work and idleness of diplomatic life. Admittedly he was talking about New Delhi, which 50 years ago was something of a political backwater.

He wrote: 'In India during my time there, there were some fifty ambassadors. They were a spectacular example of what economists call "disguised unemployment". The ambassadors of Argentina or Brazil could not have had more than a day's serious work a month. The more deeply engaged diplomat from Scandinavia, Holland, Belgium, or Spain, could discharge their essential duties in one day a week.'[5]

I had not signed up for a paid holiday at the South African taxpayer's expense so I now wondered whether as the designated ambassador to Argentina, whose remit included non-resident accreditation to Uruguay and Paraguay, I, too, was to become a member of the 'disguised unemployed'. No doubt my training crash course would yield some clues.

## A POLITICAL REUNION

DIRCO is headquartered today in a splendid, state-of-the-art, customised building in suburban Pretoria, named in honour of ANC grandee O.R. Tambo. But when my training commenced on a crisp winter morning in August 2009, the department was spread across several tired and under-furnished office blocks in Brooklyn. The 'Diplomatic Academy' was housed in a particularly ramshackle edifice showing advanced symptoms of sick building syndrome, which also seemed to have infected one or two of our more elderly instructors.

It was interesting to be reacquainted with Zola and Ngconde. We had until recently encountered each other mostly across the seldom-bridged divide of parliament and domestic politics. Zola, however, I had known from the early 1990s, when he and I were intensely involved in the high-wire dramatic negotiations in Kempton Park where South Africa's democratic Constitution was framed. Zola had been a member of every cabinet since 1994; in a country where too often the adjective 'corrupt' prefigured the name of a government department, neither scandal nor any act of bungling incompetence was attached to his name. His quiet manner and high seniority commanded respect (he was almost an exact contemporary of Thabo Mbeki and they had left South Africa together for decades in exile).

I assumed that he regarded his appointment as 'High Commissioner to the Court of St James' as surely the shiniest bauble in the diplomatic realm, a happy and prestigious reward for years of sacrifice and service. It was the wrong assumption. At our first meeting he moaned, 'I don't want to go to London. I am only going there because the Movement has deployed me.' When I pressed him further, he intimated that he found the cold weather disagreeable and would have rather retired to his home in Umhlanga Rocks on KwaZulu-Natal's North Coast. I could think of around a thousand reasons why London might be deeply agreeable, but, uncharacteristically, I kept my counsel.

However, Zola was more forthcoming when I pressed him to explain a political mystery that had puzzled me for the past few years. I had in mind the frantic run-up to the ANC's transformative (and, indeed, traumatic) 52nd National Conference in December 2007 in Polokwane. It was clear even to someone as politically and physically remote from the event as I was at the time (being in the US) that incumbent Thabo Mbeki was heading for the chopping block in his doomed attempt to retain his party's presidency.

Without the benefit of or expertise in decoding Kremlinology – apparently necessary to unlock the inner workings of the ANC – I simply took note of the voluminous South African media reports then cluttering my inbox. They all indicated that in the delegate selection process, the following wind (if not exactly the tsunami promised by some) was behind the insurgent challenger, Jacob Zuma.

'Why', I asked Zola during one of our tea breaks, 'didn't you and the other party elders warn Thabo about the likelihood of a humiliating loss?'

He told me that he had tried. He apparently advised the president's office that he wanted to speak to Mbeki ahead of the elective conference. Instead of receiving a direct hearing, he was offered a meeting with Mojanku Gumbi. She was Mbeki's formidable 'fix it' person and also his legal adviser. But, as Zola noted, she was not even a member of the ANC, being a lifelong supporter of the narrow ideology of Black Consciousness represented by the tiny political party, the Azanian People's Organisation.

'After that I washed my hands of it', Zola said.

Zola and I were at least reasonably diligent and always punctual in our attendance at the courses on offer during our much abbreviated training session. The third member of our group, Ngconde Balfour, was more notable for his absences, late arrivals and early departures. He frequently interrupted several of our instructors with the not-always useful refrain, 'I've been a government minister for years, so I know exactly how the Public Finance Management Act works.' Recently dethroned as correctional services minister, Balfour clearly bristled with indignation.

One person, however, to whom he had not apparently explained the workings and limitations of government finance and safeguards, was his wife, Thozama Mqobi. At the time of our lessons, she was in the public and press spotlight due to her suspension as Gauteng correctional commissioner because of her lavish spending on private residential accommodation (courtesy of the public purse) even when official housing had been provided. Subsequent to our time together, Balfour's wife was apparently disciplined by her department, but then successfully appealed the outcome to the labour courts and received a handsome financial settlement on her reinstatement.

Balfour, perhaps predictably, was to be the shortest-lived ambassador or high commissioner of our trio. He quit after barely five months.

## 'BULLSHIT BINGO'

As Zola and I, mostly in the absence of Balfour, went through some of the provisions of the Public Finance Management Act, I could not help but marvel, once again, at the operation of Eliot's 'shadowland'. Here was a piece of legislation with 96 sections, 6 schedules and innumerable regulations, each of which provided for good governance and stiff penalties for wasteful and unauthorised expenditure. Could there be any country where the gap between noble intention and calamitous non-compliance was as great as the case of South Africa?

I remembered at the time of its parliamentary passage, back in 1999, that my key political adviser, Ryan Coetzee, had said, a tad cynically, that the Act was designed 'to save the ANC from the ANC'. In the event, and certainly in the intervening decade since its enactment, the rigorous safeguards it provided to protect state assets and taxpayers' money had been pretty much honoured only in the breach.

But I, the major opposition voice for so many years against government corruption, would now, in terms of the Public Finance Management Act, be designated as the chief accounting officer of the South African Embassy in Argentina. Now I was to be subject to the provisions I had so strenuously argued should be applied against others. Talk about being careful what you wish or, in this case, preach for.

But while entire swaths of the government were adrift on a sea of sleaze, the department of which I was now a member was a conspicuous exception. At one of our many sessions, Asogan Moodley – a big man in all senses of the term, and DIRCO's chief financial officer – advised that DIRCO had never once received a qualified audit from National Treasury. 'And,' he added with what I thought was just a hint of slight menace, 'with your kind co-operation, we will maintain our record.'

After a brief acquaintance with this omnibus legislation we were then led, ineluctably, into sessions to explain the further requirements of the tortuously named (and even more painful in its demands, I was soon enough to discover) 'Performance Management Development System'. The PMDS – naturally, it has an acronym – is a beast with many tentacles. But, in essence, both I and every one of about 25 employees soon to be under my charge in the embassy was subject to the 'Culture of Performance'. This was not a rock opera or rocket science. It consisted of everything from 'Annual Business Plans' to 'Performance Agreements', which in turn comprised such mysteries as 'Key Results Areas', 'Outputs', 'Objectives', 'Measures', 'Weights' and 'Indicators'.

'Dear heavens,' I thought to myself, 'for thirteen years I dutifully delivered more votes and seats and influence for the party I led and never once so much as filled in a single performance audit.' But when I thought about it a little further, I suppose that the South African electorate had been my external auditor in politics and the party congresses that elected me had been the internal one. But government bureaucracy was clearly made of far more formal or exact stuff than this. At the very least, it had clearly been captured and imprisoned by an army of, doubtless well-paid, management consultants.

The 'Culture of Performance', with its endless demand for forms, weights and measures, was to be a constant and irritating companion throughout my ambassadorship. Well into my term of office in Argentina, I would devote days to filling in, with minute particularity, my diplomatic comings and goings, from high-end meetings to lowly social engagements. Completing the 'Performance Appraisal' (which had to be submitted twice a year) was way beyond my technical capacity and aggravated by the extremely user-unfriendly format provided by the department.

Apparently, certain of my ambassadorial colleagues could not even fire up a computer. Quite how they complied with the 'Culture of Performance' was beyond imagining. My secret weapon in taming this part of the bureaucratic monster was dear Michal. She could actually use the Excel spreadsheet even though the program caused lines of details to simply evaporate shortly after being typed. On one occasion, having spent an entire day at the residence with Michal filling in the form, the document seemed to disappear into cyberspace. The next day, at the embassy, my corporate service manager, André Lizamore, then had to painstakingly recover it. Doubtless, no one actually read the appraisal once it had been submitted. After two and a half years of form-filling, I had not received a single line of feedback.

It was around the time of one or another audit that I chanced upon an epiphany that so exactly explained my view of these endless processes and their relevance for the world of international diplomacy.

The enterprising, amusing British journalist and one-time junior diplomat and former MP, Matthew Parris, co-edited a volume of valedictory dispatches from HM Diplomatic Service. These 'final telegrams', where British ambassadors unburdened themselves with acidic 'home thoughts from abroad', were highly entertaining and painfully accurate. One, in particular, caught my eye and seemed to apply, with interest, to South Africa's DIRCO and the excrescences of the management age to which it was enthralled. On his final dispatch as ambassador to Rome, Sir Ivor Roberts wrote:

> Can it be that in wading through the plethora of business plans, capability reviews, skill audits, zero based reviews and other items of the management age, we have indeed forgotten what diplomacy is all about? … Well conducted diplomacy cannot properly be measured because diplomatic successes are more often than not elusive or ephemeral. The diplomat is condemned to a Sisyphean task in which as he attempts to grapple with one conflict, another one breaks out.[6]

The marvellous Sir Ivor, soon enough to become a hero in our household, dismissed the entire vocabulary and piffle of the so-called 'culture of change management' – with its reliance on 'benchmarking' and 'stakeholder empowerment' – as 'the game of bullshit Bingo'.[7]

CHAPTER 6

# MY BATTLE WITH SPANISH

In the middle of my diplomatic crash course in Pretoria, one of my ambassadorial friends, Jan Mutton, of Belgium, hosted a small dinner in my honour at his residence to which he invited several other heads of foreign missions. In full learning and absorption mode at that stage, I was eager to feast from this table of experts and professionals. During the course of the evening and in proposing a toast, Jan said that I should 'throw away all the training manuals'. Instead, he advised, I should pursue only one task: 'Learn the Spanish language.'

This necessary, not altogether welcome, advice, might well have chimed with reality. But it clashed with inner knowledge. I am a linguistic dud, tone deaf to foreign idiom and dialect. Less excusable back then was the fact that I suffered from the culturally imperialistic – and entirely wrong – assumption that the world spoke English.

There had been only one exception to my Anglo-centric ways, but this was far more localised and driven by political necessity. I had conquered the Afrikaans language. But even here the results were idiosyncratic.

'*Hy praat 'n baie sjarmante Afrikaans, maar met 'n Sandton-aksent*' (He speaks a very charming Afrikaans, but with a Sandton accent), one of my political supporters in the only-Afrikaans-spoken-here province of the Northern Cape once declared. When I entered parliament in 1989, notwithstanding matriculating in the language, followed by eighteen months in the overwhelmingly Afrikaans-speaking South African Defence Force, I could barely utter a word of *die taal* (the language). At that stage, with the National Party and Conservative Party dominating the parliamentary discourse, English was very much a second language. Thus, my understanding of Afrikaans rapidly improved even if my accent did not.

With the advent of democracy in 1994, Afrikaans, along with the political forces that championed it, was relegated to secondary status. To some ANC hardliners it was seen as the language of the oppressor.

The results of the downgrading of Afrikaans became quickly apparent and were often absurd. In the overwhelmingly Afrikaans-speaking Western Cape rural areas, for example, the police were obliged to conduct all their business in English, even though the policemen and the victims of crime and the criminals themselves mostly only spoke Afrikaans.

I became the, perhaps unlikely, champion of Afrikaans. This entirely liberal cause – supporting the underdog – also coincided with the rising support for my party among Afrikaans-speaking South Africans, white and brown. By listening every morning to *Radio Sonder Grense* and diligently reading *Die Burger*, I landed up speaking a passable, if flawed, Afrikaans.

Spanish was a horse and language of a very different colour and complexity. At the same diplomatic dinner, the Australian high commissioner advised that prior to their assumption of posts in a South American country, their diplomats were sent for months-long immersion courses *in situ,* in the case of Argentina, to the pleasant winelands of Mendoza. Only after intensive training and the attainment of reasonable fluency were their diplomats able to assume office.

South Africa's diplomatic suits were cut from far more modest cloth. Despite declarations on the importance of mastering foreign languages routinely uttered by DIRCO directors general, I discovered that my three immediate predecessors in Buenos Aires spoke no Spanish. An inspection of the budget of my new embassy revealed an extremely modest amount for language training (which future budgets would reduce even further). Perhaps the most essential guest at Jan's table that night, Argentine ambassador to South Africa, Carlos Sersale, cautioned: 'Without understanding Spanish you will never fully enter Argentine society.'

How then to square this circle – to learn an entirely new language in my fifties without the skill set to do so? In addition, I was, at that stage, frankly, overwhelmed by everything else I was trying to master in Pretoria. Aside from schoolboy Latin, I also had no linguistic hinterland to assist.

Salvation, to a very limited extent, arrived early every morning in Pretoria when the charming Cecilia Iturralde, herself from South America, presented herself for an hour's daily instruction. It all proved an uphill struggle. She was trying to explain to me the essence of the two forms of the verb 'to be' in Spanish (*estar* and *ser*); I meantime was battling to learn to count to ten, never mind trying to memorise the seven conjugations of the very few verbs I could actually remember.

I was told that learning a new language is a great bet against the onset of senility. It apparently keeps you mentally agile. My early morning encounters with Spanish convinced me that I might be suffering from a form of premature dementia. From transitive verbs to gender determinations and possessive adjectives, I suddenly realised that having established a reputation for being extremely articulate in English (I hope deserved), I actually had very little idea of the formalities of grammatical and linguistic structure – in any language. But my ability to speak and write English was so strong that I did not really need to understand the underlying rules. This was one of the many mental barriers that blocked forward progress in the language of Cervantes.

Another fact that became quickly apparent was the sprawling nature of the Spanish language itself. The simple article 'the' in English has no fewer than four possibilities in Spanish: *el*, *la*, *los* and *las* (singular masculine and feminine and plural masculine and feminine, respectively). Thus, when you read about Fidel Castro (in his heyday) hectoring the crowds with five-hour speeches from the balcony, it was not just a question of his verbal incontinence, but was also, in part, a reflection of the language of expression he used.

The other feature about Spanish that proved to be my undoing in later months when I ventured forth to torture the language in public, is that, due to my linguistic tone deafness, key words sounded just about the same to me. This proved to be particularly calamitous in one of the most high-profile events I ever addressed in Argentina.

On a balmy summer evening, in late 2010, the embassy, under my baton, had gathered 250 top Argentine guests aboard the visiting South African Navy supply ship *Drakensberg*. Adding to the glitter of the event was the performance by two young South African operatic stars, Pretty Yende and Given Nkosi.

All I had to do was provide some words of welcome. Dangerously, I abandoned my written text for one minute in order to attempt a freestyle greeting. I began, in Spanish: 'Good evening and welcome, ladies and horses.'

There was collective guffaw from the audience and I quickly realised that I had substituted the word *caballos* (horses) for the word *caballeros* (gentlemen). It will be apparent why I only continued limply with Spanish lessons for some months after arrival in Buenos Aires, until both my enthusiasm and the budget for them dried up almost in equal measure at more or less the same time.

However, due to my determination to represent South Africa with a quasi-Spanish voice, I ensured that at least part of every public address was delivered in Spanish. After my *Drakensberg* experience I used to spend many hours practising with my interpreter and using phonetic spelling whenever necessary. Even after all these checks and balances, whenever I switched my speech from Spanish to English a sort of gasp would emerge from my audience, presumably because they now realised I could actually speak at least one language properly.

CHAPTER 7

# SECRETS OF THE GUILD

Besides the various linguistic gymnastics and bureaucratic chaff, I was still waiting to discover what the real substance of my diplomatic assignment would be.

My visit to my Regional Desk (or Business Unit, in management-speak) provided some, but by no means all, answers. The director of the Mercosur–Brazil unit in which my three countries fell was Bob Cloete. He was on his way out to early retirement and was an interesting amalgam of high intelligence, severe under-promotion and world-weary cynicism. His view of some ambassadors, current and past, was breathtakingly frank.

'Many of your soon-to-be colleagues are very short,' he mysteriously declared.

'Really, how so?' I enquired.

Bob responded: 'Because no man is as short as he who stands on his dignity.'

I inferred that many members of the club I had just joined were preoccupied with issues of status and protocol. They often preferred, on this version, the dubious pleasures of attending cocktail receptions and comporting themselves in their chauffeur-driven cars, to the heavy lifting required of growing the trade flows or penning acute analysis. Soon enough, other officials retold to me – behind hidden hand – dark tales of various ambassadors tyrannising their staff (or worse); and even, in one extreme case, selling off the office furniture and equipment for personal profit.

How then would I make a real, qualitative difference as ambassador to Argentina? Here, Bob advised: 'If you are going to declare war, just ensure that you do it in the third person.' This jocular refrain was another reference to the mystifying power of form over substance. Diplomatic etiquette was to be rigidly observed in all communications and at all times – especially in the misleadingly named 'Note Verbale' (which is, in fact, a written communication from embassy to foreign ministry and vice versa). To further complicate communication in 2012 South Africa, diplomatic phraseology was still in French.

It was all a little Greek to me, however. But I was cautioned that no matter how unpleasant the message being delivered, or fundamental the objection being conveyed, each communication under my signature should commence thus: 'The South African Embassy in Buenos Aires presents its most respectful compliments to the Ministry of Foreign Relations, International Trade and Worship [note this is an even bigger mouthful than DIRCO spelled out] and has the pleasure of referring to ...'

The content that follows could then be, apparently, as disobliging as necessary, provided the communication always ended with: 'The South African Embassy in Buenos Aires would like to take this opportunity to renew to the Ministry of Foreign Relations, International Trade and Worship, the assurance of its highest consideration.'

Hypocrisy was not only the Vaseline that greased the wheels of local politics (to borrow the marvellous phrase of Pieter-Dirk Uys); it was, apparently, an international art form.

My brief initiation into the form, flourishes and rituals of my new domain was followed by a more intensive briefing on the status and nature of the bilateral relationships I would soon be supervising from the Southern Cone of South America.

Argentina was in every respect – size, influence, economic heft and South Africa's priorities – the second country of South America. Brazil held the ring as regional supremo and its hugely successful and relatively recent economic renaissance had produced a 2.5 trillion dollar economy. Its international standing was at its apogee: it was, after all, the B of BRICS – the Goldman Sachs acronym for the leading emerging powers of the world (the rest are Russia, India and China, and latterly South Africa). In all respects, Argentina lagged behind although it was very much ahead of most of its other neighbours. I was soon to discover that this irritated the Argentines mightily. A factor in aggravation was no doubt the distant memory that in 1910 its economy had been four times larger than Brazil's and today it was only a quarter of the economic size of the latter. But then again, that early twentieth century was the heyday of Argentina's global influence, when the phrase 'as rich as an Argentine' echoed across the salons of Europe.

Argentina's second-fiddle status to the Brazil behemoth meant that its economy and South Africa's were roughly of equivalent size (in the middle table of the world at around 300 billion dollars in 2009) and their populations were also in the same range (40–50 million people). While diplomatic links were sound – buttressed by a so-called 'Bi-National Commission at Ministerial Level' – there were clear imbalances in the relationship, especially on the trade ledger. In 2009, South Africa exported some half a billion rand worth of goods, mostly coal and other mineral products, to Argentina. But we imported approximately ten times that amount from Argentina, mostly agri-products.

The ambassador's job, so the desk suggested, would be to reverse – or at the very least improve – these numbers. I would doubtless learn, on arrival, what my predecessors had or had not done to turn matters around.

The other countries in my new remit were much smaller fry. Although Uruguay and Paraguay stood alongside Brazil and Argentina in a common free trade area (Mercosur), they had little of the weight of their giant neighbours.

Uruguay, which was prized for its economic and democratic stability, somewhat extravagantly dubbed itself 'the Switzerland of South America'. The only resemblance I could readily observe was its small population (only 3.5 million people). Its GDP was less than one-tenth of Argentina's. But what caught my eye in the briefing document was this tiny country's outsize contribution to peace-keeping in the world, especially in Africa, where at the time it had stationed more than 1 300 peace-keeping troops in the conflict-ridden Democratic Republic of Congo. There was also,

I remembered from a few Christmases before, a very upmarket beach resort on its coast, named Punta del Este. It had impressed me on my previous visit as a sort of Plettenberg Bay on steroids. I looked forward to more intimate acquaintance with it – the phrase 'working holiday' for some reason entered my mind.

Very much third in the line-up was Paraguay. Although twice the population size of Uruguay, it is one of South America's poorest states. It had endured a tragic and violent history, and during my readings of this landlocked country, I came across the extraordinary and to me, at least, unknown fact that it had lost two thirds of its male population during the war it commenced against its far bigger neighbours, Brazil, Argentina and Uruguay, in 1865. The literature aptly described the five-year War of the Triple Alliance as among the most devastating military defeats ever inflicted upon a nation state in recent history. At the time of my departure for Buenos Aires, it had a GDP touching just 9 billion dollars. Its terms of trade with South Africa were equally modest, providing a destination to just 0.01 per cent of our global exports, of which, I noted with some interest, the Amarula liqueur was one of the biggest items.

But in some ways, this landlocked republic was, for me, the most intriguing corner of my new domain. During my early political awakening, way back in 1974, I well remembered the visit to South Africa of Paraguay's strongman dictator and president general, Alfredo Stroessner.

Prime Minister John Vorster rolled out the red carpet and 21-gun salutes for this archetypal caudillo (strongman). He lived up, or down, to expectation with his braided powder-blue military uniform and his chest full of medals. However, the opposition-supporting Johannesburg *Sunday Times* rained on his parade. It revealed that Pretoria's new, best (and arguably back then, only) international friend had opened his country to fugitive Nazis, the most infamous of whom was Josef Mengele (the 'Angel of Death' of Auschwitz). As a bonus, the *Sunday Times* also informed its readers that Stroessner was suspected, by US authorities, of drug running.

His extraordinary political longevity was to last for 35 years until a coup ousted him in 1989. However, during his presidency, South Africa had apparently one of the largest chanceries in the capital Asunción.

I gathered from my discussions – and subsequent on-the-ground accounts – that our embassy back then essentially provided cover for a major South African Defence Force and Military Intelligence presence. It was rumoured that Paraguay was the way station for the laundering of, primarily Israeli, arms and weapon systems destined for the apartheid regime.

However, Stroessner's demise and the emergence of democracy in both Paraguay and South Africa had led to a steep decline in our diplomatic presence there. The South African Embassy had been closed and operations were now run by remote control from Buenos Aires, with energetic assistance from an honorary consul.

An interesting footnote also came to my attention. Apparently, a previous Paraguayan diplomat in Pretoria had been sent packing after his embassy was involved in a stolen car racket. This unorthodox diplomatic practice was not entirely without precedent. When Stroessner died in exile in Brazil at the age of 93 in 2006, the *New York Times* quoted the reminiscence of a former US ambassador, Robert E. White. He recalled that in his time, the Paraguayan ambassador to Buenos Aires had gambled away his embassy's entire budget! Immediately, the wayward ambassador was summoned to Asunción and handed a confession to sign. 'Then,' according to Ambassador White, 'President Stroessner promoted him to Foreign Minister. He could never have an independent thought or deed after that.'[8]

CHAPTER 8

# GETTING MY INSTRUCTIONS

In 1997, the chief of staff of British Prime Minister Tony Blair allegedly instructed Christopher Meyer, the new British ambassador to Washington, thus: 'We want you to get up the arse of the White House and to stay there.'[9]

My eve-of-departure instructions, such as they were, proved to be neither as dramatic nor as crude. But the personal encounters and atmospherics around them were quite revealing.

First up, towards the end of my training, was the Head of Missions Conference. This was a biennial two-day talk marathon at the Sandton Sun in which all 110-plus ambassadors and consul generals were gathered in the presence of the president, foreign minister and assorted cabinet bigwigs to discuss the state of the world and South Africa's role in it. That was, at least, its ostensible purpose.

My initial eager attention quickly trailed off as one after another of my new colleagues used the endless sessions either to grandstand or to complain, often bitterly, about budget cuts, protocol slights and sundry other ailments of life abroad in the service of the state. My mountain of note taking could be distilled down to two essential and useful points, both from Director General Ayanda Ntsaluba:

1. Budget cuts imposed by the onset of global recession meant that missions aboard would have to 'do more with less'; and
2. The 2010 FIFA World Cup would be front and centre of our public diplomacy.

The first item was not exactly welcome news: during my hard years in building up the Democratic Party and Democratic Alliance I became the bane of every person of wealth I ever encountered. In my self-described role as the 'debt collector of the opposition', I was a ferocious and effective fund-raiser. But I regarded the entire exercise as the 'chemotherapy of politics'. Now it would appear that I would be the chief fund-raiser of sponsorships for my new mission if it was to undertake any public activities of consequence or size.

The World Cup offered more welcome possibilities. It appeared likely (and subsequently proved) that I would hit the trifecta with all three of 'my countries' qualifying for the finals.

The gathering of South Africa's diplomatic good and great (and the bad and the ugly, come to think of it) also afforded me a chance to meet my predecessor in Buenos Aires, Peter Goosen. He had been transferred some months before to The Hague. He suggested, rather unnervingly to me, that by the time I landed in Buenos Aires at the end of September, the embassy would have been bereft of an ambassador for six months and would be 'in dire need of leadership'.

Peter was clearly part of a shrinking, possibly dying, breed: the white South African ambassador. I noticed, when all heads of mission were gathered in the hotel ballroom for the obligatory photograph with President Zuma, that only about ten of us were white – and of this small band, my party colleagues and I comprised nearly half the number.

The conference also offered a chance to catch up with Douglas Gibson (Bangkok), Sheila Camerer (Sofia) and Sandra Botha (Prague). Their immersion in foreign climes had not led to any basic change in the personalities I remembered: Douglas was relentlessly cheerful; Sandra was intelligently equivocal about her new role; and Sheila was flashing her steely determination to obtain redress from the bureaucracy afflicting her start-up mission.

Douglas, ever the shrewd observer of political power plays, commented that our new political boss, Minister Maite Nkoana-Mashabane was 'bossy but bright'. This was a useful insight as I was to encounter her a few days hence, when Zola Skweyiya, Ngconde Balfour and I were to attend a 'standing courtesy meeting accorded by the Minister before Heads of Mission-designates depart for their postings', to quote the full splendid bureaucratese that accompanied the invitation to her office.

I had only the vaguest knowledge about this relatively young – at 47 – woman whom Zuma had recently appointed as his foreign minister. Her predecessor, Dr Nkosazana Dlamini-Zuma, I knew almost too well from our frequent clashes in parliament. But I had no history with the new appointee. She had spent ten years abroad as an ambassador, first in Malaysia and then in India. By all accounts, she had performed well. It was her late husband, Norman, also an ambassador (to Indonesia), who had attracted media heat and political notoriety. The Department of Foreign Affairs, which by a curious twist his widow now headed, had found him guilty of no fewer than 22 charges of sexual harassment against an embassy staff member.

These events became even more controversial because of the sequence they followed. In 2001, after the victim, diplomat Lara Swart, laid departmental charges against Mashabane, a disciplinary board found him guilty. The director general confirmed the finding. Then, for unexplained reasons and despite her apparent feminist credentials, Minister Dlamini-Zuma overturned his conviction. Perhaps it was a case of political blood (the Mashabanes were part of a powerful ANC faction in Limpopo) overcoming ideological scruple. However, Ms Swart was made of stern stuff. She pursued Mashabane and the department through the courts and, finally, in 2006 the Gauteng High Court upheld the charges, obliged Mashabane to apologise and sent Swart's legal bill of several hundred thousand rand to the department to settle.

The Democratic Alliance, which I then led in parliament, had been at the forefront of demanding an explanation from the silent minister on her bias towards the sex offender. Mashabane died subsequently in a motor accident in Limpopo. Now I was to receive my instructions from his widow.

I had always found Nkosazana Dlamini-Zuma somewhat haughty and arrogant (she apparently thought well of me, too). Yet, at our initial meeting, her successor could hardly have been more different. She embraced me with a hug and I was struck by her open-faced good looks, ample proportions and refreshing candour.

When I suggested to her that our very brief training seemed scant preparation to take over the reins of our embassies, she waved away my hesitations: 'You three – Zola, Ngconde, Tony – have such vast political experience that you don't need any instruction, except to learn the administrative essentials.'

She was also very candid about the bureaucratic beast in whose folds we were now enveloped. Speaking with the authority of a previous ambassador, she confided: 'Sometimes out there you have to act and to do things. The Foreign Service Code [a huge tome that prescribed all matters under the departmental sun] might in fact be obstructive, as can be your Corporate Service Manager. Sometimes, you will just have to follow your instinct, do the right thing and just sort out the details later.'

Her final piece of advice appeared to be most sincere. 'If you ever need to send me a message or give advice, do give me a call or send me an SMS,' she said. When I was later to take up this invitation I would discover – as I will relate – that certain messages would not, in fact, be welcomed. But all that lay in the future.

Now, what remained was to return to Cape Town, pack up the house, the pets and the children. Buenos Aires – and a new life – beckoned.

As I stood amidst the overflowing cases on the day of our departure, I still had only a vague idea of how I would make a real difference in this, my fourth, career. But as we fiddled with last-minute arrangements, there was one Spanish proverb I did actually remember, in translated form at least: 'Traveller, there are no roads. Roads are made by walking.'

CHAPTER 9

# THE CALL OF THE PAMPAS

On the eve of our departure, a friend had thrust into my hands a book entitled *Bad Times in Buenos Aires*. The gesture was doubtless sincere, even if the title and contents were far from reassuring. On the seemingly endless flight over the vastness of the South Atlantic, I was disconcerted to read in it a description of Buenos Aires, the place that would be my home for the next several years, as 'a city stuck at the end of the world'.[10] The fact that the expatriate author was quoting the opinion of one of its residents was even more discomfiting. If indeed 'geography was destiny', then perhaps I was heading to a severely terminal destination.

Some nine hours after departing from Cape Town, the ageing Boeing 747 of Malaysian Airlines was finally overhead the huge waters of the Rio de la Plata, the muddy estuary that links Buenos Aires to thc sea. The vast pampas – the 'heartland of Argentina' and the fertile expanse of open grassland that provides cereals and beef to the world and is the backbone of my new country's (often squandered) wealth – also lay in sight.

The announcement that we were to land shortly at Ezeiza International Airport – Buenos Aires' air portal to the world – found me again rehearsing my lines for the reception party that I knew awaited me at the foot of the air bridge. My late grandmother, Ray, ever the stickler on correct etiquette, had drummed into my brother and me the imperative 'always make a good first impression – that's the one that lasts the longest'. Good manners suggested that the newly minted South African ambassador should utter his first banal words in Spanish.

*'Buenas Tardes. Soy Tony Leon, el Nuevo Embajador de Sudáfrica en L'Argentina. Encantado de Conocerte.'* (Good afternoon. I am Tony Leon, the new South African ambassador to Argentina. Delighted to meet you.)

I rather thought this line would set the right tone with the officials of the Argentine foreign ministry waiting to receive me. But just before the plane landed and I could wow the locals, I faced a far more basic problem: where were my socks? Michal and I searched the immediate area of our seats and the overhead compartment above and they were nowhere to be found. Panic! It just would not do to arrive off the plane in suit and shoes, sans hose. First impressions were now imperilled. As the plane taxied towards the terminal, our ever-frenzied sock-search party had yielded no results. There was no alternative. I would have to comport myself in the slightly vomit-yellow airline pair I had worn during the flight. Not exactly a complement to my dark suit and, far worse, a bad initial augury, my superstitious mind suggested.

I managed a sort of low trouser shuffle off the plane to disguise my footwear problem, and was disconcerted when Ariel Fernandez of the Argentine foreign ministry greeted me in flawless English and nattered away in my mother tongue, rendering my careful Spanish rehearsal redundant. Also on hand was a line-up of my senior embassy colleagues. From the outset, I was very mindful that they would be crucial in assisting, or retarding, my transformation from politician to diplomat.

On the subject of transformations, South Africa, at that stage, was undergoing its own makeover as forthcoming host of football's grand global event, the 2010 FIFA World Cup. Its imminence would see our major airports converted into futuristic palaces for aviation and consumerism. As we walked, or rather were whisked through (via the fast tracking provided to diplomats), I could not help but observe that Argentina's own hosting of this event in 1978 had left little mark today on its premier airport. Ezeiza (named after the provincial Buenos Aires suburb in which it is sited) had a distinctly third world feel to it. The cramped facilities and overstretched queues spilling out of the elderly terminal building were in marked contrast to the rather more modern and grander surrounds of the Cape Town airport we had recently departed from. Another portent of what I had left behind, I wondered?

But if not in line to win an award for its aesthetics, then my recent and intense reading of Argentine history suggested that Ezeiza had witnessed an event in June 1973 of such turbulence and violence that its name had become a synonym for a historic epoch: the return of former and future President Juan Domingo Peron to Argentina, after eighteen years of exile in Spain. Peron – the archetypal Argentine caudillo strictly speaking had not touched down at the airport that day. His triumphal homecoming, attended by an estimated and incredible 3 million people (about 20 per cent of the country back then) was marred and bloodied by a massacre at the airport when gun battles broke out between his left- and right-wing supporters, leaving an estimated 13 people dead, and 37 severely wounded. Peron wisely flew on to the safety of the nearby Moron air force base. But the 'Ezeiza massacre' became a portent for the chaos of the ageing politician's brief second presidency – he was dead within a year – and the baleful military repression that followed the coup against his presidential successor and third wife, Isabel, some three years later.

As my new chauffeur (a novel experience for me, but decidedly not for him – I was his twelfth ambassador!), the gallant Jorge Giordano expertly navigated the choked highway, where the marked lanes appeared to be utterly irrelevant to the drivers, I thought back to the parting shot of the Argentine ambassador to South Africa, Carlos Sersale. He advised: 'If you want to understand Argentina you must view it through the lens of Peronism.' He then thoughtfully added, 'And when you find out what it means, please let me know!'

As we crawled through the 45 kilometres or so separating the airport from the city, I thought about Peron and his second wife Evita. Their long political shadow still formed and dominated their country's landscape. I also did something that the guide to 'culture shock', or rather how to overcome it, had explicitly warned against: refracting your new country through the prism and personalities of the old one. It was somehow irresistible, though, to compare Nelson Mandela's release from prison, on 11 February 1990, which I had witnessed at the Grand Parade in Cape Town and Peron's return (or non-return) to the airport from which I had just departed, a generation or so before then. The comparison was not flattering for Argentina.

In 1990, early in my first parliamentary session, I had been pretty shaken that Sunday by the rioting and drunkenness outside the Cape Town City Hall as the vast crowd (by the standards of South Africa) pushed and surged and grew impatient for the endlessly delayed arrival of the country's, and the world's, most famous political prisoner. He was nearly seven hours late. And while indeed violence was to be the constant and baleful companion of South Africa's messy transition to democracy in the years that followed, I now realised that Peron's arrival home was both far more chaotic and much bloodier. In this difference of arrival lay a far profounder truth: the return of Peron (along with the embalmed corpse of his second wife and the live presence of his third wife all in the same plane – a very Argentine event) continued and amplified the ungovernability his return was intended to arrest. Mandela's release, in contrast, ushered in a genuine constitutional transfer of power within four years.

## THE SHOCK OF THE NEW

I had little time, initially, to absorb and ponder these historic truths and comparisons. *¡Hola Buenos Aires,* a useful guide for newly arrived expatriates published by the Argentina University Women's Club of the city, informed its readers that the 'severity of cultural shock varies greatly from person to person'.[11] It helpfully added that this phenomenon is the 'normal and inevitable response to a change from one culture to another, the severity in disorientation depending on the extent of the culture gap involved'.

It quickly became apparent to me that the distance between my new home and the comfort zone of my old life was as vast, if not even bigger, as the approximate 7 000 kilometres of the South Atlantic that separated Buenos Aires and Cape Town.

My initial phase in both this teeming city of over 13 million people (including the greater metropolitan area) and in my new job, suggested I had contracted this 'disease' in extreme form. I found everything utterly bewildering. I was now the commander of the 27-person South African Embassy, with an annual budget of around 20 million rand. But in truth I had only the vaguest idea of what was expected of me, no real background training, and hitherto, my greatest strength, fluency of communication, was rendered both moot and mute by the predominance of Spanish – and the almost total absence of English – in the daily life of Buenos Aires. That was the first shock: notwithstanding its cosmopolitan nature and its European pretensions, the residents of the city were in many ways inwardly focused and the default position after Spanish was, in reality, more Spanish.

Using a cellphone or an ATM became daily and, initially, dreaded ordeals: listening to voice mail, for example, led to a rapid-fire Spanish message being delivered at what sounded like 100 miles an hour. I had to listen about five times before finally cottoning on that I needed to press the number '1' and then hope that I had not deleted the software when I continued. This then led to more rapid-fire Spanish, and just occasionally, to start with, did I actually hear a welcome, and often distant, message from back home in warmly welcomed English.

The telephone exchange system itself was another mystery. Argentina had benefited from the privatisation and modernisation of its telecommunication system under the presidency of Carlos Saul Menem in the 1990s, whose zeal for free markets reform were undermined by a form of cronyism and corruption that made the ANC seem like Boy Scouts in comparison. But while the ten-year Soviet-style waiting time for a telephone, which was apparently not uncommon before Menem, had thankfully disappeared by the time of our arrival, some lingering antiquities of the old order remained. The most frustrating, and complicating, of these was the fact that cellphone prefixes changed depending where you were! Thus, from within the city of Buenos Aires, all cell numbers commenced with the digits 15; the moment you left the capital and headed into the countryside the 15 code no longer applied and had to be substituted with 011; and then again, from overseas a further and different configuration (911) was needed. It became apparent that life here would be, in the phrase of my rapidly fading Afrikaans, '*iets anders*' (something different).

## THE TYRANNY OF TIME ... AND FOOD

The second and most elemental change was in both the fixed hours of my new life and the South American pace and pulse of work and leisure. South Africa, or my working environment there, had increasingly adopted the more puritanical elements of the modern Anglo-American office routine: early opening hours, late departures and lunch either as a quick pit stop for calorie replacement or, even when more leisurely, never (at least until Friday) accompanied by anything more alcoholic than a Diet Coke. The legendary 'three martini' lunch of American yore was now confined to the TV series *Mad Men* to which Michal and I became devotees. It described an America, or South Africa, of the 1960s with booze and cigarette-fuelled 'working' lunch parties that stretched on through most afternoons. I was to learn soon enough that, like much else besides, Argentina was in something of a time warp.

Over time, I would acquire the skills of social navigation that would allow me, without giving too much offence, to leave a Buenos Aires lunch table at around 2.30 p.m., having declined the vino and mumbling an excuse as my hosts and the other guests prepared to settle into an afternoon of companionable quaffing, where no doubt some business was also contracted.

But time itself was a distinctly elastic concept over here, something that grated on my extreme sense of punctuality. 'When you get invited to a function at 8 p.m., that is the time you should leave your residence.' was the wise parting advice I received from an old Argentine hand at head office. 'Anyone who complains about "African Time" has obviously never lived in Latin America,' I complained to Michal as we found our on-time arrival at an event often preceding by some minutes the appearance of the hosting couple; the other guests drifting in up to an hour after the commencement time. I would soon rectify the errors of my earlier, punctual ways.

Harvard professor of economics, David Landes, in his impressive analysis of the global economy, *The Wealth and Poverty of Nations*, described the world as divided roughly into three kinds of nations: 'those that spend lots of money to keep their weight down; those whose people eat to live; and those that don't know where the next meal is coming from.'[12]

My early observation of my new abode was that Argentines managed to fall into the first two categories simultaneously and paradoxically, while generous social handouts and massive government intervention in domestic food pricing kept hunger levels to a minimum. In the up-market suburb of Palermo where our new home, the 'Official Residence', was located, I counted no fewer than a dozen restaurants within four blocks and the equivalent number of cafés or *confiterías*. The paradox lay in the fact that impossibly thin young women (and a few men) could be observed at all hours chewing on the sickly sweet *dulce de leche* (caramel à la Argentina) or wolfing down the home town favourite chocolate-dipped triple-layered biscuit known as the *alfajor*. How was this happy combination of high calories and low weight achieved? At the end of my stay, three years later, I guessed that the evident – in every park or public square – mania for physical culture perhaps provided the balance. More darkly, a new local friend drew my attention to the high prevalence of eating disorders that kept thousands of psychotherapists in gainful employment: Buenos Aires boasted more therapists per capita than any other place in the world.

It also did not require much research to establish that the city was not the best place to be a vegetarian. And for a Durban-born boy who had acquired an early and enduring fondness for curry, Buenos Aires was not the venue to find too many outlets for spicy cooking; but there was no shortage of beef. Indeed, the restaurant guide *Guia Oleo* proudly informed that Buenos Aires housed no fewer than 807 steak houses (or *parillas*) and each Argentine, on average, ate some 60 kilograms of beef a year, somewhat down from the record total of 71 kilograms per person recorded in 2007. Perhaps there was a link between all this red meat consumption and the fact that it was Argentine surgeons who had pioneered the first coronary bypass surgery procedures in the world some decades before.

I was also to observe, soon enough, that the glamour of the tony suburbs had its counterpoint in the vast *villas miserias* (literally 'houses of misery') or shanty dwellings and bleak, towering tenement blocks where many *porteños* lived in conditions of relative squalor. Their subsidy-collecting, track-suited residents with bulging waistlines were a study in contrast to the ultra-rich, ultra-thin glamour models, or wannabes, who populated our neighbourhood. Just like South Africa, I mused, the super elite (which globally began, around this time, to be known as 'the 1 per cent') live only a few kilometres from a sprawling underclass. But, in reality, they inhabited a different universe. I quickly observed a big difference between planet Argentina and the South African world I had just left.

Over here, just about everyone from the tycoon to the bus driver was white. Quite how Argentina became the most 'European' country of South America will be explored anon. However, I noted, perhaps appropriately for a white ambassador representing South Africa, that this southern tip of the Americas was a pretty good place to arrest any racial stereotyping that suggested, for example, that 'black' or 'African' was a synonym for 'third world'. Here, in Argentina, with its decaying and often non-existent infrastructure, its recent epoch of state terror and history of extreme violence was modern proof that underdevelopment could indeed have a pale face.

Meditations on comparative history gave way to more immediate and physically weighty matters: this related to another time shock – the tyranny of the late-night dinner. Like Argentina's imported population, this apparently had its origins in southern Europe. But whatever its provenance, Argentines had, by our doubtless parochial standards, the extraordinary and exhausting practice of sitting down to dinner any time between 10 and 11 p.m.! As we began wining and dining for South Africa, I found it challenging to stay animated and conversational when my normal bedtime was usually around the time when the first course was cleared.

A further factor in aggravation was at play here. Most Argentine enterprises, not least the foreign ministry that was my most immediate point of local contact, opened their doors at around 10 a.m. No such compensation was possible for the South African Embassy in Buenos Aires. Our need to communicate with Pretoria, five hours ahead in time, necessitated an opening hour of about 8.15 a.m. and often meant bleary-eyed mornings as the fog of late evenings enveloped my mental space the following day.

Michal and I offset the time factor wherever we could by setting home dinners, to the amazement of the local staff, for a very un-Argentine time of 7.30 p.m. When we dined out we chose to book restaurants at around 8 p.m. This meant we usually dined alone or, at best, in the presence of a few American tourists.

Quite what such strange and long hours of wining and dining meant for local productivity was an interesting question, which after three years of residence I never fully resolved. Perhaps my friend Ferdinand, who ran a high-flying financial enterprise here, was correct when he said, 'Most Argentines arrive at work very tired, and it often shows in their output!'

CHAPTER 10

# A RESIDENCE IS NOT QUITE A HOME

'Of the many sins of the apartheid government, we should credit them, at least, with the ability to buy good real estate.' Such was the thought I noted down when we entered the 'Official Residence' for the first time. Our new home was a triplex penthouse atop one of Buenos Aires's towering and smarter condominiums. It had been purchased at the time of Peron's return back in 1973 and doubtless constituted a capital gain of note, given the rise in home values since economic prosperity returned to Argentina in the 1990s.

Our new residence probably concluded, alongside language and time, the triad of initial jolts. We had hardly lived badly in South Africa. But even by the standards of our roomy and leafy home in Newlands, Cape Town, the Buenos Aires apartment was on an altogether bigger and grander scale. This was also to be – after some twenty-plus years of public service – my first, and certainly only, experience of state-subsidised living. Given that the doubtless unsuspecting taxpayers of South Africa provided every diplomat abroad with free housing, a foreign service allowance (in addition to salary) and in the case of ambassadors, two full-time, live-in domestics, it became apparent why many found such a feather-bedded life abroad so appealing.

Initially, I was overawed by the sheer proportions and features of our new abode: downstairs, on the first level, were the reception and public areas – which included a chandeliered dining room with a capacious mahogany table that could seat upwards of 30 guests; this led into an industrial-sized kitchen, replete with three refrigerators and four large ovens. A special, locked room housed, literally, the state silver and gold-rimmed dinner services. Two marble-floored lounges and a significant study completed the first floor.

Up either of two staircases and we arrived in the living quarters, consisting of an ample-sized master bedroom and vast dressing room, a small family eating area, a generously proportioned TV and recreation area, which in turn led onto a suite of four guest bedrooms. A sauna was thrown in for good measure; and only after a week or so did we discover a new bathroom off a side corridor, bringing the total number to eight! It did not end there either: the family floor opened onto a large balcony, complete with barbecue facilities. Then above it was the grand finale: the swimming pool and solarium.

Perhaps the *pièce de résistance* of this grand pile were the sweeping views afforded from all three floors: we looked out straight ahead, over the eight lanes of Avenida Del Libertardor onto the grandest park in the city, complete with a beautiful rose garden and artificial lake. Beyond it, in clear sight, was the domestic airport (plane-spotting was a cinch from the apartment), which in turn abutted the vast expanse of the River Plate. On a clear day you could see Uruguay, literally across the waters. To the north, directly over the road, was the major racecourse and across from it, the playing fields of the Campo Nacional de Polo where the Argentine Polo Association hosted the world's finest polo championship each December, the Argentine Open.

Our suburb, or *barrio,* also boasted the King Fahd Mosque, the largest Muslim shrine in Latin America, and numerous synagogues were dotted around it, where some of the city's 185 000 Jews worshipped (Buenos Aires ranks as the tenth-largest Jewish city in the world outside Israel) – two interesting instances of ecumenicalism in a country where 95 per cent of the population was Roman Catholic.

'Panoramic' hardly did justice to this visual feast. Even our most jaded Argentine guests would in future marvel that the outlook constituted 'the best view in Buenos Aires'.

But there were some obvious and yet-to-be discovered price tags attached to this apparently gilded life and lifestyle. The portraits of

President Zuma and Foreign Minister Mashabane that adorned our entrance hall were the first, and most obvious, of these. I was hardly going to remove them – indeed the official handbook decreed their prominent placement – but they served as a daily reminder that the former leader of the opposition was now enjoying an appointment courtesy of South Africa's head of state. I compensated for this obligatory portraiture by rather ostentatiously displaying in the lounge framed photographs of myself with such luminaries as His Holiness the XIV Dalai Lama, Helen Suzman and Mangosuthu Buthelezi, none of whom exactly featured on the approved iconography list of my new employers. But such minor acts of ideological rebellion yielded initially to more immediate and practical problems.

Our first night's rest was interrupted by a 'doom-de-doom-de-doom' clanging sound, which appeared to arise from somewhere in the ceiling or back wall. We discovered that the aesthetic advantage of living on the top floor of a high-rise was more than offset by the fact that somewhere in the nether regions of our apartment lay the head shaft of the elderly elevators of the building. There was – for at least the first two years of our residence – an almost nightly sleep interruption as one or another of our neighbours returned from a night's revelry and summoned the lift, which in turn lifted us from a deep slumber. Clearly, the noise suppression had deteriorated over the years, or else my predecessors in residence had been stone deaf.

We soon discovered that the first impression of the imposing nature of the residence was based, in part, on the optics or imprint created by its ubiquitous dark, wooden panelling. But living in the gloomy darkness created by it was fairly depressing. This then led us ineluctably to the chief drawback of our new arrangements and our landlord, effectively the government of South Africa. The rands that had purchased this fine abode 35 years before our occupancy had significantly reduced in overseas purchasing power. The grand facade of our residence was ill-matched by the assortment of furniture that populated its interiors. Much of it was the Argentine equivalent of the Geen and Richards ball-and-claw lounge suites beloved of my grandmother's era of haute bourgeois Johannesburg *circa* 1965. Stringent budget cutting was apparent in the over-tired and somewhat fading period pieces, which gave off the whiff of age without qualifying as antique.

The aesthetics of the interior decor was perhaps redolent of South Africa's political transition; it was an uneasy, sometimes jarring, amalgam of what might be termed 'Boere baroque' and 'African Renaissance': a brown wooden bar complete with ill-matched, beige leather stools, jutted out of one room, while garish Ndebele dolls and painted ostrich eggs adorned various mantelpieces. Given the rich and exciting offerings now available from South African artists, the residence walls displayed pictures and sketches of little distinction. 'Kitsch' was the one overall theme binding together the eras on display. I also noticed that every stick of furniture was adorned with a government barcode, probably a necessity given that one consul general, elsewhere in the world, had attempted to sell the state furniture for private profit.

We quickly dismantled the bar, sent a number of the pictures to storage and added in some of our own pieces from home (and the fine, borrowed paintings of Johannesburg artist Kevin Collins). On a limited budget we also recovered the most offensive piece, a bright pink couch, which had been left marooned, unmatched to any other piece around it, in the middle of one of the lounges.

The primary purpose of the residence was not, however, intended for the personal indulgences of the resident ambassador and his family. It was meant to showcase the country and provide an appropriate venue to entertain locals and visiting dignitaries. Whoever had chosen our apartment had obviously been impressed by its size and scale – the downstairs area could comfortably accommodate more than 150 standing guests. However, they had overlooked the rather material issue of conveying them: there were two very small (and, as indicated above, noisy) and slow elevators into which no more than five people apiece could be accommodated.

I worked out that it would take around two hours to get the guests upstairs for a large event; hence in a crucial aspect our quarters were unfit for purpose. I soon enough began to suffer from a form of 'residence envy' as I attended rather swish national day events at my diplomatic colleagues, who in their back gardens managed to fit upward of 300 guests, while we had to hire an infinitely more expensive and blander hotel for the same purpose.

Even smaller events could be a challenge. My corporate services manager cheerily recounted the saga of the Springbok rugby team visit some four years before my arrival. The weight of mighty Kobus Wiese, plus a few other front-row forwards, had squeezed into one of the elevators, which had promptly broken under their combined weight. An equally hefty bill for its repair had been sent to the embassy for settlement! Finally, there was the no small matter of nature and its calls: for all the fact that we now inhabited a home of endless bathrooms, only one of them was located in the downstairs entertainment area. This meant that beyond twenty or so guests, the 'loo queue' would be endless. At the outset of my mission I was, however, more interested in plumbing the depths, or at least the surface, of my new environment than over-concerning myself with the plumbing of our residence. Buenos Aires beckoned below and we set about exploring it.

CHAPTER 11

# DISCOVERING BUENOS AIRES

'Let's meet at the grill room of the old Plaza Hotel – it is a bit like Argentina itself – possessed of a sort of shabby grandeur and remembered more for its noble past than its current pre-eminence.' Thus read the e-mail invitation that I received from Carlos Rosenkrantz, an early contact, who headed the prestigious private university, San Andrés, one of Argentina's finest. Actually, the dinner was far better, and the surrounds more salubrious than he had suggested. But Carlos was onto something. As we started to discover Buenos Aires – its landscape, monuments, streets and people – we could also glimpse from the sights, sounds and snarling lines of impatient drivers and frenzied pedestrians, something about the city and country's history, people and prospects. But first impressions were often as concealing as they were revealing.

The first was the sheer scale of the place: fully a third of the country's 40 million people live in the capital and the boundless dormitory suburbs that surround it. Yet, it was misleading in the sense that the vast hinterland of the country was, by comparison, almost empty: its second- and third-largest cities (Rosario and Córdoba) were about ten times smaller than the capital with populations barely more than 1 million people apiece. Standing in the middle of the multi-laned Avenida 9 de Julio, the widest boulevard in the world in downtown Buenos Aires – whose size and expense (it was built in 1937) rendered it the finest road in all of Latin America – it was easy to forget that half of the country was desert or semi-desert. Indeed, the Argentine landmass of some 3 million square kilometres was the eighth biggest country in the world, or as

Michal put it 'the size of India minus 1.16 billion people'. Argentina's biodiversity ranged from the semi-tropics of the Chaco to the beginnings of the Antarctic in the far south in Tierra del Fuego. In between, the lush pastures of its huge provinces provided the soy and cereals that fed some 400 million people across the world.

Yet, walking across this and other monumental roads and viewing the belle époque mansions that dominated the chic suburbs of Barrio Norte and Recoleta, was I suppose as much, or little, of a clue to the history and current prosperity of Argentina as concluding from a stroll down Victoria Road, Camps Bay, that you had distilled the essence of South Africa. The founding wealth and elegance of Buenos Aires appeared when you looked up and around at some of its fine buildings. One of the first that I entered, to present a copy of my credentials to the foreign minister the day after my arrival, was Palacio San Martin. It was, literally, palatial; yet it had been built back in 1909 as a 'town house' in the French style of a vast *petit hôtel*, with sweeping staircases and monumental colonnades, for a wealthy family whose estates in Anchorena provided the wherewithal for such an indulgence.

Even more impressive in scale was the neo-classical Teatro Colón, whose grand re-opening Michal and I were privileged to attend some months after our arrival. Originally built in May 1908, it was reputed to be, after La Scala in Milan and Covent Garden in London, the finest opera house in the world. Its *balcones* and *palcos* were packed that night with well-heeled and finely coiffed locals, as we marvelled at its stained glass dome and the busts of Wagner, Rossini and Beethoven in the imposing foyer. It was not a stretch to imagine when Stravinsky, Toscanini, Pavlova, Nijinsky, Nureyev and Callas had graced its stage. We were later to attend a magnificent concert series there starring the maestro conductor, Argentine-born Daniel Barenboim. He was a flamboyant and towering reminder of the country's cultural talent, both past and present.

But for all such architectural splendour, there was an even money chance that you would trip up on a broken paving stone, step in ubiquitous dog poo or be accosted by the outstretched hand of a street beggar. In a city where the iconic Recoleta Cemetery – dubbed the 'world's greatest necropolis' – was its number one tourist attraction, there was indeed something very much both current and more attractive about the grandeur of its past, than its somewhat frayed present and perhaps uncertain future. It brought to mind my late German friend Otto Graf Lambsdorff's put-down of Thabo Mbeki after meeting him during his presidency: 'He is burdened by too much history.' The same seemed to apply to my new city.

## A QUESTION OF IDENTITY

Another feature that the city landscape revealed was the almost complete absence of any of the old architecture of colonial Spain. This was in contrast to capitals such as Quito in Ecuador, which I was to visit later on during my stay. Early in its urban evolution, Buenos Aires decided to emulate Haussmann's Paris, as was apparent, buildings aside, from the grid system on which the 12 000 city blocks were arranged. Extraordinarily, my chauffeur Jorge seemed to know every one of them.

As I gazed from my unaccustomed perch in the back of the ambassadorial BMW at the unpredictable, haphazard and very fast manoeuvring of the drivers, I reminded myself that this was the land of Juan Manuel Fangio, who dominated the first decade of Formula One racing in the 1950s; while the winner of the 1972 South African Grand Prix (back in the days when South Africa hosted such events and I followed them) was the Argentine Carlos Reutemann, currently one of the country's leading politicians.

The gargantuan traffic jams of Buenos Aires were aggravated by the almost daily political demonstrations that stalled or severely disrupted the chaotic movement of millions of cars, and probably necessitated a degree of desperado driving. Indeed, it seemed as though normal traffic laws were treated with a splendid disregard by the motorist. Life as a pedestrian was not exactly easy either, since drivers seem to regard a zebra-striped pedestrian crossing as an excuse to gun their cars directly at the hapless person, including me, who dared to attempt to cross it. I would discover soon enough that disobeying the rule of law was not confined to the road. In fact, the early history of the Buenos Aires settlement had been one of 'bootlegging and smuggling', which apparently provided the origins of the local expression '*hecha la ley, hecha la trampa*' (where there's a law there's a loophole).[13] I immediately resolved that Michal, accustomed to the aggression of traffic in Tel Aviv, would be, in Jorge's absence, our designated driver.

The differences with the rest of South America went beyond architecture. Shortly after my arrival, one of our South African diplomats was preparing to return home. I asked him what had been his most difficult experience of life in Argentina. 'Being black', was his simple but disconcerting reply. It brought to mind the disturbing dialogue that Paul Theroux recorded in *The Old Patagonian Express* of his encounter with Argentina's foremost man of letters, Jorge Luis Borges, at the latter's apartment in Buenos Aires in 1979:

> I had read that a quarter of Argentina's population had once been black. There were none to be found now. I asked Borges why this was so.
>
> 'It is a mystery. But I remember seeing many of them ... They were cooks, gardeners, handymen,' he said. 'I don't know what happened to them.'
>
> 'People said they died of TB.'
>
> 'Why didn't they die of TB in Montevideo? It's just over there, eh. There is another story, equally silly, that they fought the Indians and the Indians and Negroes killed each other. That would have been in 1850, but it isn't true. In 1914 there were still many Negroes in Buenos Aires, they were very common ... They didn't work very hard. It was considered wonderful to have Indian blood, but black blood is not such a good thing, eh? There are some prominent families in Buenos Aires that have it – a touch of the tar brush, eh. My uncle used to tell me, "Jorge, you're as lazy as a nigger after lunch." You see they didn't do much work in the afternoon.'[14]

Was there more authenticity in the racist ramblings of Argentina's eminent author than in the subsequent and impeccably politically correct acts of Argentine governments? To express its abhorrence against racism, for example, after the restoration of its democracy in 1983, Argentina quickly broke diplomatic links with apartheid South Africa.

Whatever the real answer, the question of identity and a pejorative attitude to race had informed and shaped much of the country's history. The result was apparent wherever you looked: the country was the 'whitest' in South America, almost entirely absent of the Hispano-Amerindian mixture, which makes up much of the population in the rest of the continent. In fact, fewer than 10 per cent of Argentines were mestizo (or mixed race) and barely over 1 per cent were indigenous (Mapuches and Tobas Indians).[15] Argentine historian Felix Luna put it equally bluntly:

> Let's be quite honest: we are hardly Latin American at all. The Mexican novelist Carlos Fuentes says that 'The Mexicans came from the Aztecs, Peruvians from the Incas, and Argentines from the ships. In fact, Latin America only starts to appear (in Argentina) somewhere north of Córdoba where the chapels, faces and songs take us back to our pre-Hispanic origins ...'[16]

I discovered, as I dipped into the country's history, that this was not simply a matter of demographic accident. Almost from the founding of the country, or the cities of its earliest settlements – Córdoba, Santiago del Estero, Tucuman and Buenos Aires – in the late sixteenth century by the Spanish viceroyalty, to be a criollo (a native born of Spanish blood) was to be placed in the winner's circle. In contrast, life as a mestizo (which meant, literally, 'crow coloured') could be, in the parlance of Thomas Hobbes, 'nasty, brutish and short'. But for the early settlers and native-born Argentines, and the slaves who followed in the wake of the Spanish conquistadores, the country held very much second-fiddle status to Alto Perú (today's Bolivia) and its city of Potosi, the mineral riches of which made it the wealthiest place in the Americas. Only gold and silver counted for the rapacious Spanish colonisers and Buenos Aires had neither. Indeed, a Spanish royal accountant described it as 'the poorest city in the Americas'.[17]

But over the following 200 years, as the Argentines began to discover the techniques to exploit the agricultural resources of the sprawling pampas that surrounded Buenos Aires, fortunes began to change. Its first wheat exports were in 1878, and a year later a ship containing a piece of new technology appeared in the port of Buenos Aires, which was to be a game changer: the French vessel *La Frigroique*, with its refrigerated cargo holds, would export the first tons of frozen Argentine lamb to Europe and the world. Beef followed and in such quantities and fine quality that the country quickly assumed its place as a leading economy in the world: Argentina, just 100 years ago, was one of the richest countries on earth with a GDP per capita comparable with those of France and Germany. Back then it had four times the wealth of its giant neighbour Brazil. Quite how it fell so precipitously in the decades since then would absorb much of my ambassadorship as I would observe first-hand its unerring ability to both continue with failed policies of spectacular economic folly, and throw in some new ones for good measure, all of which conspired to eviscerate its natural bounty. To put matters into current perspective, by the time of my arrival in 2009, the Argentine economy had shrunk to a quarter of its surging neighbour Brazil, which by then had ousted Great Britain as the sixth largest economy in the world – some 30 places ahead of Argentina and South Africa (see Chapter 7).

But, during the golden years of its growth and influence, roughly from the mid-nineteenth century until the 1930s, Argentines believed that prosperity was their destiny, oozing the conviction that 'God is a criollo and a couple of good harvests will see things right'.[18] Little time or effort was apparently spent in building up institutions for good and durable governance. Instead, the early rulers of independent Argentina (it declared independence from a disintegrating Spanish Empire in 1816) spent prodigious energies first fighting among themselves – especially the rulers of Buenos Aires against the interior provinces. However, in its various factions, the new ruling elite were apparently of one mind, and iron resolve, in Europeanising their vast land. In 1879, General Julio Roca, one of the many caudillos who would dominate its politics, set about 'pacifying' the Indians in the vast southern interior. His infamous desert campaign, Conquistada del Desierto, was a somewhat romanticised title for what many regard as racial genocide. His destruction of the Patagonian Indians left a huge hinterland open for settlement, which would be filled initially by Irish and Welsh sheep farmers. Later, and of some significance to my mission a century or more afterwards, they would be joined by Boer *bittereinders* fleeing the victorious British after the conclusion of the South African War in 1902 (see Chapter 34). There was no end to the attraction of Patagonia's desolate remoteness for fugitives – from Butch Cassidy and the Sundance Kid to Nazi war criminals.

One of the bloodiest pages in the book of South American history was the absurd and lopsided war of the Triple Alliance (1865–70), where megalomaniacal Paraguayan President Mariscal Solano Lopez declared war against the combined might of Argentina, Uruguay and Brazil. This futile bloodletting decimated three-quarters of the male population of Paraguay. Argentina emerged victorious, with its territory expanded and as the regional super power. In terms of 'whitening' the country, the war saw the virtual disappearance of its African (slave-descending) population, which the army deployed as its front-line troops. Most of them were, literally, wiped out.

At around the same time and into this racial void stepped Argentine President Domingo Sarmiento, who coined the slogan 'to govern is to populate'. He set about with great energy, although with decidedly uneven result, to create a new population. Apparently, he was enthralled by the example of the US, which at the time of his rule was attracting European emigrants with – in Sarmiento's opinion – their habits of 'work, thrift, and respect for authority'; all the characteristics that he believed to be lacking in his own country. Yet, as the historian Felix Luna noted, when Sarmiento observed bearded Hassidic Jews, bedraggled Syrians and sundry Eastern Europeans disembark in the port of Buenos Aires, they were 'far from the ideal Anglo-Saxon emigrant he had in mind'. The president apparently was moved to observe, 'These aren't the immigrants we were looking for.'[19] But no one was turned away, and millions of Europeans poured into the new country over the next 60 years, with a disproportionate number arriving from Italy, especially from that country's impoverished south. Borges was onto something when he described Argentina as 'an imported country – everyone here is really from somewhere else'.[20]

One of the consequences of this emigrant melange was explained to me, after arrival, by a new Argentine friend. He described the national identity in the form of a joke: 'An Argentine is an Italian, who speaks Spanish, acts like a Frenchman, but secretly wishes he were English.'

The French influence, architecture and urban planning aside, the most notable and lasting legacy was the tango. This dance, alongside football and Evita, probably defined the image of Buenos Aires in most foreign and local minds. However, its origins lay in the brothels and bars of Paris, something that apparently appalled the snobbish upper crust of Argentine society. The writer and diplomat Enrique Larreta sniffed, early in the twentieth century, 'it is never danced in the drawing rooms of the well born'.[21] However, its importation into Buenos Aires, initially into the seamy whorehouses of the working-class La Boca waterfront area, transcended class and creed, so that it could be rightly claimed, as indeed local scribe Osvaldo Bayer did, to be 'our national anthem'. There was much in the dance, particularly in the legendary life story of its most famous singer, French-born Carlos Gardel, which accentuated both the cross-cultural origins of the country with which it became most famously associated and the sombre mood of its earliest settlers.

The word 'tango' is thought to derive from African origins, linked to the *tambour* or drum, while its roots are apparently Cuban, and when it emerged from the shadow of the brothel into the light of the dance halls, these so-called *milongas* came from a local rural tradition. Since I had difficulty even dancing at my own wedding, I was not exactly a prime candidate to master its difficult and sophisticated steps. Michal and I attempted a lesson at a typically run-down studio, but never returned as participants. A bit like a visit to a game reserve in South Africa, every foreign tourist, including the many we were soon to host, felt it obligatory to 'go to a (highly touristic and high-priced) tango show'. I tired of accompanying them soon enough – appropriately perhaps, since the theme of most tango song and dance routines was ennui overlaid, according to the experts, with the music of 'bitterness, melancholy, betrayal and jealousy'.[22] Not my idea, exactly, of a happy night out!

CHAPTER 12

# THE FORGOTTEN COLONY

Given my fluency in English and daily battles with *idioma Español*, I found the British stamp on Argentina both a more hopeful and, much like the country itself, somewhat baffling aspect of the place. The deserted and boarded-up Harrods shop frontage (one of the few overseas outposts of the eponymous Knightsbridge department store) still dominated the pedestrian mall, Calle Florida, adjacent to the South African Embassy in downtown Buenos Aires. Both its presence and current desertedness underlined the once powerful reach of the English influence and its later decline. Without having ever formally colonised Argentina, despite a few fitful military attempts to do so early in the nineteenth century, there were still plenty of signs of Albion about. For many years, until the Second World War, the British dominated the Argentine economy and used the country to extract vast resources back to London, particularly in terms of agriculture, banking and transport (the British laid the first railway network in Argentina). Perhaps appropriately, a chronicler of the English impact, Andrew Graham-Yooll, entitled his study of it *The Forgotten Colony*.[23] Even the fact of, and furies resulting from, the Falklands War of 1982, between Britain and Argentina, had not entirely dimmed the Anglophile tendency, especially in elite circles.

My first intimation of the lingering pervasiveness of the English influence came in the cheery form of my 'social secretary' at the embassy, Lizzie Schiele. Although into her early sixties when we first met, and having lived her entire life in Argentina, she spoke a cut-glass form of the Queen's English, with far better elocution than the Estuary form of the language that today predominates in Britain. I was amazed when she told me that her family had first settled in Argentina in 1850; from her accent I would have assumed she was only just off the boat. Like others from this interesting, one-time dominant, currently declining, substratum of the elite, Lizzie had spoken English at home, before she learnt Spanish.

I soon noted other manifestations of the reverence for things and matters English. The most visible and anachronistic of these was the Argentine elite's obsession with London-style clubs. While South Africa's expression of the same phenomenon, the Rand Club for example, appeared to be battling to survive financially, no such ailments were afflicting the Argentine equivalents. The most ostentatious example in Buenos Aires was the Jockey Club. It was a sumptuous Recoleta palace, which dazzled with a splendour not matched by anything I had seen in either St James or Pall Mall, the headquarters of London's club land. Although my diplomatic status entitled me to honorary membership, I quickly tired of its boarding-school-style fare and sexism (women could not be members or lunch in the rather splendid dining room, unaccompanied by a man). But my custom was unimportant. There was a waiting list for membership, which required a cool 50 000 dollar joining fee. Little wonder then that for many poor and disaffected Argentines, this club was a hated symbol of exclusion. In the 1940s, Peron's supporters had burnt down the first version of the club.

A far more practical and welcome remnant of one-time English dominance came in daily form to my front doorstep. The *Buenos Aires Herald* had been published for over 130 years by the time of my arrival. It was, literally, my initial life saver: the ability to scan all important domestic events and politics in my home language – coupled with a generous dose of international news – allowed me a pretty direct insight into the events shaping my new environment. Its slightly dishevelled, acutely intelligent editor, Michael Soltys, usually attired in an off-white jacket to offset his shock of white hair, looked as though he had stepped directly from the pages of a Graham Greene novel. He was to prove a helpful guide in navigating the complex, often bitter, politics of his own country, and flattered me by quoting back to me remarks I had long forgotten, but which he had thoughtfully read up from my own autobiography. It was, in fact, this relatively small newspaper – tiny in terms of both circulation and influence compared with the mighty *La Nación* and *Clarín* – which had played an outsize, even heroic, role during the darkest days of Argentina's military junta. During the country's Dirty War it fearlessly published details of the *los desaparecidos* ('the disappeared') and helped to save the lives of many so-called subversives whom the pitiless regime would otherwise have murdered (see Chapter 28).

I took early note of two impeccably English sources for a key to unlocking aspects of the Argentine character and the nation's characteristics. In 1925, the Prince of Wales, later to ascend the throne as the ill-starred and short-reigning King Edward VIII, paid a visit to Argentina. His princely observation, in a letter home to his father, King George V, provided an interesting insight: 'These Argentines are queer people – v. Latin in their touchiness and excitability but also human and cheery tho' with quite a heavy veneer of pompousness. Their official and ceremonial stunts are very ostentatious, but absolutely lacking in organisation and time means nothing to them.'[24]

Another uncensored and highly undiplomatic observation appeared in the valedictory telegram of the British ambassador, Sir Michael Hadow, in 1973:

> All I knew of the Argentines before coming here was that they were generally disliked by all other Latin Americans as unduly pretentious, snobbish upstarts. Their pride in their 'Europeanness' is certainly justified if it means that they are white and lack the essential mixture which goes to make up the basic Latin American. They are a melting pot of European races … [but] they have not found a sense of nationality or patriotism except through vocal outbursts of xenophobia. They are probably desperately unsure of themselves yet want to be admired and loved. Politically, they yearn for a strong leader and admire totalitarianism but at the same time they yearn for no governing hand at all.[25]

## COMPARATIVE HISTORY – AND SOME SHOPPING

Did the prince's and ambassador's observations constitute cartoon-style caricatures or objective analyses? A bit of both I discovered as I spent the next few years trying to unravel the complexity and contradiction of the so-called 'Argentine national character'. But, however elusive and frustrating and often maddening I found the process, I always reminded myself that South Africa itself was a country that grappled, on a daily basis, with the issue of identity – our mooring on the southern tip of Africa often in danger of being untethered by aspects of our European identity; our de facto leadership of our continent also often invited the resentment and jealousy of peers and neighbours. South Africans, like Argentines, also had a tendency towards self-congratulations and often a reverence for the things that they had got right in the past, rather than dealing effectively with the many challenges confronting the present.

'Tread cautiously,' I mentored myself, 'lest in the mirror of Argentina, you do not find the reflection of your own country staring back at you.' Indeed, both countries, in the second decade of the twenty-first century, could well have borrowed and transposed Massimo d'Azeglio's famous description of Italy in the mid-nineteenth century: 'Italy has been made; now it remains to make Italians.'[26]

But the big difference between my home country and the one I was now an emissary in, was that Argentina, for the reasons detailed above, lacked any of the racial, ethnic or linguistic fault lines that had made South Africa's democratic attainment so improbable and so admired. Yet, despite its comparative advantage here, Argentina's history had been marked by 'frictions, violence, and a 50-year series of military coups d'état'.[27] Its current achievements did not include any apparent long-term vision for the future, or much trust or respect for the national institutions that could take the country forward.

Contemplations on matters of comparative history again yielded, initially, to far more practical and essential matters. Going shopping was one of them. My first experiences left me little doubt that as far as modern consumerism was concerned, Argentina was stuck somewhere where South Africa had been in the 1960s, often still with the chronic disorganisation observed by the Prince of Wales more than 85 years previously. For example, one Saturday morning, shortly after arrival, Michal and I were strolling through one of the cypress-lined avenues of upscale Recoleta, admiring the Doric porticos of its fine buildings, when we spied an attractive delicatessen and decided to purchase a few *medialunas* (Argentine's answer to the croissant).

This simple transaction took a full half hour to conclude: the first step was to obtain a paper number from a dispenser (a much-loved feature of practically every shop, government department and clinic). Then we joined the first of two queues snaking out of the shop. In the first, shoppers lined up and selected, at a leisurely pace, their intended purchases; the next and more significant line consisted of customers waiting to pay for them. An electronic barcode scanner was nowhere in sight: instead an elderly gentleman, adorned in a grey dust jacket, was painstakingly writing out every purchase in an order book in a faint blue ballpoint pen. By the time our minor transaction was concluded, the charm of this quaint *confitería* had given way to impatience and irritation. In fact, 'mom 'n pop' stores, a fading childhood memory of sleepy Durban, still held the consumer ring in today's Buenos Aires and were far more ubiquitous here than probably in any other modern city of equivalent size.

This led to another early, and lasting, discovery. For all their fabled Latino impatience, Argentines seemed to have an almost endless endurance for long waiting lines and chronic lashings of bad service. I vowed never to complain again about these matters back home. South Africa, by comparison, was like Singapore or New York.

Then there was the mystery of money. To describe 'cash as king' in Argentina would be a masterful understatement. '*Solo efectivo*' (Cash only) was not simply a sign in a shop window; it was often the required means of payment for even the most advanced or sophisticated services. Visits to the dentist or doctor would require me to arrive with, literally, a brick of money. I had, quite wrongly it transpired, assumed that Argentina – like South Africa – would be a place of the cashless electronic transfer. No such luck. And it was not simply a question of cheating the taxman, although in this sport Argentina appeared to be alongside Greece and Italy in the Olympic finals. The distrust of the banking system and belief in hard currency had recent, and more baleful, roots. The

2001 economic meltdown had, literally and overnight, wiped out most of the value of people's bank savings, and the government's 2008 nationalisation of private pensions had further diminished a jittery population's trust in formal institutions.

Before too long, I also discovered that the colour of money here was also not what it always appeared to be. First encounters suggested that passing off counterfeit notes was something of a national pastime. The purple 100 peso note was a particular favourite. I was ripped off, soon after arrival, at a foreign exchange outlet. However, the taxi driver – in a city that boasted more than 40 000 cabs – was often the prime culprit. A visiting friend, Tara Forster, had such an encounter that left her both fuming and several pesos poorer, and her experience was, alas, fairly typical. The scam was masterful in its simplicity: she proffered a 100 peso note to pay for the fare. The driver took it, examined it and returned it to her, complaining that it was a forgery. But what he had done, while allegedly examining it, was to switch her genuine note for the counterfeit one. At her expense, I learnt always to carry lower denominated and less easily forged notes on all such journeys.

Fascinating though these initial observations were (to me at least), they were not the essential reason for my presence in Argentina. An ambassador is both his or her nation's chief diplomat in the country of accreditation and its head of mission there. Thus, I set about discovering what mysteries awaited behind embassy walls.

CHAPTER 13

# BEHIND EMBASSY WALLS

Jorge navigated the silver BMW with its tinted windows through the choked and narrow city-centre street – Avenida M.T. de Alvear, named after a former Argentine president. I was about to set foot, for the first time, in the building that housed my new office, the South African Embassy in Argentina.

Not for the first time in my life, I contemplated my status as an 'outsider-insider', and the constant tension between, in Ian Buruma's words, 'my affinities chosen or inherited'.[28] Thinking back on my life and career to date, I considered some of its contradictions: I had been one of a handful of Jews at a Natal (as it was formerly known) Methodist boarding school; I had entered parliament opposing the Democratic Party establishment's preferred candidate and went on to become the English-speaking leader of a predominantly Afrikaans-supported political party, the Democratic Alliance. I had been 'a white politician' (to borrow Thabo Mbeki's put-down) in an essentially black parliament. Now I was about to cross a new threshold: representing a government I had resolutely opposed.

I told myself as I entered the building that now was my chance to walk, or at the very least work, the talk I had often proclaimed: drawing a line between state and party, firmly reminding myself that I was here to represent the 'people', not simply the state of South Africa. Or was this simply self-serving sophistry – the proverbial distinction without a difference? I would soon find out.

My first impression of my new working environment was favourable: the marbled floors and mirrored wall in the reception area, offset with gentle spotlights, exuded a calm elegance, and the gold lettering on it proclaimed 'Embajada De Sudáfrica/Embassy of South Africa'. But, as I was to discover, appearances in my new post often flattered to deceive.

Once I had entered through the heavy security door, I noted the stripped-down interiors, with institutional lino-tiled floors, pale peach-painted walls on which hung, in somewhat uneasy balance, posters of both the struggle and tourism sort, and decidedly elderly, public works-style furnishings. Functional economy rather than luxury was the key here, and my first acquaintance with our ever-shrinking budget provided the explanation.

Some months later, during his stay with us, my former parliamentary counsellor, Gareth Morgan, described the three floors of our embassy as reminding him of the 'interior of a provincial hospital' – a painful, but accurate, observation. At the very least, I rationalised, visiting taxpayers from home would see that their hard-earned rands had not, in this far corner of the world at least, been squandered on ritzy and sumptuous fittings.

As a backbench MP, my first four years in parliament had been spent in the office equivalent of a windowless cell – and by these and other standards at least, the large, comfortable corner office reserved for the ambassador suited me just fine. It looked out on to a tree-lined city square, Plaza San Martin, named after Argentina's most famous son, General José de San Martin, who had plotted and led the downfall of the Spanish Empire across the Andes in the early nineteenth century. Directly across from the embassy was the Hotel Plaza, which at the time of my arrival was celebrating its centenary as 'the most traditional and elegant hotel in Buenos Aires'. Having already been introduced to the culinary delights of its grillroom, I was intrigued to later learn that it was there, by chance, in 1917, that the world's two most famous ballet stars, Nijinsky and Pavlova, met each other.[29] Of more practical relevance was the hotel's gym, whose treadmills would provide me with some offset against the heavy wining and dining, which seemed obligatory in my new job.

'Would the ambassador be willing to address the staff – we have arranged a small tea in your honour?' my corporate services manager, André Lizamore, both enquired and advised. It dawned on me that titled deference was to be my new accompaniment. It was very different, indeed, from parliamentary life, where everyone from the cleaners to colleagues, and even my deadliest political enemies, had addressed me as 'Tony'. In my new life and position, I would never once, no matter the informality of occasion, be addressed by any of my staff as anything other than 'Ambassador' or 'El Embajador'. We might, in the best Argentine tradition, hug and kiss each other, but this formalism prevailed in every circumstance.

## THE CREW

The embassy staff awaited me in ranked order downstairs. Since I had very little idea of what it was they did or, more crucially, how I would be spending my time over the next few years, I shook hands, uttered a few boilerplate banalities, sipped some tea and fled back to my office to consult the business plan and budget and work out what it was that ambassadors actually did and how they went about their business.

This was to prove much more difficult than I had imagined. In the absence of an ambassador for the six months preceding my arrival, the embassy appeared to have run on semi-autopilot mode. The South African diplomat who had acted as head of mission was reaching the end of his posting and, I gathered, his mind was far more focused on his imminent return home than on the detailed intricacies of the bilateral relationship, or explaining it to me. His amiable disposition clearly cheered the staff, but did little to provide me with the nuts and bolts of where precisely we were in terms of implementing our objectives. When I enquired about the progress of one or another project, he would, somewhat disconcertingly, hit his head with his fist and mutter something about his 'connections in Luthuli House', a reference to the ANC headquarters in Johannesburg, whose relevance to my enquiry I never quite fathomed. But while not a pillar of enlightenment in my quest to do the work at hand, he, like all the staff, treated me with exquisite deference.

Further down the food chain I was to discover that I had been gifted with some excellent officials, both South African ('transferred' in foreign service argot) and Argentine (locally recruited personnel or

LRPs was the accurate, if decidedly unglamorous, official title for this component).

Through a process of one-on-one discussions, furious readings, panic calls to head office and chance encounters, the fog of my initial bewilderment and incomprehension started to lift. It seemed to me, and events were to confirm, the ambassador's job – distilled to its essence – consisted of: implementing foreign policy; acting as the South African lead representative to my three countries of accreditation; and running the embassy. In truth, the latter was largely supervised, some two floors below my office, by André Lizamore, the highly intelligent and bureaucratically savvy head of administration ('corporate service manager' in department-speak). But as head of mission, I was the chief accounting officer, and thus, accountable for any 'wasteful' or 'unauthorised' expenditure, to quote but two of myriad sins for which I was now responsible. So I would keep my nose in the books and my eye on an ever-shrinking bottom line over the next few years. Midway through my term, André returned home and his replacement, Mardi Pather, continued to run the administration with a capable and can-do attitude, and his wife, Rhoganee, thoughtfully provided us with some marvellous morsels of Indian cuisine, a commodity much absent in spice-averse Argentina.

Actually, it was in the lower reaches of my new kingdom that I discovered another insight into Argentina, which still held sway, even if it owed its provenance to the fierce labour protectionism championed by the Perons, whose *descamisados* (literally, 'shirtless ones') had lifted Juan and Evita to power some 60 years before. Shortly before my arrival, a minor employee of the embassy had been caught, more or less red-handed, stealing some cash, which he was meant to deliver to the office from the bank. The onerous and employee-friendly provisions of the disciplinary process prescribed by local legislation had all been scrupulously implemented, and he had been found guilty of theft and his dismissal ordered. As I sat reviewing this matter, I was startled by the final recommendation of the DIRCO representative who had adjudicated the case. There appeared to be a disconnection between the weight of damning evidence against the accused and the final sentence, which read: 'Therefore it is recommended that the employee be dismissed *without cause*.' 'Why on earth is it without cause?' I demanded of a bemused-looking André. 'It seems to me that we had every cause in the world to fire this scoundrel.'

'Ambassador,' he responded in his quiet way, 'let me show you the side-opinion which we obtained from our labour lawyers here. It makes it quite clear that under Argentine law, if in fact we cite theft as the reason for his dismissal, he will immediately take us on appeal at no cost to himself, tie us up in years of litigation and tribunals each of which are stacked in his favour, and the overall cost to the embassy will vastly exceed, even in the unlikely event that we ultimately prevail, the one year's salary we will pay him out for the "dismissal without cause".' So to protect the interests of our taxpayers, we were stitched up in an effective legal charade.

My innocence started to wane and the beginning of wisdom commenced. I was to learn from this, and later brushes with Argentine labour law, that my fevered opposition to the Congress of South African Trade Union's accommodation in every nook and cranny of our domestic labour law appeared overblown in comparison. In Argentina, it was almost impossible to lose your job, and for those in work there were a staggering 22 days of public holidays to ease the burden of the working year. Things got even more generous when it came to such exotica as 'mental stress', to which Argentines seemed disproportionately prone: here the ever-beneficent provisions of local legislation went into overdrive, mandating several months of paid leave for recovery. When I related these nuggets to Frans Baleni, influential secretary general of the South African National Union of Mineworkers, when he paid a later visit to us, even he seemed intrigued!

Happily, none of the staff under my baton pursued us through the labour courts during my term – and indeed proved to be, largely, centres of excellence and unbounded motivation. A constant and irritating background noise to my political leadership had been the refrain that 'Tony Leon surrounds himself with white men', neither accurate nor, in my view, especially illuminating (or damning, come to think of it). 'If they could see me now!' I thought to myself as I set to work 'selling South Africa' (in the approving phrase of Tim du Plessis, editor of *Beeld* newspaper, who would shortly visit as a guest) with an almost entirely female crew of Argentines and a South African contingent who represented the best and brightest of the 'rainbow nation'.

The replacement for my disengaged, and soon to depart, number two was an experienced department hand, Mbulelo 'Shoes' Mtilwa, who was to prove effective, loyal and decent as the political counsellor. In our young first secretary, Mziwanele Langa, I discovered a true gem of a public servant – conscientious, intelligent and proficient in Spanish to boot.

The consular work, an essential core of our function – from issuing passports and visas to dealing with 'distressed South Africans' (another euphemism that covered all manner of ailing or deceased citizens marooned in Argentina, from the sick, to the impecunious and, in the final instance, the dead) – was headed by Lorato Legotlo. She was also a young career diplomat of skilful efficiency, who balanced her role of mother to a young daughter with an endless and efficient application to a variety of tasks in the embassy. Her ever-changing hairstyles and impeccable fashion sense brought to mind the Jewish princesses of my Wits University days except, among several differentiating facts, Lorato hailed form Mafikeng in the far-off North West province. For everything that was wrong with the public service in South Africa, I had lucked in to head a mission containing that which was right with it.

My Argentine crew were cut from similar, albeit distinctively Latino, cloth: my new social secretary, in effect my personal assistant, Clara Miri, had a gazelle-like elegance matched by proactive competence; Maria Isabel ('Mony') di Liscia was charged with bolstering our political and cultural ties, which she did with zeal interspersed with spiritual and yoga meditations. Mony's bright passion was infectious and often lit up the dullest event.

The efficiency of our trade section (the diplomatic area to which I ascribed the most 'weight' in the dread performance agreement and on which I expended the most effort) was attributable to the most remarkable young Argentine woman, Florencia Achcar. In just two years she managed to give birth to two children and simultaneously help me and, more importantly, South Africa achieve by 2011, a record 1.3 billion rand export total to Argentina, an increase of 80 per cent compared with the previous twelve months. In the same year, the World Trade Organization had branded the country 'the most protectionist in the world', making our accomplishment go against the grain.

Completing this sterling quintet were Nadia Volonte and Laura Wilson, the latter quietly (an unusual characteristic in our often boisterous office) steered Argentine tourism arrivals to South Africa to new heights, ensuring our entry onto the South African Tourism 'watch list' as one of the best new markets in the world. For reasons readers would have gleaned by now, my translator, the sensitive and intelligent Nadia Volonte, was to prove utterly indispensable.

## THE MULES

A singular irony struck me when I investigated the services our embassy provided. Part of Lorato's remit was to 'provide consular assistance to imprisoned South Africans'. She had no shortage of clients. During my three years as ambassador we had no fewer than 50 South Africans either convicted or awaiting trial in various penitentiaries of Argentina. Each of them – and they covered the racial spectrum and age and gender divides (the youngest was just 23 and the oldest, incredibly, was 65) – had been arrested, usually at the airport, for transporting drugs (cocaine being the narcotic of choice and South America was, of course, the home of the coca leaf). But, and here lay the paradox, most of this motley – often financially desperate – collection of South African drug mules had been arrested by another official of our embassy, our energetic South African Police Service officer, Captain Mike Dunlop. Thus, we had two officials, out of seven South African diplomats, deeply engaged in both ends of the narcotics trade – a capable policeman who interdicted the offenders and a consul who, with equal efficiency, provided them with legal representation, arranged prison visits and attended to their medical and financial needs!

The policy of prohibition and the practice of interdicting, known as the 'war against drugs' (first declared by President Richard M. Nixon in 1973), was a combat zone without winners. In mid-2011, the *Financial Times* reported:

> Though the fight [against drugs] has cost billions of dollars and thousands of lives, the trade – and its effects on those who take the products – has barely been dented. Production has been increased and global consumption with it. Of an estimated 272m users of illicit drugs worldwide, about 250 000 consumers lose their lives every year.[30]

One afternoon, I congratulated Mike on another of his and the Argentine police's drug busts – and this one was pretty spectacular: two baggage handlers at the Ezeiza Airport had just been arrested, some 45 minutes before the South African Airways plane was to take off to Johannesburg. Using false passenger names and printed luggage tags, they had attempted to place two suitcases containing 40 kilograms of cocaine, with a street value of approximately 20 million rand, into the hold of the aircraft. Mike ruefully acknowledged: 'Thanks, but you know we probably don't catch more than 10 per cent or 15 per cent of the smugglers.'

Many of our weekly management meetings dealt with lurid reports on the darkest side of this illicit, but highly profitable, trade. During my tenure, three South Africans died ingesting the drugs they were couriering. 'Swallowing' liquid cocaine was thought, erroneously, to be a detection-free method. In one case, the unfortunate mule had a fatal heart attack on a flight between Buenos Aires and Frankfurt, forcing the aircraft to make an emergency landing in Recife, Brazil. Another died in a bus on the forlorn border between Argentina and Bolivia, a regional centre of the coca industry. The third corpse was found, several days post-mortem, in a fleapit hotel in downtown Buenos Aires. It also did not pass unnoticed by us that the desperado South Africans we variously arrested, assisted or, *in extremis*, arranged to cremate, were simply in the lower reaches of the trade; the kingpins were seldom apprehended and were, apparently, mostly Nigerian.

As one of only two air portals between Africa and South America (São Paulo being the other), Buenos Aires was an obvious drug smuggling 'hot spot'. But there was another reason why we had so many South African traffickers on our hands. Some years before, while an MP, I had interrupted a vacation in Thailand to visit a South African drug mule there, Alexander Krebs, at the urging of his sister. For a relatively small amount of heroin (1.2 kilograms), he had received the death sentence at his parody of a trial, later commuted to 100 years (he went on to serve out eighteen years of his sentence before being recently deported to South Africa). And the Bang Kwang prison where he was serving his sentence seemed, in its squalor and misery, to approximate the eastern reaches of Dante's Inferno. By contrast, the sentencing regime in Argentina was remarkably light: for the equivalent and even for greater amounts of trafficking cocaine, the average sentence was just four years, with most South Africans being expelled and sent home after serving half their sentences.

One afternoon I decided to visit some of our 'customers' and duly presented myself at the Ezeiza Penitentiary, close to the Buenos Aires airport. I met about ten South African prisoners there, each with their own story of entrapment or stupidity and one or two proclaiming their innocence. Interestingly, none complained seriously about conditions of imprisonment, which, at a superficial glance, seemed infinitely more benign than the prison hellholes of South East Asia or the 'universities of crime and recidivism' that well described the bulk of correctional facilities back home.

By the time of my departure in late 2012, many serious voices in Latin America, noting for example the staggering 50 000 people killed in Mexico since its government launched an all-out assault against drugs in 2007, questioned the efficacy of current policies and practice. The former president of Colombia, Cesar Gaviria, to mention one influential source, declared the war on drugs a '*fracaso*' ('crashing failure').[31]

CHAPTER 14

# THREE PRESIDENTS, THREE CEREMONIES AND ONE POLITICALLY INCORRECT ANTHEM

Before I could delve further into the substance of my new perch, I had to yield to the imperatives of protocol. Ahead of an ambassador becoming operational, he or she needs to 'present the Letters of Credentials to the Head of the Receiving State'. The evening of this ritual, shortly after my arrival in Buenos Aires, found me in very unfamiliar territory: being driven at high speed, flanked by motorcycle outriders, in the Argentine equivalent of the frightful South African 'blue light brigade', albeit that mine was a one-car entourage!

Immodestly, I quite enjoyed my 'fifteen minutes of fame' as the traffic parted and we swept through the streets leading to the Casa Rosada, or 'Pink House', the official seat of the Argentine president. Appropriately, given the origins of the country, the building is a blend of French and Italian Renaissance styles, although with no trace of the architecture of the Spanish Empire. I was a little disappointed to note, as I was escorted through the front portico of Casa Rosada, that coloured spotlights were now used to heighten its famous, eponymous rose colour. Apparently, back in the eighteenth century, ox blood mixed with whitewash was used to achieve this effect.

Perhaps the most famous aspect of the presidential palace was the balcony that faced onto the Plaza de Mayo. It had been used by Madonna in the 1996 movie *Evita* when she famously belted out 'Don't Cry for Me

Argentina'. Her appearance there was directly facilitated by star-struck Argentine President Carlos Menem, who infamously stated that 'he wanted carnal relations with the United States' – perhaps an apt phrase for this self-styled playboy. From the same spot in 1986, the bad-boy hero of Argentine football, Diego Maradona, had held aloft the World Cup he had won for Argentina, virtually single-handedly. More significantly the balconies of the Casa Rosada had been the essential backdrop for every major presidential appearance in Argentina's turbulent history – from the Perons to Leopoldo Galtieri. This military strongman, as head of the country's junta, had proclaimed from there, back in April 1982, the invasion of the Falkland Islands, of which ill-fated adventure much more anon. And, of course, the Plaza had been the scene for, and given its name to, the Madres de Plaza de Mayo, the brave mothers and grandmothers of the *los desaparecidos* (or 'the disappeared'), the thousands of young people abducted, and in many cases murdered, by Galtieri and his cohorts. Wearing white headscarves, their weekly silent vigils, outside the Casa Rosada, had switched the world spotlight on the Argentine Dirty War of 1976–83 and helped illuminate some of its horrors (see Chapter 28).

The president I was about to meet and present with my 'Letters', Cristina Fernández de Kirchner, was both a Peronist (the popular moniker for the ruling Justicialist Party) and a populist. But at the time of our meeting, she was far from popular. She had been elected just two years before and her big mandate was thought by many to be attributable to her predecessor, who also happened to be her husband, Nestor Kirchner. He was credited with the resurrection of the Argentine economy from the crater of the debt default and meltdown in 2001. Many thought he still wielded the real power.

But whichever half of the couple really governed, in October 2009 the Kirchners appeared to have spent most of their political capital. After picking, and losing, a fight with the country's powerful farming sector and falling out with her vice president, the president's party had recently lost control of congress in the mid-term election. She was widely considered a one-term lame duck, with her popularity recorded at just 22 per cent. However, events would soon prove her presidential obituary writers grievously wrong. Her storming comeback over the next two years would feature prominently in my reports back home, but on the night of our first meeting I was more struck by her appearance and frankly by her sex appeal.

'The lips of Angelina Jolie,' I thought to myself as we shook hands in the gilded chamber of the presidential reception room on the first floor of the Casa Rosada, within spitting distance of Evita's balcony. Overall, she cut an alluring and demure figure: perfectly arranged Titian hair, her silk lilac shirt offset by a handsome string of pearls, which showed her perfectly unlined face to best advantage. Given that she was some four years older than me (making her 56 at the time) there was little doubt that like many of her fellow country women (and men) she had enjoyed the benefits of cosmetic enhancement, which doubtless also accounted for the outsized lips that had so attracted my attention. She was also to Botox her political image to great effect in the following months and years, however improbably her flawless and expensive appearance contrasted with the mass of her poor and lower middle-class support base.

The ceremony itself was efficient, brief and ritualistic: I handed over my letter of appointment and my predecessor's letter of recall, signed in the original by President Zuma. Warned by the protocol officer not to try to engage the strictly unilingual 'Cristina', as she is universally known, in my mangled Spanish, we exchanged a few banalities. (I said, for example, 'It is a great honour to meet you.' She responded, via her brilliant young interpreter who made the entire exchange seamless and looked around twelve years old, 'South Africa is so important to us.') Not exactly the stuff of a nuclear summit, but sufficient for the purpose. The entire 'audience' with her lasted about three minutes.

Some months later, as I relate further on, we had a more substantive encounter. That evening, the person with whom I had a far more engaged discussion, in flawless English, was her deeply impressive foreign minister, Jorge Taiana. He possessed what in South Africa would be termed approvingly as 'struggle credentials', having spent seven years in prison, without trial, during the era of the military junta. His ascent to the heights of the Peronist party was also doubtless facilitated by the fact that his father had been the personal physician to party founder and national icon, President Juan Domingo Peron.

His considerable knowledge of Argentina's relationship with South Africa and his flattering observations about my own role in our democratic progress suggested a person on top of his brief and possessed of a reservoir of charm. I dutifully wrote up, and sent back, an enthusiastic report to Pretoria. Not for the first or last time, I was to learn that as with all courtiers, service and retention in the court of 'Queen Cristina' was governed by arbitrary whim and thus easily terminated. Within months of our meeting, Taiana was forced out of office, having apparently displeased his regent.

A similar fate soon befell another key official, Central Bank president, Martin Redrado. With film-star good looks and a hugely impressive grasp of economics, as well as an honest assessment of his own country's strengths and significant weaknesses, it was difficult not to be dazzled by him, as I duly was at our first fairly extensive and agreeable meeting. At Redrado's urging, I used my long-standing relationship with Pravin Gordhan, then starting off as the South African minister of finance, to pass on some personal and political messages. Whatever hopes we had that this access could translate into a more effective partnership between our countries in shaping the agenda of the G-20 were dashed soon enough: barely had I sent off my last mail on the subject than Martin was also fired (or forced to resign) for refusing, on impeccable constitutional grounds, to hand over bank reserves to pay off government debt and thus free up funds for the president's further handouts to her ever-expectant voters.

The dismissal of a cabinet minister is a routine occurrence in any democracy, however ill-considered. But my internal alarm clock rang (and was more loudly sounded by most local and some international economic and media commentators) when the supposedly independent head of the reserve bank could be so easily dispensed with in effect for doing his job, i.e., safeguarding the country's reserves! This was the first of many jolts that suggested that, like a contrived movie set, Argentina had the appearance of a modern democracy, but it was illusory – the substantive core was either missing or had been hollowed out.

Although by the time of my appointment entire swaths of the South African machinery of state had, literally, seized up, the wheels of my new department still turned, but at an exceedingly glacial pace and often with eccentric results. It thus took a further six to seven months after my ceremonial with Cristina to complete the same process with the presidents of Paraguay and Uruguay. The 'Letters' for these countries had yet to arrive. Matters were further delayed when someone in Pretoria managed to misspell the president's name on the one letter and, in the other, the predecessor president was named as the incumbent. Sorted out, eventually, one evening in April 2010, I took off from Buenos Aires and headed due north to destination Asunción, capital of landlocked Paraguay.

Since there are over 100 accredited heads of mission resident in Buenos Aires, receiving new ambassadors there is more of a chore than a major occasion for the head of state. But in poorer, and more off-the-track Paraguay, with perhaps only two dozen resident embassies, the arrival of an ambassador was an event on which some stardust was sprinkled with far more ceremony and presidential face time than I had anticipated.

My first impressions of the capital, on the humid morning of my event, were not favourable. Counterfeit DVDs and fake watches seemed everywhere on sale in the dusty and undistinguished streets of low-rise and sprawling Asunción. I was bemused to see a trestle table slapped right in front of the foreign ministry, where the vendors conducted brisk business in contraband, undisturbed by the numerous policemen standing guard there.

I was even more amazed to find multiple copies of the movie *Invictus*, just recently premiered by our embassy in Buenos Aires, and on current cinematic release in Asunción, on sale on the table for just 2 dollars! On the ground, Paraguay seemed to live up to its unhappy title as the 'headquarters for smuggled goods in South America'. Fortunately, future visits, augmented by the formidable charm and hospitality of our honorary consul, Angel Auad, would offset this unpromising start. But it was *Invictus*, Clint Eastwood's Hollywood treatment of our 1995 Rugby World Cup triumph, which actually provided the conversational basis for my imminent meeting with President Fernando Lugo.

Pomp and flummery preceded this presidential encounter and the

Paraguayans put on a rather fulsome show. Back home, as Democratic Alliance leader, my appearance at party rallies had been accompanied by all the hype and hoopla associated with modern political theatre plus some South African characteristics – kwaito music, strobe lighting, chanting crowds, confetti cannons and sometimes even an excited praise singer. My ambassadorial inauguration in Asunción that morning was from an entirely different world, if not century.

First off, outside the Palacio de Gobierno, or presidential palace, I reviewed the crisp uniformed honour guard, replete in gleaming white tunics and braided trousers and was saluted with drawn sabre by the company commander. I then stood to attention as a military brass band played the national anthems. All seemed to be going well, in fact rather splendidly I thought, until the playing of the South African anthem commenced. I immediately had an uneasy frisson of pre-1994 déjà vu. The Paraguayan version of our national song on offer that morning consisted solely of 'Die Stem'; the preceding and rather crucial musical verses of 'Nkosi Sikelel' iAfrika' were absent. Since we were in the middle of the ceremony and I was ramrod-stiff in attention-mode, there was nothing to be done. I recoiled inwardly and thanked heaven for the absence of any South African media representatives. Afterwards, I had a quiet word with the honorary consul to ensure the correct version was made available for future use.

Fernando Armindo Lugo Méndez's road to Paraguay's presidency had to rank as one of the more unorthodox and unusual journeys undertaken by any head of state. Most of his life had been spent as the Roman Catholic bishop in one of his country's poorest dioceses. This background gave him both a constituency and an understanding of the poor and the landless in a country where two thirds of its agricultural heartland is held by fewer than 10 per cent of the population.

But Fernando Lugo's decision to enter politics, and stand for election to the presidency in 2008, incurred the displeasure of Rome. South America was the theological nursery for what became known as 'liberation theology' – a radical movement particularly popular in the continent in the 1980s, which proclaimed the church as an instrument for social change and as deriving its legitimacy and theology from, and articulating the needs of, the dispossessed.[32] Lugo's fallout with the Vatican was hardly surprising given Pope John Paul II's conservatism and his strenuous opposition to this tendency. More surprising and salacious was the fact – as the local tabloids had published in excruciating, lurid detail – that while still a priest, Lugo had fathered a number of, needless to say illegitimate, children!

Discomfiting his life further on the morning of our first meeting had been the recent bouts of chemotherapy he had undergone to treat the non-Hodgkin lymphoma with which he had been diagnosed. None of these travails, present or past, were evident during my encounter with him. Instead, as we sat in vast, throne-like gold-brocaded chairs (mine, appropriately, being at a lower height to his) set upon a plush red carpet, we engaged in a detailed discussion on South Africa's road to democracy and reconciliation, of which he was both a student and an admirer. Lugo asked me if I had seen *Invictus*. On responding affirmatively, he went on to tell me that he thought the book on which it was based *Playing the Enemy* (*El Factor Humano* is the Spanish title) was even better than the movie, but which he had enjoyed watching. I thought better than to mention that pirated versions of it were on sale down the road. But he was much intrigued when I informed him that its distinguished author, John Carlin, was a friend and that – not a difficult feat admittedly – John's Spanish was considerably better than mine, assisted by the fact that he had spent his early years growing up in Buenos Aires as the son of a resident British diplomat.

After a fairly informed discussion about the roles and legacies to history of Nelson Mandela, Desmond Tutu and F.W. de Klerk, our conversation, which lasted over a half hour, turned to the more immediate matter of football and South Africa's role and expectation as host nation for the forthcoming FIFA World Cup. I advised the president that I was due back in Asunción in a few weeks' time to support and host our national squad, Bafana Bafana, which was scheduled to play a friendly against Paraguay as part of its training preparations.

His response was immediate and unexpected: 'Well, of course, Ambassador, you must accompany me to the match, which I will now definitely attend.' In this matter, he proved to be a politician of his word.

Not only did I watch the game a few weeks later in his company (which happily resulted in an exquisitely diplomatic 1–1 draw) but he also graced the reception party that I hosted for our boys. He seemed genuinely delighted when the team presented him with their soon-to-be world-famous yellow and green jersey.

Lugo's charm did not extend to his many political opponents in the country's legislature: in June 2011, he was unceremoniously, and barely constitutionally, impeached by the senate and was replaced as president by his deputy.

The final panel in this presidential triptych was Uruguay's José 'Pepe' Mujica. Of the three heads of state, his background of armed struggle, as a leading member of the Tupamaros armed insurgency against Uruguay's authoritarian military rulers in the 1970s, including his imprisonment for fourteen years, most closely resembled the biographies of many ANC one-time struggle activists now governing South Africa. But as I read copious background notes on Mujica, in preparation for our meeting, a singular difference leapt out from the pages of his biography.

In contrast to the riches acquired, and deference expected, by many in my country's ruling elite, Mujica's election in late 2009 as president had not led to any change in his admirably austere ways and lifestyle. Apparently, he continued to live with his wife, a fellow former guerrilla, on a very modest farm on the outskirts of Montevideo and recorded as his only asset an 'elderly' Volkswagen Beetle. He also donated the bulk of his presidential salary to charity. At one level, his exemplary modesty was in keeping with what was to become my impression of his people: although just a 30-minute flight (or three-hour hydrofoil ride across the River Plate) from boisterous Buenos Aires and the somewhat boastful *porteños*, Montevideo and the Uruguayans were in every respect smaller, quieter, apparently more serious-minded, and possibly therefore duller than their outsized neighbour. On the streets of Montevideo on the morning of my meeting with the president, I was somewhat nonplussed to see so many people clutching thermos flasks. On enquiry I was advised that these contained an infusion called *mate,* a unique South American beverage, hugely popular in Uruguay, roughly approximating a bitter version of green tea. It was often drunk communally by friends and colleagues from a shared gourd also called a *mate,* through means of a metal straw known as a *bombilla.* In the interests of cultural diplomacy I tried it once, but that was enough!

When we met later in his appropriately no-nonsense office in a modern downtown high-rise, President Mujica did not offer to share his *mate* with me. But in every respect he resembled a description I had read of him in *The Economist*: 'A roly poly former guerrilla who grows flowers on a small farm and swears by vegetarianism.'[33] Elderly, short, tieless and indeed podgy, he reminded me more of a benign uncle than a head of state. Could there be a president anywhere in the world, I wondered to myself during our interesting and remarkably informal encounter, less affected by the trappings of office than this man? His rattling cough and rheumy eyes were a reminder of his 75 years and some of the ravages of time and doubtless also the torture to which he had been subject when imprisoned. Like President Lugo, he also expressed close interest in, and much admiration for, the 'South African experience' and the lessons it offered to other deeply cleavaged societies, including, he added, 'my own'.

CHAPTER 15

# THE SMALL GERM OF A BIG EVENT

From these high-level encounters and from other initial discussions, I had another light-bulb moment. I realised that the image of South Africa, even among the best informed and worldly of my interlocutors, was akin to a sepia-tinted photograph. The portrait on display more or less consisted of the following tableau: two statesmen (Mandela and De Klerk) had negotiated over a divide of centuries of racial struggle and fashioned a modern democracy and, through a process of 'truth and reconciliation', had forged a nation (with the assistance of Archbishop Desmond Tutu, another hero in this corner of 'the South') at peace with itself and the world. Winning the 1995 Rugby World Cup, against the odds with a mostly white team, inspired by its most ardent cheerleader, the sainted Madiba, had put the seal on the 'negotiated miracle'. Our imminent hosting of football's greatest tournament seemed a just reward for such an admirable and globally admired country.

None of the more inconvenient, and recent, truths then pressing in on South Africa appeared to have washed across the South Atlantic. Of the excavations being dug under our constitutional foundation, or the siren calls for nationalisation then being sounded by Julius Malema and his youth league, or the intense and coarsening race-baiting evident in the current debate back home, and the coils of corruption strangling the state and its ability to deliver, little was known or had been heard in my new domain. If South Africa had been a movie rather than a historical snapshot, then this version – highly romanticised as it undoubtedly was – ended for most South Americans in about 1996.

This somewhat outdated picture actually suited a number of my personal and diplomatic purposes. From an ethical standpoint I could with sincerity, and as a first-hand participant, describe the process of our democratic evolution and incipient nation-building. Sticking to that theme would also avoid me having to advance or defend the more recent, often ominous, developments, with which I was in fundamental disagreement.

'South Africa's Route to Democracy and Reconciliation' became the subject, and stump speech, for my multiple future forays and lectures, at schools and universities, on TV shows and to think tanks. I was practising and implementing my own version of what the business plan rather pompously termed 'public diplomacy'.

Primarily, however, this epiphany seeded in my inventive and ever-restless mind the germ of an idea for a hugely ambitious project: bringing to my new domain key political actors from my old one and some of the sporting and cultural greats who could recreate the magical moments from South Africa's recent past and provide fine exemplars of its creative future.

A year after my arrival, in November 2010, we mounted just such an event, or rather a series of diverse offerings, before capacity local audiences, under the banner of 'The South African Festival in Celebration of the Argentine Bicentenary'. This rather long-winded title captured the fact that 2010 was the 200th anniversary of Argentina's journey towards independence. Its staging in November that year allowed us to glide further on the huge following wind South Africa's hosting of the FIFA World Cup had created in July, and around which our embassy had staged a series of high-profile events.

We kicked off with a movie festival, featuring some of South Africa's best contemporary productions. It was immediately followed, at the prestigious Museo Nacional de Bellas Artes (National Museum of Fine Arts), by the display of the Nelson Mandela Photographic Exhibition, expertly curated by Christopher Till, who arrived from the Apartheid Museum in Johannesburg for the purpose. We then inspanned the services of the

South African Navy supply ship *Drakensberg*, in local waters at the time for joint sea exercises, to serve as a stage for a wondrous operatic performance by two of the brightest stars in South Africa's operatic firmament, Pretty Yende and Given Nkosi. Michal had conceived this part of the festival and we flew in the two singers, after endless logistical obstacles, fresh from their training and performing in Milan and Tel Aviv respectively.

Two nights later, the historic home of Argentine rugby, Casi Club in the northern suburb of San Isidro, was the venue for a rugby match that we dubbed 'Spirit of Invictus', and for which we airlifted from home 25 former Springboks, the South African rugby legends. Led by Joost van der Westhuizen, whose outsized role in our 1995 Rugby World Cup triumph had been captured in the movie earlier in the year, they played in front of 3 500 excited rugby fans, against a distinguished and energised team of former Argentine national players, Pumas Clásicos. Although I thought the Puma one-point win was attributable to a questionable refereeing decision, this result conspired to please mightily the locals, which was the essential idea behind the whole festival.

The *pièce de résistance* of the month-long series of events occurred the day after the rugby: a public seminar in Buenos Aires, before another capacity audience, featuring F.W. de Klerk and senior ANC leader, and soon to be appointed presidential spokesperson, Mac Maharaj, and myself – representing three strands of South Africa's democratic quilt and the hazardous journey to its construction. The debate on the topic 'South Africa's Road to Democracy', and the big political beasts we imported from home to address it, garnered acres of respectful newspaper coverage over the next few days. It also shone attention on the existential and dramatic thing South Africa had got right more than a decade and a half before, rather than on the many murkier, perhaps smaller, things that had gone wrong since then.

My own creative juices and a lifetime's worth of contacts back home, amply supplemented and often exceeded by the imaginations and practical inputs of embassy colleagues plus Michal, conceived and choreographed and, with very few glitches, delivered a very successful festival. We would go on, over the next few years, to showcase other aspects of the South African offering, from tourism expositions, to trade fairs and wine festivals. I always reminded my staff of the wise injunction, 'we're only as good as the next thing we do'. There was no shortage of ideas or areas to showboat. The problem was with money or, more precisely, the lack of it.

I was much amused when a fellow ambassador remarked, after attending one of our exhibitions, with some combination of wonder and envy: 'If only I had your budget to put on the sort of events which you do.' The brutal truth was, in fact, that I had pitifully few funds from my department for such purposes. Of our annual budget, which was never upwardly adjusted to account for local inflation of about 25 per cent per annum, only approximately 3–4 per cent of it was available for so-called 'discretionary projects', which rather mystifyingly were allocated under a line item called 'venues and facilities'.

More than nine-tenths of our yearly allocation from head office was ring-fenced for local salaries, rentals, travel, educational costs for diplomatic children, accounting and legal fees, and other charges.

It was to exasperate me at our heads of missions' talkfests how the minister and other bigwigs would boast on the one hand about the fact that South Africa now had 110 diplomatic missions in the world, and bemoan, simultaneously on the other hand, the problem of having to cut key projects from the budget – as though there was no connection between the two.

In fact, an embassy is a cost, rather than a profit, centre, in terms of projecting and promoting the country. As our budget illustrated, once all the fixed expenses and outgoings had been met, practically nothing was left over for the core purposes of public and trade diplomacy. My suggestion, at one such event, that we in fact close down and rationalise the proliferation of diplomatic outposts and establish a core of big missions in key centres on each continent and deploy diplomats on a satellite basis into neighbouring domains was met with stony silence.

'Of course what you said is logical, but you are trampling on too many vested interests and careers,' I was cautioned by a senior colleague during the tea break.

When I first started dreaming up the festival event, about ten months before its execution, I realised that my back-of-the-envelope costs for it came in at about 150 000 dollars, exceeding by well over 100 000 dollars our entire budget allocation for projects for the year.

At around this time, I was also grappling with how to convert my predecessor's deeply impressive, but highly theoretical, project from idea to execution. Ambassador Peter Goosen had won departmental accolades (and a transfer to The Hague) for initiating a voluminous 'trade study'. Simply put, and with a welter of data to back it up, derived from an intense study by a local economist of the harmonised commodity description mandated by the World Customs Organization, the many loose-leafed folders containing its findings reached a singular conclusion: South Africa exported, at a more competitive price, many of the goods and components that Argentina was then importing, at a higher price, from other countries.

This had particular application in the manufacturing sector, notably the local automotive industry and also in the supply of inputs for local mining and agriculture. If we managed to switch some Argentine importers from the third party countries and companies they were currently buying from to South African exporters providing the same, but cheaper, items then we could start to dent the terms of bilateral trade then running at about 10:1 in Argentina's favour. After flipping through its contents, I discussed its findings with Florencia Achcar. Since she and I – plus one administrative assistant – constituted the grand total of South Africa's official trade and investment presence in the three countries of accreditation, our mutual understanding was essential. So I asked her the crucial question, 'Tell me, Flor [as we all called her], how many of the Argentine companies which the study has identified have been visited by the embassy?'

'Not one yet,' she replied. It became immediately clear to me that to achieve any of my evolving objectives, from funding festivals to selling South Africa's trading advantages to the barons of local business, and even to measuring, accurately, the country's political temperature, I would need to get out of the embassy and build a web of personal relationships. As I surveyed the exceptionally modest list of contacts I had been bequeathed, the parting words of Cape Town businessperson and friend Philip Krawitz, chairperson of Cape Union Mart, rang loudly in my recall: 'Your net worth is your network, and vice versa.'

CHAPTER 16

# THE NETWORK

He looked like an Italian fashion model – an elegant, avant-garde suit hugged his lithe and tall frame and his raffishly long hair completed the impression of cosmopolitan trendiness. In fact, the appearances, again, deceived. He was Johannes Jurgens Roets, head of personal and business banking of Standard Bank of Argentina, 70 per cent owned at that stage by the eponymous South African financial giant. He awaited us at the entrance of the gleaming spire of high finance, which headquartered Standard Bank in the Puerto Madero waterfront area of Buenos Aires. I was 'his ambassador', as he rather charmingly put it, and Michal and I were there, newly arrived in town, to open our local bank accounts.

This commenced, by far, my most consequential relationship in Argentina. Johan, at one level, had long ago slipped the bonds of his early life as a farm boy, growing up near Parys in the Free State. His outward appearance and his worldliness also betrayed little trace of the archetypal chartered accountant, which in fact he was by qualification. On the back of a highly successful information technology business, which he had sold in 2002, he entered into the senior management of Standard Bank, and had been running the operations in Argentina since 2006. Adding to his taste for the exotic was his striking and glamorous blonde Russian wife, Irina Zyrianova. She had been the principal dancer at the St Petersburg Ballet, and the couple had met in 2005 when she transferred to the State Theatre in Pretoria.

In terms of achieving our diplomatic objectives, and funding some of our key projects, Standard Bank was by far the biggest, and certainly most generous, South African entity operating in Argentina. Their support also made business sense: the better South Africa was promoted and the more our embassy could produce high-level ministers, officials, sports and political stars from back home, as we duly did, the more obvious it became to their high net worth Argentine clients that the bank was an important bridge between the two countries, where it operated with consummate professionalism. (Toward the end of my term, Standard Bank Argentina would be sold, at great profit, to the largest bank of China, ICBC.)

Johan and I hit it off immediately. He was not simply a fount of funding, but became a key co-architect of many of the events that would shape my ambassadorship. But Johan met another deeper need. The only South Africans in my immediate orbit were Michal and the embassy officials. With my staff, I maintained extremely good personal relationships and, outside of work, ensured that we socialised several times a year. But I was keenly aware of the fact that I was also their boss, and responsible for professionally assessing their performances and, on extremely rare occasions, pulling one or other of them up for some significant slip. In any event, if I became too friendly with one, another could claim favouritism. In the very small ecosystem of our mission, success and survival meant maintaining a fine balance between the professional and the personal. And while Michal was perhaps now more than ever a rock of dependency and intimacy, she was as foreign and green as I was to this strange new country we had so recently entered.

## OF *CHANTAS* AND *BARRA BRAVAS* ...

Johan was the one person with whom I could share my concerns and frustrations and receive counsel based on his own experiences as a South African in Argentina, which were far deeper than my own. Johan's prowess on the polo fields and golf courses of Argentina also gave him useful insights into and access to the local elite, for whom both such pastimes were de rigueur. We were to watch each other's backs over the next few years, something of a necessity in a country where it was sometimes difficult to know whether your charming local interlocutor was what he proclaimed to be, or was in fact a *chanta,* a word and a type I was to encounter early on as it fitted several of the characters I would meet. This unusual noun was well defined by the historian Jill Hedges, thus:

> ... an Argentine word describing a condition so familiar to Argentines that it has no real translation in either English or standard Spanish, charlatan being not too far off the mark. Although the style of the *chanta* differs from province to province, he is a universal figure in Argentina. Though decent Argentines may pretend contempt for the *chanta,* there is a cultural tendency to harbour at least a sneaking admiration for a successful one.[34]

Several favour-seeking *chantas* initially crossed the threshold of our embassy, but after a few such encounters, Clara and I managed to filter out, or fob off, most of them. However, on one occasion, just after the conclusion of the 2010 World Cup, our by then well-developed deterrence mechanism failed.

The background to this incident was the vigorous and anticipatory security measures South Africa had applied to keep potential troublemakers away from the football finals. Argentina's infamous *barra bravas* – the violent gangs that exercised great control and influence over the local game (see Chapter 35) – were determined to be present in South Africa. Our immigration authorities, basing their intelligence on lists of the most dangerous *barra bravas* supplied to us by the Argentines, were equally determined to deport them before they could set foot on South African soil, or create mayhem in South Africa. Those on the proscribed register never got beyond passport control at O.R. Tambo Airport and were sent back to Buenos Aires on the next flight.

I had already experienced a backlash as a result of the expulsions – a note of protest from the Argentine foreign ministry, which enclosed a complaint from the lawyers of some of the 'brave fans' (being the literal translation of *barra bravas*, although 'football hooligans' was a more accurate description) alleging that their clients' 'human rights had been offended' and demanding an appeal. There was something deliciously Argentine about this charade: one arm of the government provided us with a list of people to deport, while another protested the deportation!

I duly ignored the note and simply sent it to Pretoria where, doubtless, for once, a bureaucratic non-response would be appropriate. I thought nothing more of the matter until one lunchtime I was alerted to a commotion in the seventh-floor reception area where our embassy handled applications for passports and visas. In terms of our security arrangements, the guards on the ground floor of our office building had strict instructions not to admit anyone to the eighth-floor reception (which admitted visitors to the diplomatic section, where I was sequestered) without checking both the credentials of the visitor and phoning upstairs to ensure the person was authorised to enter. Obviously such measures did not apply to the fairly regular stream of visa-seekers and others requiring consular services, who were sent up to the seventh floor. In any event, it was impossible to enter the embassy from the seventh floor without breaching a massive security gate that was only opened from the inside. But now in the seventh-floor reception was a young man in the company of a middle-aged woman, loudly demanding that they would not leave the premises until she had a 'personal audience with the ambassador'.

It transpired, after the receptionist correctly refused her admittance, that he was an expelled *barra brava* (and an indicted criminal, we later discovered) and she was his lawyer. They were there to 'demand justice'. The fact that they had conned their way into the embassy by claiming to the guard downstairs that they were visa applicants did not seem to trouble the attorney's sense of legal ethics, which were obviously more flexible than those I had been taught. But I certainly was not about to engage her in a debate on lawyerly conduct; in fact I was determined not to engage with them at all. But how were we to remove them since it was apparent they were determined to stand their ground, doubtless hoping to emerge as causes célèbres to their comrades and clients?

The local police were called but claimed, mystifyingly, that they could not act without clearance from the foreign ministry, and our contacts there were, literally, out to lunch. The impasse was resolved, after some time, when Mike Dunlop, our South African Police Service officer, went out to the reception and very persuasively insisted that the football hooligan and lawyer were trespassing on foreign territory. Whether he was exactly right in terms of the Vienna Convention was far less relevant than the fact that at 6 feet 2 inches he cut an imposing and, doubtless to the now less than brave fan and his lawyer, highly persuasive figure: they agreed, amidst protest, to depart. Immediately after their exit, I rushed over to the foreign ministry – now back from lunch – and received an assurance that police guards would be placed outside the embassy and residence, as they duly and promptly were for the next few weeks. We heard nothing further from the *barra bravas* or their lawyers.

## ARGENTINA'S RICH AND POWERFUL

Argentina's football hooligans were at the bottom end of a stratified society. By contrast, in the more rarefied atmosphere at the top of it were some truly impressive and even inspirational figures: men and women of high accomplishment, exquisite manners and cultural sensitivity. But the standout feature of the local upper crust was how they leavened their great wealth and achievements with huge dollops of warmth and were to bestow on us generous hospitality. In my experience, this positively distinguished them from the financial and landed aristocracy in colder, more northern climes.

Leo Tolstoy famously wrote in the opening line of *Anna Karenina*: 'All happy families resemble one another, but each unhappy family is unhappy in its own way.'

While I never found a local equivalent of the TV programme *Lifestyles of the Rich and Famous*, over time I obtained personal access to, and the friendship of, several Argentine families who could easily have starred in such a reality show. Superficially, at least, each wealthy Argentine family appeared more or less the same: they had a multiplicity of financial holdings and interests, usually originating from the land, but spun off now into a web of overlapping commercial and industrial enterprises; very often three generations of the same clan commanded different aspects of the family business; their suburban villas and beautiful apartments were for weekday use – since weekends were traditionally enjoyed on a sprawling ranch in the *campo* (countryside); the wives were generally chic and chiselled; the children were exceptionally well mannered and attended one or other of the fine, expensive private schools in Buenos Aires, modelled on Eton and with instruction in English; crisply uniformed maids served the canapés and champagne at the many receptions they hosted, often in support of a charitable cause; holidays were spent on the beach in Punta del Este and in Europe, while the big shopping was done in Miami. Most of them wisely, given the volatile history of their homeland, held the bulk of their wealth offshore. And, like all Argentines across the divides of class and wealth, the extended family was front and centre of all activity.

This generalised but broadly accurate portrait could, of course, also capture – with a few substitutions – the upper reaches of South African society. But the big difference is that in Argentina most of the country's wealth is both generated and held by private families or in opaque instruments under their tight control, rather than by and in listed investment corporations where the bulk of South Africa's patrimony publicly trades. This point was well made at an afternoon seminar we hosted featuring Dr Lyal White, one of the few South Africans who can claim real knowledge and understanding of South America. He is an impressive and passionate champion of what his centre at the Gordon School of Business Science at the University of Pretoria terms 'dynamic markets'. In his presentation, Lyal produced a compelling statistic to dramatise the difference: in 2008, the market capitalisation of listed companies on the Johannesburg Stock Exchange, as a percentage of South Africa's GDP, was in the region of 200 per cent; in Argentina, by contrast, the figure was only 16 per cent.[35]

The Werthein family was in every respect part of Argentina's winners' circle. Their business empire included telecommunications, financial services, gas and energy, real estate and land – of which they owned a great deal, reputedly over 100 000 hectares in three provinces and 45 000 head of some of Argentina's best beef and dairy cattle. I was introduced to them, in a roundabout way via a well-connected Argentine in New York (whom I incidentally never met, but as the result of one telephone conversation, received from him a treasure trove of local, hugely influential contacts). They quickly embraced Michal and me in their circle of family warmth and influence. Only after meeting and socialising first with Darío Werthein, did I discover that his two uncles, Adrian and Gerardo, owned 20 per cent of the shares in, and were directors of, Standard Bank of Argentina. And this was not the only point in common. My forebears, a common trait shared by most Jewish South Africans, came to South Africa as part of the great wave of migration commencing in the late nineteenth century until the First World War, from the Pale of Settlement – the ghettos (*shtetls*) contained within a vast swath of Russia and Eastern Europe where Jews were confined. The push factor was the waves of pogroms and persecutions, which, between 1881 and 1917, forced 2 million Jews to leave Russia. One family, the Drusinskys, left the Crimea and landed up in Johannesburg in 1896. Their infant youngest child was my maternal grandmother Tamara. On the other side of the world, a few years later in 1904, the Werthein family arrived, from Bessarabia, in southern Russia 'with nothing' and settled in the rural province of La Pampa in Argentina. Common origins and a shared culture immediately created an affinity between us. The Wertheins were to be generous sponsors of some key embassy projects. But more fundamentally and endearingly, they opened the door for us to enter, and at least glimpse, the super class of Argentina at work and play.

One night found us at a seat of honour at Adrian's 60th birthday. Adrian, a bear-like man with a fondness for Havana cigars and fine wines and a penchant for outsized black hats, lavished on us an epicurean feast, replete with dazzling bands and performers, and endless buffets of food and the finest champagnes, shared with 1 000 of his best friends, who ranged from devout rabbis to major politicians and included, happily, a few select ambassadors. We did not quite last for the grand finale of this sumptuous event, which was lamb on the spit served at 5 a.m.!

The Werthein ring of influence seemed boundless. Back in 1997, I had shared the tea table in South Africa's parliament with President Bill Clinton. But my then proximity to the 'most powerful man in the free world' was due to my leadership of a political party. Fast-forward fourteen years and Bill Clinton is long out of power and looking much sleeker and greyer than in those far-off days in Cape Town; and we shake hands again, this time at the Hilton Hotel in Buenos Aires. The Werthein family was hosting the former president to address some 200 of their friends and business associates. Clinton might be long out of office, but he has lost none of his elan or insight. He delivered two or three memorable 'take-aways', which I scribbled down on a paper napkin. Seated on a platform, between Adrian and Gerardo, Clinton amusingly described himself as 'the lost Werthein brother'. He then went on to suggest that whatever else ailed Argentina and the world (then about to record its seventh billion birth), 'everyone has got to eat and this country with its twenty feet of topsoil in the pampas, provides enough food for at least half a billion people every year'. He also noted that he had won re-election as president in 1996 on the back of delivering a balanced budget and near-zero unemployment, which, to put it at its mildest, was a vastly different situation from that confronting his successors on the world stage that evening as they stared into the pit of the worst global economic crisis since the 1930s. Clinton suggested that the only way to address the myriad challenges and crises was to stay focused on what he termed 'the future business' and not to be enthralled by the past.

I found his insights fascinating, but whether they were worth the rumoured 250 000 dollars apparently paid to Clinton to deliver them and rub shoulders with us was not a question I had to answer.

Gerardo Werthein came to my rescue in another social and business context. In March 2012, Mary Slack arrived, plus entourage, in Argentina. Mary, her late father Harry Oppenheimer and her mother Bridget had been generous and loyal supporters of the Democratic Party in the very difficult times when I first led it, at a stage when few other donors were prepared to raise their heads above the parapet or reach into their pockets to fund the South African parliamentary opposition. My association with the family was warm and my regard for Mary considerable. She was in town to visit land she had recently acquired on the coastal plain near Mar del Plata, where she intended to establish a stud farm, based on her expertise and passion for horse racing and the excellence of Argentine thoroughbreds.

Over an exceptional dinner, and fuelled by generous amounts of the finest Malbec wines, I rather rashly suggested to Mary and Jehan Malherbe, one of South Africa's best bloodstock agents, that it would be 'no problem' to arrange a get-together between them and some leading members of the country's horse industry. Perhaps lunch at our residence on Sunday, some five days later? I received confirmation shortly that Mary and her group would be 'delighted' to attend.

The only problem was that my Rolodex of local contacts did not include anyone from the country's horsey set, or so I thought. But with some long-distance encouragement from Johan Roets, via phone from South Africa, I was reminded that Gerardo had once been a distinguished showjumper, a trained veterinarian and also happened to be at the time president of the Argentine Olympic Committee. Miraculously, he was free that Sunday for lunch.

Another 'emergency acceptor' for the lunch, to borrow a racing expression, was Eduardo Novillo Astrada and his delightful wife Veronica. We had met at a dinner a few months previously and I had been charmed by 'Taio' as he was universally known. In my utter innocence in all matters relating to polo, the passion of Argentina and a sport they play better, by far, than any other nation on earth, I had simply assumed that Taio was a quietly spoken business leader, since I knew he was the head of a major chain of cinemas. As I was scrambling to put together my equine lunch, it was suggested that he would be an ideal guest. Only then did I discover (he had been utterly silent about his prowess when we had previously met) that Taio had been – in his heyday in the 1970s – one of the best polo players in the world.

Into the bargain, the Novillo Astradas, which included his five sons who comprise the ace La Aguada polo team, is, in an overcrowded field, one of the finest polo families in the country. For example, one of the sons, also Eduardo, is a 'ten-goal handicap' player – there is no higher ranking in the world of professional polo, and it is held by perhaps only a dozen other players on the planet. Their family had provided to this sport a dynasty as distinguished, and understated in its own realm, as the Oppenheimer name and legacy had bequeathed to mining.

The lunch, anchored by such impressive guests, was a great success. But, on the business side – Mary and Jehan's quest to export South African broodmares to Argentina – I was less optimistic. On all matters – from horses to harvesters – Argentina expected unhindered access to the markets of the world but saw no contradiction in erecting high barriers against any equivalent imports. This imbalance was to prove one of my greatest challenges. As I relate in Chapter 32, I would strain every sinew to right-size it, with decidedly mixed results.

It was actually the Werthein-sponsored chat with Bill Clinton that triggered in the trade-side of my mind another meeting and friendship. Gustavo Grobocopatel had been dubbed by the media as 'Soy King of South America'. But as his small plane bounced through the air pockets caused by the thermals of the vast pampas below us, I quickly discovered there was nothing regal about one of the world's most successful agribusinessmen. Red-haired Gustavo wore his accomplishments very lightly, and appeared far more interested in finding out about South Africa than he was in telling me his own remarkable story.

We were headed to Carlos Casares, a small farming town several hundred kilometres north-west of Buenos Aires, in the wheat and soy heartland of Argentina and headquarters of the family company, Los Grobo. The origins of the family, and the company, were as impressive as their achievement. The Grobocopatels had arrived in Argentina on a similar trajectory as the Wertheins. In their case, however, they arrived in Carlos Casares as part of a Jewish agricultural colony pioneered by Baron Maurice Hirsch. They were quickly dubbed, perhaps appositely, the 'Jewish Gauchos'. But Gustavo and his father, Adolf, were living and breathing proof of the adage, 'you must honour the past, but you cannot live in it'. They had pioneered the use of modern business methods, biotechnology and resource-sustainability to create one of the largest soy and wheat empires in the Mercosur region (Argentina, Brazil, Paraguay and Uruguay), the area that produces 70 per cent of the world's soy crop.

In between explaining his passion for folk singing and showing me the old Jewish cemetery in the town, Gustavo gave me a crash course in why this humble protein bean contains in its seeds, literally, the future well-being of the world. As the earth's rapidly spiralling and urbanising population is projected to reach over 9 billion people within the next twenty years, double its size from 1990, the single most important challenge will be to feed everyone. Soybean products, primarily soymeal and vegetable oil extracts, are the cheapest and most essential form of protein for animal feeds – beef, poultry and swine. Of the many dazzling statistics Gustavo flashed on the PowerPoint that day in Carlos Casares, two, in particular, stood out: China, which absorbs over 40 per cent of the world's soy imports, has moved from a per capita meat consumption of just 7 kilograms in 1975 to 50 kilograms in 2010; Argentina and Brazil have increased their annual production of soy by 300 per cent in just the past ten years. The key to this dramatic rise lay in the technology that Los Grobo and other world leaders had adopted. I was about to experience it first-hand.

We left the modern conference centre of Los Grobo for the field just outside. Somewhat warily, I was placed on a harvester and was now to witness that which I had read so much about – the 'no till cultivation' method that had revolutionised crop production here and elsewhere in the Americas. Of course, to my untutored eye, one piece of agricultural equipment looks much like another. But, as Gustavo explained to me as the harvester made its stately progress across the pasture, the one I was on had been adapted to seed the field directly without disturbing the soil. This form of tillage decreased erosion dramatically and increased the nutrients and water in the soil, since the process minimally disrupts its surface by retaining the crop residues from previous harvests. My outing that day converted me into something of a 'no till' proselytiser back home. It was obvious to me, and increasingly to the many visiting delegations I bored on the subject, that for our country, and particularly for Africa – home of the largest uncultivated agricultural lands in the world – 'no till' could be a game-changer in terms of future food security.

Gustavo was an obvious choice for a keynote speaking slot at a seminar our embassy organised a few months later on the theme 'Argentina and South Africa: Gateway Countries to Continental Opportunities'. The large and influential audience we mustered for the event at the historic Palacio San Martin, a venue hospitably provided by the Argentine foreign ministry, were as impressed as I had been with Gustavo's presentation of Los Grobo's profitable marriage of high-end technology to Argentina's natural riches and its lessons for the world. A further speaker I arranged for the event was the head of another eminent and hugely successful Argentine agricultural family company, Luis Otero Monsegur.

The company, SA San Miguel, was one of Argentina's biggest producing and exporting citrus enterprises. Argentina is the headquarters for their lemon production and Uruguay for naartjies (or tangerines). Happily for both the seminar and for my ambassadorship, Luis and his son Martin had recently decided to invest a cool 100 million rand in the Sunday's River Valley, near Port Elizabeth. They had identified South Africa as the global centre for their orange production. It was the largest single foreign direct investment from Argentina during my tenure and, into the bargain, the Otero Monsegurs and I became my good friends.

There is an even money chance that most tourists to Buenos Aires will at some stage step inside one of the city's prestigious modern shopping centres. They are at the other end of the consumer scale from the plethora of down-at-heel mom 'n pop stores described earlier. The owner of the greatest of these consumer palaces – Buenos Aires Design, Patio Bullrich, Galerías Pacífico and Alto Palermo – is Eduardo Elzstain.

Inevitably my rapidly expanding network led me to the warm embrace of this real estate mogul. Eduardo was not simply a businessperson of consequence. He also had the power of persuasion: it was his doing that ensured that one of his Buenos Aires shopping centres housed the only McDonald's in the world outside Israel that flips strictly kosher hamburgers. Eduardo was devoutly orthodox and held the number two position in the most important global Jewish organisation, the World Jewish Congress.

I would spend many hours with him as he tutored me through the labyrinths of his country's economic complexity and also signed up to support some of my embassy projects. When one of South Africa's leading young entrepreneurs, on a flying visit to the city, asked me whether I knew of a home where he could spend a traditional Friday night (Sabbath) dinner, Eduardo graciously and immediately did the hosting at his impressive home. It was a far more appropriate venue, in terms of religiosity, than the very secular fare on offer at our residence.

It would prove ironic, given the deep freeze that was to settle shortly on our own personal relationship (see Chapter 36), that Helen Zille, my successor as party leader, provided us with our first pair of friends in Argentina. Helen's mother had migrated to South Africa from Germany to escape the looming horrors of the Nazi Reich. One of her mother's sisters had arrived, for the same reason, in Argentina. The sister's son, and Helen's first cousin, Roberto 'Bobby' Herzfeld and his ebullient wife Erna were to be our boon companions as they shared with us the culinary, cultural and touristic delights on offer in such abundance here in the far south of the world. My brother Peter, impeccably connected through the International Bar Association and no mean networker himself, introduced us to Michael Rattagan and his enchanting wife Marie-Jo Cardinal. We would happily spend Sundays with them at their country retreat, appropriately named 'La Linda', a tranquil counterpoint, replete with horses and a polo field, from the urban grittiness of Buenos Aires.

Marie-Jo placed Michal firmly in the centre of her impressive circle of friends, and we were quickly absorbed into a new Argentine and internationally minded social set. But they did not just enrich our personal lives. Michael's standing as one of his country's leading mining and resource lawyers enabled me to provide instant local expertise to visiting South Africans seeking opportunities in a country that was as rich in minerals as it was complexly governed and whose rule of law was often a moveable feast, especially for the unwary foreign investor.

On the subject of feasts, the *asado* (barbecue or braai in our language) was the hinge on which so many of our pleasant social gatherings revolved. After frequent encounters with this Argentine carnivore heaven, I realised that my attempts as a weekend braaier back home were decidedly amateur by comparison. An *asado* is a ritual practised everywhere, especially at Sunday lunch, from urban slum dwellers using a grass verge off a highway to elite gatherings where a professional *asador* expertly turned the meat on the manicured lawns of a country home. In South Africa we have the habit of cooking the fare altogether on a Weber or gas cooker. Here in the land of perhaps the best beef in the world, there is a qualitative difference. First, the cuts of meat are entirely different – sliced through the bone and muscle rather than across them. The Argentine barbecue is cooked slowly by means of an iron rack over an open fire contained within a clay outdoor oven. Accordingly, each such piece of meat is served separately, and so an *asado* is a leisurely event, lasting several hours, and consisting of many courses. It usually commences with the *achuras* (offal), followed by two types of sausage – the *chorizo* (beef or pork) version and the *morcilla*, or blood sausage, an acquired taste that I never did acquire. These, together with a delicious cheese grilled on the braai (*provoleta*) and some *empanadas* (pastries containing meat or vegetables) are simply the appetisers, although in reality are enough for a hearty meal on their own. The main course comes with a profusion of different cuts, served consecutively: the *asado* itself (a form of brisket); then ribs *(tira de asado)*; the grand finale consists of at least three versions of steak – *lomo* (a form of fillet), *vacío* (flank) and, my all-time favourite, *bife de chorizo,* not to be confused with the eponymous sausage, but the local equivalent of either sirloin or entrecote.[36] Python-like, one retires from such a session sufficiently full, if not bursting, and not really requiring further food for the next few days.

It would become apparent almost immediately upon our arrival, however, that we were not simply to be beneficiaries of the kindness and companionship of a new and ever-widening circle of friends and contacts. We would be expected to play host to an army of arrivals from South Africa, from family and old friends to virtual acquaintances and for a plethora of visiting dignitaries. Each seemed fascinated to discover where, and in what style, the Leons were now living.

CHAPTER 17

# THE VISITORS

On hearing of our posting to Argentina, Michal's friend Tova Herzl, previously Israeli ambassador to South Africa, wrote: 'You will never know how many good friends you had until you are an ambassador to an interesting country with a good residence.' We more than complied with Tova's menu, and could add a further item: South African Airways flew directly thrice weekly between Johannesburg and Buenos Aires. Our new life would be fully shared, in instalments, with a battalion of visitors and guests.

The plus side of the official residence, a veritable 'house [or, in our case, multi-floored penthouse] of many rooms with room for all' was that it operated as a sort of private hotel. While we were personally responsible for provisioning it with food, drink, towels and bed linen, the state provided and paid for our two live-in domestic workers, Angela Gonzales and Alicia Vera. They gamely coped with our endless stream of lodgers, from the one-nighters to those who settled in for longer stays. On the eve of our own final departure, I totalled up more than 80 guests who had shared our residence with us in just three years. Our visitors' book reflected that in December 2010, the apartment was top-heavy with a record twelve people accommodated simultaneously, with the younger set sleeping in the solarium on the pool deck.

By and large it was a bonus and an inoculation against homesickness for us to share our new life, in such an exotic locale, with those who had so enriched our previous lives and careers. However, browsing the tacky for-tourists-only wares on display at the vast street market of historic San

The send-off: I receive my instructions from the man who had just appointed me ambassador, President Jacob Zuma, in August 2009.

At Plaza San Martin, Buenos Aires, laying a wreath on the evening of presenting my ambassadorial credentials.

Credentials ceremony: I present my diplomatic credentials to the president of Argentina, Cristina Fernández de Kirchner, at the Casa Rosada in October 2009. Behind her stands Jorge Taiana, the foreign minister with whom she later fell out, forcing his departure from public life.

Great support: With Michal and my excellent embassy staff celebrating Freedom Day in Buenos Aires in 2010.

At a high-level meeting with the Argentine foreign minister, Héctor Timerman (left), and the South African trade and industry minister, Rob Davies. Trade tensions were a running issue during my tenure.

The myth of the cocktail party: Every embassy function, happily including our own, always attracted a big attendance.

The Africa Group: With my fellow African ambassadors in Argentina, commemorating Africa Day.

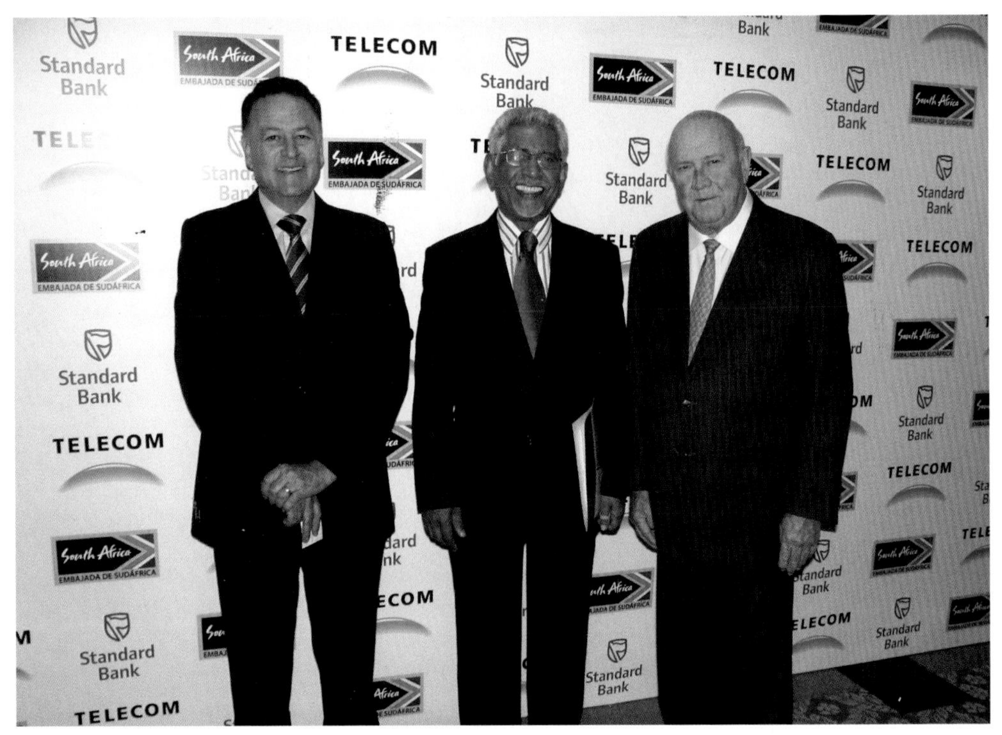


Three versions of South Africa's democratic journey: One of the highlights of our South Africa Festival in 2010 was a seminar in Buenos Aires featuring former president F.W. de Klerk (right) and senior ANC leader Mac Maharaj. Between the three of us, we covered much of the table of the South African transition.

Opposition minds: Mauricio Macri was the high-powered mayor of Buenos Aires and leading figure in the country's fragmented opposition. Doubtless, my opposition credentials endeared me to him.

A cabinet of curiosities: Nearly a dozen South African ministers came calling during my ambassadorship. Here we accompany the high-profile minister of human settlements, Tokyo Sexwale (third from left), and his children to a reception hosted by our good friend and near neighbour, US ambassador Vilma Martínez (centre).

Good steward: Pravin Gordhan (centre), the South African minister of finance, impressed the Buenos Aires audience. I invited him to address because of his reputation for fiscal prudence – in sharp contrast to the eccentric economics of Argentina.

Selling South Africa: The unflagging efforts of my colleagues and I saw a record rise in South African exports to Argentina and tourism arrivals from there.

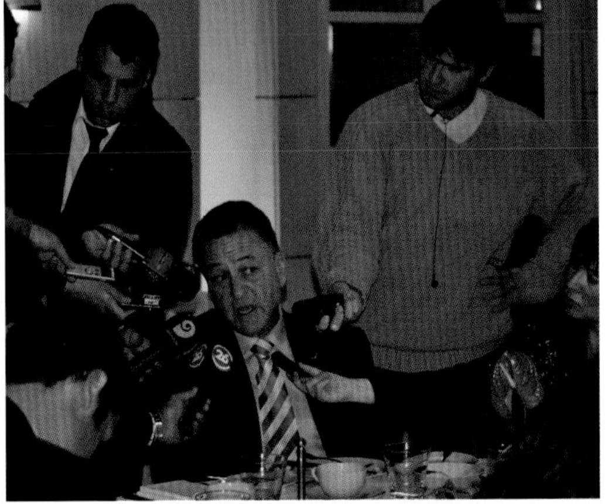

A press conference in Spanish: My battle with the Spanish language never inhibited my zeal to use the media to project South Africa's image.

Pomp and circumstance: I am saluted by the Argentine navy on parade in Buenos Aires.

South Africa operatic supremos Pretty Yende and Given Nkosi came to Buenos Aires as one of the many highlights of our South Africa Festival in 2010. Here they perform aboard the visiting Navy ship *Drakensberg*.

The entrance of the South African Embassy in Buenos Aires.

Football and the World Cup: South Africa's hosting of the global football festival in 2010 was a golden moment for our public diplomacy. The great Lucas Radebe (centre) flew in to lend support to our efforts. Seated next to him is Toxozile Xasa, South Africa's deputy minister of tourism.

Football crazy: To understand Argentina you needed to go to a football match. Here I attend one in the company of visiting South African former star Dr Khumalo (centre) and my first secretary Mziwanele Langa.

Asunción, Paraguay, is the home of the South American Football Federation. I visited its futuristic museum and left behind Zakumi, our 2010 FIFA mascot.

Looking ridiculous for a good cause: We blow the vuvuzela on the eve of the World Cup in Buenos Aires, June 2010.

F.W. de Klerk, Michal and I attended a memorable match between the South African Rugby Legends and the Pumas Clásicos.

Sports diplomacy: With the Springbok rugby team in Mendoza on the eve of the 2012 four nations championship test between South Africa and Argentina.

The playing of the national anthem before a capacity crowd in Mendoza. We leveraged a significant number of events around the Springbok presence in Argentina.

Hard work: Behind every big event lay a great deal of work and careful planning. Some of my embassy staff are pictured here just before the Springbok versus Puma test in Mendoza. From left: Mardi Pather, Rhoganee Pather, Lorato Legotlo, me, 'Shoes' Mtilwa, Frank van Rooyen and Sonica van Rooyen.

Out and about: Michal and I enjoying the perfect beaches of Praia de Pipa in the north of Brazil.

Visiting Sprinkbok legend Joost van der Westhuizen holds our newly acquired dachshund Argentino Julio. Both Joost and Julio have arresting eyes.

With some of our many visitors on a typical outing in the oldest part of Buenos Aires, La Boca. Pictured here from left are Dandre Lerm, Geoff Engel and Mark Witney.

Córdoba is the centre of Argentina's history, learning and classical Spanish architecture. Michal and I were on tour following my participation in an agricultural seminar.

In the Galapagos Islands: I regard this spectacular archipelago as the gold standard of the natural world.

Michal and I on horseback during our gaucho experience at a magnificent estancia in the province of Buenos Aires.

I get to grips with that most Argentine of institutions: the *asado*.

Telmo on a Sunday, or attending yet another late-night tango show lost some of their appeal after the 27th such outing! We eventually armed our visitors with guide books and Michal's excellent customised must-see list (included as an appendix to this book) and sent them out and about to explore the city and countryside on their own.

All these stay-overs, bar one, passed off remarkably smoothly and our friendships were intact, and usually enhanced, by the time we bade fond farewell to our visitors. The exception happened one Friday afternoon in November 2011 at the juncture of two visits and during one of my busiest periods at work. Ryan Coetzee, one of my closest political associates, was in residence for the second time. The previous December, he and two other members of the 'boys' club', as the press had dubbed them, but in fact two of the key lieutenants from my party leadership days (Nick Clelland and Gareth van Onselen) had spent some R&R time with us to decompress from the much weightier positions they now occupied in both the Western Cape government and in the Democratic Alliance. At a poolside *asado* expertly prepared by Gareth, we toasted ourselves as the 'government in exile', a phrase that would doubtless have unsettled the real premier for whom they now worked, Helen Zille.

But on the current visit, Ryan, now installed as Zille's special adviser, was leading a delegation from the Western Cape to explore options for twinning that province (a formalised process for interprovincial co-operation) with two I had identified as suitable in Argentina. We were on the eve of heading off to Mendoza for this purpose. Two days later, the British-South African academic and major scourge of the ANC, R.W. 'Bill' Johnson, and his wife Irina were due to move into the residence as our guests. Meanwhile, later in the next week, the day after our return from Mendoza, our headline public event for the year, a major bilateral trade seminar, featuring trade and industry minister Rob Davies from home and Argentine foreign minister (Taiana's replacement), Héctor Timerman, was to be launched in Buenos Aires. As part of this event we were scheduled to host at the residence a cocktail function for some 150 of the good and the great from both countries (a vastly optimistic reach given, as previously mentioned, the modest capacity of the elevators). The multiplicity of events and comings and goings was more reminiscent of my previous frenetic campaigning schedule than the more leisurely pace at which I found diplomacy was conducted.

So much for the grand plans and tight schedules: on the Friday morning in question, we awakened in the residence to no electricity, no water and no shortage of panic from Angela and Alicia. While we had slept, a fire had broken out in the electrical centre of our residential building, and the elevators had been knocked out, along with all the other utilities. We were now marooned, and literally in the dark, on the 22nd floor. Ryan and I duly huffed and puffed our way to the basement down a dangerously unlit backstairs fire escape to get to our scheduled appointments.

A few hours later I was delivered further good news from the building administrators: the elderly and noisy elevators, bane of my nightly sleep, had finally given up the ghost. The electricity stoppage had permanently incapacitated them, and it would now, we were informed, take 'a few days' (Argentine-speak for at least a week) for them to be restored, as the new parts had to be imported! The imminent visit of Bill Johnson presented a seemingly insuperable challenge: some two years before, while swimming in a lagoon near his holiday home on the KwaZulu-Natal South Coast, a minor cut in his foot had led to a horrifying, and near fatal, infection of necrotising fasciitis, which had resulted in the amputation of his leg. Bill had in the interim made an impressive recovery and, with the aid of a prosthesis, had learnt to walk again. However, even the most turbo-charged limb would not easily manage to scale the stairs to our rooftop penthouse.

There was no alternative: we decommissioned the apartment for the next week, and moved into a downtown hotel, where Ryan and the new arrivals would also have to stay. When we advised the Johnsons of this unsettling development they were game enough about it, except when they left Cape Town for the long haul across the ocean to Buenos Aires, Bill forgot the charger for his hi-tech prosthesis – an expensive, potentially ruinous, omission since if left uncharged for more than a day or so, this artificial limb is permanently incapacitated.

Ryan and I were already in the winelands of Mendoza, when Jorge drove Michal and the Johnsons to an outer suburb of Buenos Aires where the right charger was finally secured at an exorbitant price. Shortly thereafter, both Bill and Irina fell ill, just to cement their first impressions of a vacation *chez* Leon. We also, simultaneously, had to find an alternative venue for the post-seminar cocktail function and deal with a myriad ancillary changes while we camped out of the residence for the next several days.

Rather gallantly, I thought, after the unwelcome start to his Argentine odyssey, Bill wrote to us at its conclusion: 'Well, it would be possible to see our visit here as an uninterrupted chain of disasters, but in fact it was a lovely and deeply memorable stay.'

## JEMIMA AND JULIO

Often during the height of one or another political battle, while dealing with some act of deviousness or flagrant insincerity or worse, I would ruefully quote the wise observation of the great US president, Harry Truman: 'If you want a friend in politics, get a dog!' I was fortunate that I had made and kept some sterling friends in a fairly long and often turbulent political career and it was a pleasure to unfurl the tattered red carpet for them in Argentina. But I had always, even before politics, been a signed-up member to the Harry Truman school of friendship, and surrounded myself with dogs.

Since the arrival of Michal's children in my life, and especially my stepson Etai, we had become a strictly dachshund family. We eventually had a trio of them – George, Gina and Jemima. Before our departure to Argentina, George had sadly ascended to the great kennel in the sky. The children's location at various universities meant that Gina and Jemima would move with us across the ocean. They were duly dispatched, some months after our arrival, in a small wooden kennel, strapped down in the cargo hold of South African Airways. They arrived seemingly none the worse for the journey and we went about introducing them to their new abode and their new city. Their pampered existence would continue unaffected, but with one big difference: instead of having their Cape Town garden in which to frolic and, more crucially, ablute, they would have to come to terms with apartment-style living, interrupted with frequent visits to the large park across the road.

Between Michal, the two maids and I we established an informal roster. My nightly duty was to escort the dogs for their parkside constitutional. More a pleasure than a burden, I much enjoyed our outings under the big crimson and scarlet sky as the city headed towards nightfall and the dogs and I explored the enchanting park. Then one night, a few weeks after the dogs' arrival, disaster struck.

Dogs, especially the dachshund breed, have great characters and quite individual personalities. In our case, Gina was disciplined, fearless and seemingly indestructible (she had already survived, back in South Africa, two major spinal operations and a near-death experience with rat poison, not to mention numerous emergency drives to the vet to force her to vomit whole pizzas and similar stolen foods). Jemima, whom we had rescued from an animal shelter, was hugely affectionate, but very timid. This combination had lulled me to believe that no harm would come when I unleashed them in the park. And so it had proved, until the terrible night when it all went wrong.

We were walking along the lake in the park when, as per our normal routine, I took them off their leads to allow them to run about. Suddenly, Gina cocked her head and barked, and rushed off to chase a swarm of geese that had gathered behind the fenced-off section of the lakeside. She managed to insert her dwarfish body under the railings and disappeared from my view. And then, quite against the grain of her normal placid nature, Jemima scooted off in hot pursuit and also disappeared. I called and shouted and rushed to the fence but, peering over the railings in the rapidly fading light, saw neither dog, only a gaggle of now highly excited geese. I waited and called some more, but received no response. I now was very agitated. The park is very large, perhaps 8 kilometres in diameter, and is crisscrossed by many busy roads. How would I find the dogs? How could they not be harmed?

I rushed back across the road to collect reinforcements – Michal and our friend Roy Eskapa visiting from London. When we quickly returned to the spot from which the dogs had disappeared, there was Gina, waiting unperturbed for our arrival. But of little Jemima there was no sign at all. We persuaded the guard to open the fenced-off section, and when we entered we found neither Jemima nor the geese. We then, with mounting concern, divided up the park between the three of us, and scoured the area. After a long and fruitless search and having left all our details with the park attendants, we headed disconsolately back to the residence. There, Michal, via the Internet sourced several animal rescue organisations (Buenos Aires is one of the most canine-friendly places on earth, and there was a profusion of sites) and posted the details of our recent loss. In the early hours of the following morning, the fateful telephone call came: a drowned dog, answering Jemima's description, had been found, washed up on the lakeside of the park.

We were all utterly devastated and I was guilt stricken, and Gina was now alone. The only solace I felt was to know that at least for her entire, relatively brief, life with us Jemima had been cosseted and happy, which I suppose was a comfort, or rationalisation, of sorts. To offset the gloom that had temporarily settled on our lives and over the residence, a few weeks after our loss I furtively (being very unsure of Michal's response) arranged for Mony at the embassy to check out where we might acquire a dachshund puppy.

A few Sundays later we set off to the rather unpromising *barrio* of San Miguel, some 30 kilometres north-west of our residence. I had used a combination of heavy nagging, sweet reason and elementary emotional blackmail ('just look how miserable Gina looks without a companion', etc.) to persuade Michal even to undertake this journey to an unknown dachshund breeder here in an area suffering the extreme ravages of urban blight and decades of neglect. Happily the GPS of the BMW delivered us to the right address and fortunately it did not contain any personal safety warning. When I told a local friend, a few days later, of our adventure into the sticks his response was along the lines of 'San Miguel? It's so dangerous, you were lucky you weren't hijacked'. 'Come to South Africa!' I thought, but being its ambassador, did not utter, in response.

If the suburb was dodgy, then the breeder's home was positively dismal – a sort of ramshackle ruin of a structure, one or two tiers up the housing scale from what we would call, back home, a shack. But inside was a dachshund lover's heaven: all manner, types and colours of the hound were running about. As we sat chatting to the breeder in the lounge a tiny puppy attached himself to me. He had the colouring of an Nguni cow:

dappled or piebald and sporting a weird, but striking, Josephesque coat of many colours – grey, white and with tan tips around the most extraordinary eyes I had ever seen (in either a human or a dog), the one blue and the other grey-brown. I was now seriously in love, and it appeared from his nuzzling of my leg that it was reciprocated. Michal also melted; and in my exuberance I barely noticed that I parted with some serious money (about the equivalent of 2 500 rand) for this 2-kilogram bundle of joy. So it came about that this miniature *salchicha* (sausage dog) – technically a double dapple dachshund – 'Argentino Julio Leon' entered our lives.

His name is an inversion of a famous late-nineteenth-century Argentine president, Julio Argentino Roca. At the risk of anthropomorphising him, he evinced many of his nation's best and worst characteristics: friendly, happy, passionate, good-looking, vain, stubborn and ill-disciplined. My old friend, Mark Witney, visiting us later from Cape Town, observed 'this is not a dog, but a cartoon'. He also duly fell in love with Julio, as he became known, but the latter was, and remains, notably promiscuous with his affections. I have no idea whether or not this was a particularly Argentine characteristic!

CHAPTER 18

# OFFICIAL GUESTS FROM THE 'CABINET OF CURIOSITIES' AND ELSEWHERE

The desolate arrivals area of Ezeiza Airport at about 2 a.m. on an icy-cold mid-July morning is not calculated to lift the spirit or nourish the soul. But protocol requires that the resident ambassador be on hand to meet and greet the arriving minister. So there I stood awaiting the much-delayed flight (an on-time arrival or departure in Latin America is an extremely rare event) due to deliver science and technology minister, Naledi Pandor, into my tender clutches. Our embassy had done a lot of heavy lifting in the preceding months, from vetting hotel rooms to choreographing the appointments to ensure a successful and hassle-free visit. Naledi was in town to sign an agreement on nanotechnology with the Argentines and engage in other, lesser works of ministerial minutiae.

I wondered, as we sat chatting in the back of the car, at about 3 a.m., how much of my rapid-fire briefing on the political economy of Argentina her jet-lagged mind could absorb. But early the next morning, we met again and set off for a full day of back-to-back meetings followed by a dinner that I hosted for several of the local eminences that evening. In the best Argentine tradition, the evening started late and finished in the small hours, yet Naledi appeared unflagging and engaged. During our many years together in parliament, I had never doubted her intelligence and application, but we had never enjoyed anything approaching a warm relationship – the political divide and history separating us was simply too great. But here we were, together, advancing the bridges of biotechnology research and related areas of bilateral engagement.

Naledi and a slew of other ministers and their deputies I would shepherd around Buenos Aires were always on their best behaviour, generally well informed and appreciative of the embassy's efforts to provide them each with in-depth briefings and meaningful engagements. I, of course, kept reflecting on the irony of my past and current roles – sort of akin to the poacher who becomes a gamekeeper. But I did not enquire whether any of our ministerial guests held any views on this paradox.

The plus side to my previous jousts with the governing elite back home, in terms of my new diplomatic role, revealed itself in November 2010, when Lindiwe Sisulu, minister of defence and military veterans, came to town. Any government minister was, I suppose, objectively, a paladin of the state – a charmed and chosen member of the inner governing circle, for whom both title and the expectation of deference were important. Lindiwe Sisulu was, in ANC terms, a full-blown princess, and not just in their estimation of her and her lineage (her father was the struggle hero Walter Sisulu) but also in terms of her own healthy self-assessment. We had clashed in parliament when she had served as minister of housing – not a job I thought she had performed with conspicuous success. I had also found her prima donna haughtiness and disdain for accountability grating. But, in an admittedly not overcrowded field of her sometimes dowdily dressed and often inarticulate colleagues, I always gave her top marks for her stylish sense of fashion and cutting repartee.

About a year before her arrival, I had actually written to her, at the urging of our hard-working but exasperated defence attaché, South African Navy captain, Lesley Johnson, who was attached to the embassy. The letter was occasioned by a meeting to which Lesley and I had been summoned by the chief of the Argentine Navy. In his excessively polite, even slightly baroque, manner Admiral Jorge Godoy expressed disappointment that more than two years had elapsed since drafts had been exchanged on a proposed 'memorandum of understanding on defence co-operation' between South Africa and Argentina, with no final response from our side. After this gentle dressing-down, Lesley and I on return to the office drafted and sent a fairly sharply worded letter to Sisulu, under my signature. In it I concluded: 'The meeting proved to be an embarrassment for myself, for the defence attaché and, in my view, for the image of South Africa. The Argentines are clearly losing confidence in the promises that South Africa is making in the defence area. I would greatly appreciate if you could take the necessary steps to expedite this much-delayed memorandum.'

I had no great expectations for a response and in this I was not to be disappointed, initially at least. But a few months later, the defence bureaucracy lumbered into life and we received word that indeed a draft had received final approval. The minister, plus a significant top-brass entourage, would arrive in Buenos Aires in November to sign it.

With all this background, and our own personal history, as I stood in my normal perch at the foot of the air sleeve awaiting Lindiwe, I did not expect from her more than – in Damon Runyon's arch phrase – a 'medium hullo'. I could not have got it more wrong. Elegantly dressed as ever, she embraced me warmly on arrival, duly announcing, 'I am here because of *that* letter!' As I squired her around and through the signing ceremony and a whirlwind of other events during her 24-hour visit we exchanged a warm and easy banter, something that had been notably absent from previous encounters. On her departure, preceded by a braai on the rooftop of the residence in the company of the visiting Springbok Legends' rugby team, she wrote in the visitors' book, 'Congratulations Tony – you are doing a fantastic job.'

From its inception, I had judged Jacob Zuma's government in its make-up and personalities to be something of a 'cabinet of curiosities'. Two final examples from the ministerial visits I hosted confirmed my initial impression. I did not, in any true sense of the term, 'host' Tokyo Sexwale's visit to Argentina. It would be more accurate to say that the reverse happened during his stay in early 2012. I had received word, 'as a courtesy' from his office, that the minister for human settlements (the somewhat grand rebranding that the plain old ministry of housing had undergone) would be in town on a private visit to accompany former US vice president and Nobel Prize laureate Al Gore on a visit to Antarctica.

Uncharacteristically for such an eminence soon to be in our midst, his office assured me that the 'minister requires no assistance, but would be glad to meet with you if you have the time during his stay'. Tokyo and I had, in contrast to certain other ANC personalities, a warm and long-standing relationship. Back in the fraught, but I suppose – viewed now through the misty lens of retrospect – golden age of constitutional negotiations in the 1990s, we had respectively led our province (Gauteng), he on behalf of the ANC juggernaut and I for the very much smaller Democratic Party.

Sexwale lived and travelled in a highly rarefied stratosphere inhabited by the multi-billionaires of the world, of which tiny club he was, even in US dollar terms evidently, a member. This was apparent on his arrival – he came in his own Gulfstream jet, accompanied by his two personal pilots, his two impeccably well-mannered children and sundry assistants. After an enjoyable drink or two on the night of his arrival I suggested that Michal and I lead the group on a Saturday tour of Buenos Aires. He agreed with enthusiasm and we set off the next day on an abbreviated visit (in view of time constraints) of the many highlights of the city.

While touring the famous Bombonera football stadium, home to the fabled Boca Junior team, Tokyo announced, 'My only requirement is that we have lunch at the best steak restaurant in Buenos Aires!' I knew just the place. But I also realised that lunch for our group of ten at El Mirasol in Recoleta would, at about 100 dollars a head, absorb a tenth of my entertainment budget for the entire year! I duly made the booking and, not for the first time in my life, decided to 'spend in faith'. After a suitably sumptuous feast of Argentina's finest beef, washed down with copious amounts of its best Malbec, the moment of truth arrived when the bill was placed squarely in front of me. Before I could move, Tokyo swept it up and placed 1 200 dollars in crisp new notes on the table.

He said, with a flourish, 'Please note, Tony, I never use the government credit card.' I immediately responded with plain-speaking appreciation, 'Well, Tokyo, you are probably the only minister who doesn't need to!'

That evening we accompanied the Sexwales to a small reception, hosted by my good friend and near neighbour, US ambassador Vilma Martínez, for Al Gore and his Antarctic explorers, who included Virgin founder Richard Branson and Hollywood movie star Tommy Lee Jones. One of the advantages of my diplomatic activity in the preceding months had been a deep immersion in the intricacies of the climate change conference, which South Africa had hosted in December 2011 in Durban on behalf of the United Nations (COP 17). Although its outcome contained, in the words of one observer, 'more shoulds than musts', Gore was gracious enough to thank me, as the South African in his presence, for its 'successful outcome'. Vilma then advised the one-time presidential candidate that 'Tony provides me with all my information on American politics'. Gore laughed and somewhat awkwardly gripped my arm, but there was something stilted in his body language, which seemed to underline his weakness as a public figure and which gave the clue, perhaps, to his defeat in 2000 at the hands of the apparently more likeable, although perhaps less intellectually nimble, George W. Bush.

On the latter point, however, a pleasant dinner some months before in Buenos Aires with Bush's one-time White House speech-writer disabused the conventional wisdom. David Frum told us in answer to a question by my brother Peter who was visiting us at the time: 'I can tell you two things about George W. Bush: he is not nearly as stupid as people think he is, nor nearly as nice.'

The month before the high-profile and high-living Sexwale descended upon us, I played host to a cabinet colleague of decidedly lower wattage. Bathabile Dlamini, the minister of social development, was in town to represent the government at the inauguration of the recently re-elected Argentine president Cristina Fernández de Kirchner. Over drinks (or in her case, tea) at the residence she reminded me that we had been colleagues together in parliament. I had thought her name and face familiar, and then the penny dropped.

Before her ascent to ministerial office, she had been one of my many colleagues fingered in the 'travelgate' scandal in 2004. So many other abuses of high office had since been revealed that even the most conscientious corruption-watcher might have forgotten this particular mark of Cain that had done so much discredit to the institution of parliament. I had not, and after she repaired back to her hotel, Mr Google confirmed that she had pleaded guilty to one count of fraud for abusing the parliamentary travel voucher system, to an amount of 250 000 rand. She had, under generous plea-bargain arrangements, been sentenced to a fine of 120 000 rand or five years' imprisonment.[37]

Clearly, in the morally flexible, perhaps ethically challenged, Zuma government this had not impaired her subsequent upward march to high office. But whatever her past sins, Ms Dlamini proved to be an uncomplaining and undemanding guest at the following day's endless, thoroughly exhausting and poorly organised ceremonials arranged to honour and herald Cristina's second presidential term. In fact, the only specific request that Dlamini made during the weekend of her visit was to purchase some memorabilia of Ernesto 'Che' Guevara, an easy find the next day in the flea market of San Telmo, especially since this hero of the Cuban Revolution had in fact been born and raised as a scion of the Argentine middle class in the city of Rosario.

This impressed the minister who, in her note of thanks, wrote to me: 'I must say that I felt very emotional when we landed here because it is the place of Che Guevara, one of the sons of the soil who have dedicated themselves to all humanity.' I was not certain that the victims and families of Che's infamous 'revolutionary justice' in the early days of the Cuban Revolution, especially his presiding role in mass executions at La Cabaña Fortress prison in Havana, would have shared her sentiments.

## A PRESIDENTIAL CLOSE-UP

Attendance at her inauguration in December 2011 had provided me with only the most distant view of President Cristina Kirchner. Strangely enough, of all the visitors I invited and received, it was the long-retired F.W. de Klerk who provided me with direct access to this centre of power in Argentina. In a country where political, economic and state interests were highly personalised and tightly held, face time with the president was the most valuable coin, by far, in the currency of the realm. Time and distance had erased the rancour that had once characterised my relationship with F.W. when, some ten years before, he had supported the machinations of his successor, and my deputy leader in the Democratic Alliance at the time, Marthinus van Schalkwyk on his route out of our party to the ANC. His presence in Buenos Aires in November 2010, along with his formidably charming wife, Elita, and Mac Maharaj, was – as mentioned previously – to preside as a keynote speaker at our public seminar on 'South Africa's Road to Democracy'. Considerable political controversy later attached itself to the last white president of South Africa when, in 2012, in a clumsy interview with CNN he was perceived to be defending the apartheid system of homelands. But there was no denying the fact that his singular act of political bravery in 1990 had – alongside the moral leadership of Nelson Mandela – inaugurated the constitutional settlement that had made South Africa one of the most admired countries in the world, not least here in Argentina. Happily, this visit would also reset our friendship with F.W. and Elita.

De Klerk's reputation and standing secured us a late-night (by our standards, not hers) meeting with Cristina at the Casa Rosada on a Monday evening. Her all-powerful husband (and presidential predecessor and presumed successor as well), Nestor, had died, quite suddenly, of a massive coronary just three weeks before. This event, as related elsewhere, was personally devastating but politically helpful to his widow. That night she was appropriately dressed in black, although I noted the silk taffeta frills on her sombre outfit indicated that mourning had not entirely erased her keen sense of fashion. She rose from behind her desk to greet us and gestured us to sit with her at the top end of an ornate conference table, whose intricately carved chairs were as elegant as they were uncomfortable. Aside from her interpreter, we were alone with the most powerful person in the country. A framed miniature replica of a street poster then mushrooming across the city was the only table adornment. Across a photograph of the Kirchners embracing, it proclaimed: 'Nestor is with Peron, the People are with Cristina!'

Entirely absent from our 40-minute encounter were any of the histrionics and stridency that typically characterised her public addresses. Up close and personal, the president was the soul of warm intelligence: the public Valkyrie replaced by the private schmoozer. After she thanked De Klerk for his expression of sympathy on her recent bereavement, she told him, 'I feel as though I am sitting next to history.' The vigorous-looking 73-year-old F.W. immediately riposted, 'I hope that I am not yet history, Madame President!'

After an exchange of further pleasantries, including De Klerk noting that this was his third visit to Argentina, we were then treated to

Cristina's view of the world *circa* November 2010. She told us that she had much enjoyed sitting next to President Zuma at the recently concluded G-20 summit in Seoul. She added:

> Developed countries cannot continue as before. Einstein reminded us that it is 'sheer madness' to do the same things again and again and expect different results from them. The fall of the Berlin Wall was meant to ensure the triumph of American capitalism. But then there was 9/11 just a few years later, and just two years ago Wall Street itself fell. This has not been 'the end of history' predicted by some at the conclusion of the Cold War.

She told us that at the G-20 meeting she had recently attended, how striking it was that US president, Barack Obama, was a somewhat 'diminished figure'. 'Previously everyone wanted to crowd around him, now he remains an important figure, but only one among several. I noticed how German Chancellor Angela Merkel practically opened the door for the President of China. The world and its centres of power are shifting.'

This led her, inevitably, to a robust defence of her controversial 'model of economic development'. She launched forth with a vigorous elucidation of its many achievements: 'Our model has helped boost aggregate domestic demand and found a way to ensure that money and savings don't simply accumulate in banks, but that they are productively used by companies and the government to boost demand and retain jobs.'

De Klerk was far too tactful to raise with her an issue on which I had briefed him, namely the government seizure of private pension monies and central bank reserves for this purpose. But he did gently raise with her the flip-side of her model, the galloping inflation rate of Argentina then charging along at an annual rate of an estimated 25 per cent.

Cristina flicked her hair away from her face and responded: 'We measure over 400 products in determining shifts in prices. Only beef, which Argentines anyway eat far too much of, has registered any real price inflation. Attempts are being made to use inflation as a political weapon by my opponents. Inflation is a fabrication of the media.'

And you, Cristina, I thought silently to myself, suffer from the well-known disease that afflicts powerful leaders who shut out contrary voices and views, namely political autism. When I wrote up a report on the meeting for head office, I commented, more diplomatically, on her mythologising of inflation:

> There is little credence here for the president's depiction of inflation as a 'fabrication'. It should be noted that the current wage and salary negotiations have seen increases of around 25–30 per cent being recorded. The widely discredited inflation statistics provided by the national statistics agency (INDEC) which posts inflation at around 11 per cent have little credibility in reputable economic and civil society circles.

## NOBEL ENCOUNTER

De Klerk's visit and the access it provided to President Kirchner was a highlight in an overcrowded schedule of visiting political panjandrums and personal friends. Nine months later another, far more reclusive, South African Nobel Prize winner arrived in Argentina and my encounter with him was in its own way even more fascinating and affirming. This was despite the disastrous choice of restaurant that I selected for our encounter.

J.M. Coetzee had been awarded the 2003 Nobel Prize in Literature and had twice won the Booker Prize. In my highly inexpert view, he was the towering giant of South African letters; in his exacting and extraordinary prose, so much 'richer than all his tribe'. The embassy was advised that this prince of literature was about to arrive in Buenos Aires as guest of honour for a literary festival, and the organisers thought perhaps the South African ambassador would care to meet him? Indeed the ambassador would be most honoured to do so, we quickly responded. However, at the outset two problems seemed to present themselves: I utterly disregarded the first of these, namely that Coetzee was now – technically – no longer a South African citizen, having a few years before immigrated to Adelaide and very publicly and ceremoniously assuming citizenship of Australia. The second issue appeared more intractable, and was evidenced by the means of our initial direct communication, or lack thereof. The author had a famed reputation as an ascetic recluse: according to one colleague he had seen him laugh 'just once in a decade'; while a social acquaintance described a dinner party where the great man had 'not uttered a single word'. The festival organisers made it clear to us that we could not, apparently on his instruction, communicate directly with Coetzee and certainly could not have access to his e-mail address. It reminded me of a visit that I had once paid to the king of Sekhukhuneland in the desolate hinterland of Limpopo province. Although I was seated in the same room as His Majesty, protocol required me to address him through a medium, and he responded indirectly to me through the same person. Setting up a meeting with J.M. Coetzee appeared to be the electronic equivalent of this, and I had little expectation that he would accept the (indirect) invitation I had sent him to join me for lunch on his arrival in Buenos Aires. I was so pleased and surprised to receive, via the conference organiser's e-mail, a warm and affirming response and positive acceptance to 'Dear Tony', signed off breezily by 'John', that I gave no attention to selecting the venue for our lunch date. I merely told Clara 'just book at the normal place'. This was shorthand for the Plaza Grill, a famed home of the outsized steak.

Instead of having fixated on my guest's apparent social diffidence, I would have done well to have remembered that he was also one of the world's more illustrious vegetarians, as a cursory glance at the title, never mind the contents, of one of his books *The Lives of Animals* made clear. And who could forget the vivid scenes of euthanasing dogs in *Disgrace,* which many regard as his finest work? With a sinking feeling I recalled, far too late, this rather obvious background fact as my tall and trim famous guest's piercing blue eyes rather quizzically studied the menu in front of him. But 'John' very quietly asked for a pasta dish (off the menu but happily available) and waved away my apology for my very undiplomatic choice of restaurant.

We then proceeded to discuss all topics under the sun, from diplomatic work, to the intricacies of Spanish, some rather well-known politicians and especially rugby, of which his expert knowledge was so much greater than my own. I presumed to ask him why he had chosen to relocate to Adelaide. 'It is the perfect place if, like me, you enjoy a quiet life in a small-sized city,' he easily and, contra-reputation, laughingly responded.

I did not, however, in our most agreeable two-hour get-together, feel emboldened to ask him anything about his literature, intuiting that this might be an off-limits subject. He also did not ask me, directly, about my political career.

Two nights later, I had a front-row seat in the packed-to-the-rafters Malba Art Museum auditorium as Coetzee read one of his spellbinding short stories, 'The Old Woman and the Cats'. He made some pleasant opening remarks in rather good Spanish and then proceeded to read his beautiful 45-minute tale of rationality versus emotion in pitch-perfect English. I felt privileged to bear witness to this event, and deeply proud that South Africa had produced such an extraordinary and austere talent.

Perhaps the most remarkable feature of the evening was how the normally boisterous *porteño* audience was utterly still throughout his reading; clearly as mesmerised as I was by this encounter with greatness. They rewarded him with a huge ovation at the end of his reading. I did not manage to say goodbye to him as, again contrary to reputation, he patiently sat at a table on stage and signed copies of his books clutched by a vast queue of his admirers snaking through the venue.

However, a few mornings later I was profoundly moved to find in my inbox an e-mail of thanks from 'John', which in an encomium of praise stated, 'I always admired you for the job you did as leader of the opposition, never (at least to an outsider's eye) allowing yourself to be disheartened in the face of huge odds. I think you should look back on that phase of your life with great pride.'

I noticed at the top of the note that it had been sent from his private e-mail address.

CHAPTER 19

# THE AMBASSADORS

'An ambassador is someone who thinks twice before he says nothing.' This sage advice was rendered by Rengaraj 'Vish' Viswanathan, the pint-sized, but hugely effective, Indian ambassador to Argentina. We were sitting in his high-rise office with its sweeping views of the port of Buenos Aires, where container ships and cargo vessels lined up to discharge and receive the shipments of exports and imports, which were one of the key measurements of any diplomatic mission's success.

On closer acquaintance, Vish did not, happily, entirely practise what he preached. In fact he blogged, tweeted and offered a platform of useful insights as an old South American hand, whose sign-off line, on numerous electronic missives was 'Passionate about South America'. Early on, I decided that while the code of *omertà* (the shroud of silence, originating in the south of Italy) might well apply to the more cautious and prudent members of the diplomatic community, it was ill-suited to my own more outspoken disposition. However, I was not so crassly undiplomatic as to directly criticise the multiple examples of misgovernance, which I soon observed in my host country or which continued to emanate from South Africa. I saved my inner critical thoughts on happenings in Argentina for the 'weekly report' that our mission dispatched every Tuesday to head office and in my occasional notes of protest about South African foreign policy to the minister of international relations, Maite Nkoana-Mashabane, of which more anon.

My appointment with Vish, shortly after my arrival in Argentina, was part of my outreach to divine from more seasoned colleagues the secrets of the guild I had so recently joined. Like a sort of Freemasonry, were there specific rites and practices in international statecraft to master? My meetings with fellow ambassadors yielded different results.

The pecking order of diplomatic protocol is determined by the arrival date of the ambassador in his or her post. In this sense, ambassadorial seniority was very similar to the seating plan of parliament, where front-bench allocations were allotted on the length of parliamentary service. Once again in my new life, I was, in September 2009, a backbencher, just as I had been exactly twenty years before when I first arrived in parliament. I forged an immediate bond with my fellow new arrivals, the ambassadors with whom I had presented my credentials to the president. We were a decidedly mixed bag, but quickly became fast friends as we fathomed the depths of our new environment.

Mexico's Francisco del Rio was a man of immense charm and high intelligence and a seasoned diplomatic hand. Naela Chohan of Pakistan, also a foreign service professional, brought to our group a combination of warmth and graceful elegance. In her and her husband Musa's company it was easy to forget the cruel caricature of their conflict-ravaged country as a 'failed state with nuclear weapons'. Like me, Mario Boyd of Panama had been recruited to diplomatic service from politics, and shared with me an amused scepticism about some of the pretensions and puffery inherent in our new profession. But, on any objective measure, the most important member of our neophyte band was the US ambassador, Vilma Martínez.

Few relationships are as important and fraught with complexity as the link between Argentina and the US, or in fact the bonds between Latin America as a whole and the hemispheric giant, the US. Ever since the Monroe Doctrine of 1823, the US had regarded South America as its unique sphere of influence, if not dominance. The blowback from this was the many populist movements in Latin America, which had been fuelled on high levels of 'anti-gringo' sentiment. Fifty years before Vilma's arrival in Buenos Aires, President John F. Kennedy had proclaimed an ambitious 'alliance of progress' between North and South America and promised to pump billions of dollars into the region with the pledge to build a hemisphere 'where all people can hope for a sustainable standard of living to live out their lives in dignity and freedom'.[38]

These high-sounding words and aid dollars were seen, accurately, by many South Americans as a cover for a stringent US-backed anti-communism, which the US executed, replete with covert aid for regime changes of left-leaning governments on the one hand, and by providing support for traditional authoritarian governments in Argentina, Chile, Brazil and elsewhere on the continent on the other hand. A more cynical, and to many anti-American critics accurate, view was provided by President Richard Nixon, who apparently advised a young Donald Rumsfeld in 1971, 'Latin America doesn't matter. People don't give one damn about Latin America now.' He told the future American defence secretary about which part of the world 'to avoid if he wanted a brilliant career'.[39]

But Latin America mattered 'more than a damn' to the current US president, Barack Obama. While the region was by no means its largest trading partner, by 2009 trade to Latin America (excluding Mexico) had grown by 82 per cent compared to 1998, with the total flows nearly three times those between the US and Africa, for example. At the time of my arrival as ambassador, American exports to Argentina stood at just under 10 billion dollars, in comparison to the very modest total of about 150 million dollars of South African goods and services exported to Argentina in the same year.[40] Whereas I had about seven major South African investors to worry about, Vilma's embassy was responsible for the interests of some 500 US companies with operations in Argentina.

Our embassies reflected the difference: hers, in the post-9/11 world, resembled a fortified bunker in suburban Buenos Aires and housed some 350 US diplomats and agency officials as opposed to the grand total of 27 employees (the cook and cleaners included) under my baton. The controversial presidency of George W. Bush had inflamed the anti-American cheering gallery, led by Cuba and Venezuela, and which had been echoed to some extent by the populist Kirchners in Argentina. However, the advent of Barack Obama, an avatar par excellence of American exceptionalism, was hugely popular in this corner of the Americas, and his election held the prospect of a fundamental reset in hemispheric relations.

It had not gone unnoticed in the capitals of Latin America that the large Hispanic, or Latino, bloc in the US had played a pivotal role in Obama's 2008 election. Vilma, his personal choice as ambassador to Argentina, was a leading member of this community and, like her president, had risen from modest emigrant (in her case, Mexican) origins to the pinnacle of legal practice in Los Angeles. She had a very distinguished record in public life, especially in leading the battle for Mexican-American legal rights.

Vilma, like me, was a stranger to diplomatic ways. But, while the new South African ambassador to Argentina did not attract undue or outsize attention, in Vilma's case she had barely unpacked her bags before she was in the midst of serial and very public controversies. This had nothing to do with her quiet and courtly demeanour. It was, as in the rest of the world, the result of her being the resident embodiment of the world's hyper-power (albeit somewhat in decline) and the globe's biggest economy. The first fire she had to douse was a vicious and violent strike launched by militant local trade unionists against the US food giant, Kraft. Almost before an uneasy peace had been brokered between management and workers there, then the notorious Julian Assange struck, or rather WikiLeaked, against her with nearly calamitous results.

Among the 250 000 US-purloined diplomatic cables that Assange's WikiLeaks organisation published online were several unvarnished opinions and reports on local intelligence-gathering emanating from the US embassy in Buenos Aires. They appeared at the height of an escalating confrontation between President Kirchner and various media groups. So, naturally, two of the newspapers concerned, *Clarín* and *La Nación*, delighted in providing their readers with acres of details on the questions raised in the confidential (and I thought extremely well-written) reports on such matters as the mental stability of President Cristina Kirchner and widespread allegations on the dubious origins of her family's current multi-millionaire status.

As a matter of practice, every US embassy cable, whether personally inspired by the ambassador or written by a lowly official, appeared under the signature of the ambassador. Before the conflict that now existed between Vilma's embassy and the Casa Rosada could heat up any further, she wisely arranged a telephonic apology, soon followed by a personal visit from the secretary of state, Hillary Clinton, to calm the waters between Argentina and the US. I suggested to Vilma that being the US ambassador to Argentina (or anywhere else in the world, come to think of it) reminded me of the famous South African definition on the difficulty of editing a newspaper under apartheid restrictions: 'It's like walking through a minefield blindfolded.'

But the advent of WikiLeaks brought home to me the tension between my new role as a diplomat and my own preference for transparency and open dialogue, especially acute in the vulnerability, read accessibility, of digital recording. I quickly discerned there was, in fact, no contradiction. At one of our endless heads of mission conferences, the South African foreign minister had harangued us: 'I receive far too many reports, the contents of which I can view on CNN.' I took this to mean that any cables from our embassy should, where possible, contain insider information and a frank, sometimes even brutal, assessment on the issue being reported on from the country in question. There was no shortage of government critics in Argentina and there was, in fairness, much to criticise about the increasingly eccentric economic course and political polarisation championed by the country's president. I decided early on to 'report and be damned'. But obviously there is the world of difference between a frank assessment provided on a confidential basis to inform Pretoria's policy-makers and sharing these views with the entire world!

Happily, Mr Assange and his gang of cyber-leakers had bigger fish to fry than exposing South Africa's viewpoints on South America. However, whatever WikiLeaks claimed it achieved for openness, its advent probably did inhibit or chill the writing of cables from some key embassies, and thus did considerable damage to the uninhibited and robust commentary that any worthwhile diplomat should provide to his or her head office.

Another early friendship I struck up on my diplomatic rounds was with the British ambassador, Shan Morgan. She was a career diplomat of personal warmth and steely professionalism. She required both attributes in spadefuls, since her job in Buenos Aires was even more challenging than Vilma's. This all related to the 'F. word' or the Falkland Islands, which in Argentina had to be referred to as Islas Malvinas.

As I relate in Chapter 29, the dispute over the sovereignty of this windswept and (in my opinion at least) God-forsaken archipelago some 460 kilometres off the coast of mainland Argentina was a constant, running conflict between Argentina, which claimed them, and Britain, which governed there, with the support of the islanders. Argentina's invasion of the Falklands in 1982 and the subsequent war to recover them launched by Britain meant that the UK envoy in Buenos Aires had a hard time of it, especially since in a country where practically every issue was disputed, the rallying cry '*Las Malvinas Son Argentinas*' (The Malvinas are Argentine) was one of the very few themes that united this fissiparous nation. But Shan, in the best British stiff-upper-lip tradition, managed her post with sangfroid, which I found deeply admirable.

Whatever Argentines thought about the issue, their strong attachment to British ways and the magnificence of Shan's official residence, whose luxuriant gardens I thought resembled the biblical description of Babylon's, ensured that her dinners and lunches attracted the who's who of Buenos Aires society. I was happy to be frequently included on the guest list at her über-elegant soirées.

Compared to the headlines that the Anglo-American diplomatic missions attracted in Argentina, South Africa's bilateral relationship with Argentina was less controversial and of a lower profile and generated far less background noise. I spent considerable energy, some of our meagre resources and raised generous sponsorships to amplify our voice and views in the local media and in the mindset of the Argentine government and people with some success. But the one area where South Africa held the ring in Buenos Aires was as chief representative of Africa. This was admittedly not an overcrowded field in Buenos Aires but it did lead me to the somewhat somnambulant 'Africa Group' of resident heads of diplomatic missions.

CHAPTER 20

# THE MYTH OF THE COCKTAIL PARTY

The dean of the Africa Group at the time of my arrival was the ambassador of Angola, a certain Mr Fernando Dito. All ambassadors meet periodically in geographic groupings and as the newly arrived South African emissary, and thus most junior member of the Africa Group, I presented myself early on to my dean. 'Ambassador,' I politely enquired of the Angolan, 'what is the best practical advice you can give me on operating here most effectively?'

I was a little taken back by his response: 'Have a two-hour nap every afternoon; it's the only way that you will cope with the late hours that the Argentines keep,' he solemnly advised.

Of course, Ambassador Dito was referring to the social circuit of endless cocktail functions and dinners, invitations for which flowed onto my secretary's desk by the sack full. And it has to be said that old Fernando (for he was in truth quite antique at the time of our meeting) threw a helluva party. His last Angolan national day, just before his recall home, at the sumptuous Alvear Palace Hotel, undoubtedly the finest and certainly the most expensive hostelry in all of Argentina, if not in South America, was a sight to experience and a wonder for the hedonist epicurean. 'Never underestimate the price of oil!' I mumbled to a colleague as we munched on the caviar and the prawns, washed down with vintage champagne, freely available at the event.

Apparently, certain of my diplomatic colleagues spent a lot of their time agreeably gliding between various national day receptions and some or other cultural offering, which, if assiduously attended, would leave little time, and certainly no energy, to do what I thought to be the more essential tasks of diplomacy. I was not alone in my view. The great John Kenneth Galbraith – like me, as mentioned, a transient member of the diplomatic community – used his corrosive pen to shatter the myth of the cocktail party, which still lubricated embassy life and living in Buenos Aires, some 50 years after this observation was drawn from his own posting in India:

> I never learned anything at a cocktail party or a dinner that I didn't know, or needed to know or wouldn't soon have learned in the normal course of business. The emphasis that diplomats of all countries and in all capitals accord to entertaining is the result of a conspiracy by which function is found in pleasant social intercourse and controlled inebriation.[41]

I became a convert to his school of thought, and would make fleeting appearances at those cocktail and other functions I deemed absolutely core to my diplomatic business. I was often amused when one or another diplomatic colleague would say, 'Tony, we haven't seen you around recently. Where have you been?' Decoded, this meant, of course, I had not attended the last twelve cocktail parties or musical evenings arranged by the Association of Diplomatic Spouses. I never did answer with the truthful response, 'Actually, I have been doing my job.'

I was not surprised to learn from the corridor gossip in my embassy and at head office that several South African ambassadors were inebriates, one of whom, I was reliably informed, would insist as early as at the 10 a.m. meeting that his sober and conscientious colleagues join him for a stiff drink before the business of the meeting could be commenced. Another apparently was interdicted dancing semi-naked down the streets of a major European capital, clutching a champagne bottle.

Unsurprisingly, DIRCO had a Wellness Centre, one of the aims of which was to assist South African diplomats to overcome substance-abuse problems. This was hardly unique to South Africa, as Galbraith observed of his fellow diplomats in India so many decades before.

Clearly, alcohol was then and remains today a powerful, but potentially destructive, lubricant of diplomatic work and life.

But inevitably the job, however workmanlike I intended to be in it, did involve hosting functions, dinners and even dreaded cocktail parties. By the time our mission ended in Buenos Aires, Michal and I had presided over at least 50 such gatherings. Were they simply 'conspiracies', as per Ambassador Galbraith, for 'controlled inebriation' or did they serve a more useful purpose?

Whatever my own view, it was abundantly clear that locals delighted in an invitation embossed with a country's coats of arms and issued in the name of the ambassador and his señora. It mattered little whether it was obscure Bulgaria or mighty Brazil that was hosting a diplomatic event. The same crowd of Buenos Aires socialites, dressed up in their finery, well coiffed and bejewelled, would queue for hours to shake the hand of the hosting diplomat (happily, a fast track was usually arranged for fellow ambassadors, allowing a quick entrance and, in my case at least, a fairly rapid exit).

This, again, is a universal phenomenon. When Clara, my embassy personal assistant and 'social secretary', was recounting to me one day a call she had received from a Buenos Aires social lioness in high dudgeon at her non-invitation to our Freedom Day reception, my mind cast back to my time as parliamentary leader of the opposition in South Africa. I had just announced the reshuffle of portfolio allocations to the members of our caucus when I received an agitated visit from a senior colleague. Renier Schoeman's political flexibility – he was at that stage briefly passing through the Democratic Alliance en route between the National Party and the ANC – was matched only by his social ambitions (in this matter, he was more a mountaineer than a climber). He complained bitterly that he had been omitted from membership of the parliamentary committee on foreign affairs, on which he had long served but which was now completely outside his new responsibilities. When I pointed this out he responded: 'But if I am not on that committee I will not be invited to any diplomatic functions in Cape Town!' I admired his somewhat uncharacteristic candour, and duly surrendered and reinstated him.

CHAPTER 21

# 'OFFICIAL ENTERTAINMENT'

Three imperatives informed my own view of 'official entertainment' as described in our own, relatively modest embassy budget. The first was a consequence of the perversity of government financing, or what could be dubbed 'the use it or lose it' principle. I quickly discovered that far from incentivising savings, public finance practice actually penalised thrift.

If any item on the annual budget had not been spent up to at least 97 per cent of the allocation, an assumption was made that the unit, in our case the diplomatic mission, in question was incompetent, dilatory or poorly managed. Not only would the ambassador and his corporate services manager be carpeted, but the next year's budget would be shrunk accordingly!

So whatever my views on the merits or otherwise of spending the ring-fenced amount of about 100 000 rand on a national day celebration, for example, I could not allocate it for another purpose. And not to use it at all would be to invite the penalties described. However odd the rule book, there was no limit placed on imaginative use of such functions. This led to my second principle for entertaining: align the event to some strategic purpose. Thus, for example, we propagandised the 500 people we assembled for a very liquid breakfast at a Buenos Aires hotel for the opening ceremony of the FIFA World Cup in June 2010, with endless videos highlighting our majestic tourism offer in South Africa. The huge spike in our tourism arrivals from Argentina after this global event (continuing to this day) could be, in part, attributed to such relentless marketing.

The third rule was enabled and enforced by Michal: use every culinary event to showcase South Africa. This proved to be both a challenge and a home-grown lesson in the upside of globalisation, or the borderless world. We were hosting a dinner at home for Argentine and international guests and Michal had decided to serve samosas with the drinks and bobotie as the main course. Here we had to make a virtue out of necessity. In import-averse Argentina, not much beyond some form of very basic Indian ingredients were possible to source locally and even then they were hard to find. Fortunately, we had placed in our luggage and container some essential spices and chutneys. But our cook at the residence, Angela Gonzales, who originated from Paraguay, was bilingual only in the sense that she spoke Spanish and Guarani (an indigenous Indian language much used in her native country). She certainly could not read a South African recipe and had never hitherto apparently extended her culinary repertoire into preparing such exotica.

Shortly before the dinner, I discovered Michal scouring the Internet for the best and simplest bobotie recipe, and then meticulously translating it into Spanish and relaying the information to Angela in the kitchen. None of our guests on the night in question imagined that my Israeli wife had inspired and translated an ancient Malay–South African recipe, which was cooked to perfection, for her first time ever, by our Paraguayan chef in an Argentine kitchen. Accompanied by some of Jean Engelbrecht's finest Rust en Vrede estate red wines, the *postre* (dessert) of malva pudding rounded off a perfect evening. Dinners thereafter became progressively easier to prepare, and often we used an outside caterer, also subject to the cooking-in-translation method.

Back home I had always been a very hands-on host, fussing around my guests, filling their glasses and assisting to serve and, if necessary, clear the courses. That is what I always regarded (and learnt from an early age) to be my role at the home dinner party. Being an ambassador presiding at an official dinner in the 'official residence' was to become a very different sort of host – the hands-off variety – and something of a difficult habit for me, the ultimate micro-manager at work and at home, to learn.

I do not know the context that led to the famous Woody Allen aphorism that 'the secret of much of life is just to show up'. But its author could have been describing my new and unfamiliar role as 'mein host' at one of our official events. Aside from choosing the guest list and selecting the wines, I simply had to pitch up at my home at the appointed hour. Everything else, apart from conducting the conversation along agreeable lines, was performed by a small army of chefs, waiters and maids. I kept reminding myself that when this gig ended, I would resume my hands-on role at the dinner table and in the kitchen after my return to South Africa. But, while in my Buenos Aires posting, I did not underestimate the cachet that an invitation to an embassy dinner table held for even the most blasé and well-heeled local. Perhaps the British ambassador to Norway (himself the son of an ambassador) was onto something when he wrote, 'My father used to tell me that the quality of an ambassador was determined by the skill of his cook.'[42]

In order to both lend lustre to our guest list and to reciprocate hospitality we would often mix Argentine guests with fellow diplomats, a usually agreeable and winning combination. Despite Michal's Israeli origins, we numbered among our diplomatic friends several Arab ambassadors and their spouses, even those who were still, officially at least, in a state of war with the Jewish country. We thought this fact pleasant and unremarkable, if not somewhat ironic. One Saturday night however, the potential hazards embedded in such a relationship surfaced. It was about half an hour before the start of a dinner at our residence, and I was called to the phone. The usually amusing and animated Afaf Hadman, wife of the Lebanese ambassador, who was among the invited guests expected shortly, was on the line. She sounded anxious and edgy.

'Tony,' she commenced nervously.

'Is everything all right, Afaf?' I responded.

'Well actually, Tony, I hate to do this, but I do need to ask you an important, perhaps rude, question before we arrive ...'

I was completely mystified about what this enquiry could be about and urged her to proceed.

'Tony, we need to ask you whether the Israeli ambassador is among the guests tonight. Because if he is, Hicham [her husband, the ambassador] and I cannot attend as our country laws prohibit any contact with Israeli diplomats.'

When I assured her that the Israeli ambassador to Argentina was not among the guests invited that night by my wife, she sighed with relief and announced, the danger averted, they would be present shortly.

It was clear that as far as Israel's Middle Eastern enemies were concerned, Michal's South African status operated as a sort of River Ganges washing away the perceived sin (in the somewhat myopic view of official Arab policy) of her Israeli identity.

The other members of our Africa Group of Heads of Mission, as we were called for official purposes, were certainly entranced by the minutiae of hospitality. Most of our meetings seemed to revolve around matters social, not political, or, heaven forbid, geo-strategic. Endless hours would be spent on determining how many dollars were needed for an Africa Day celebration or which restaurant would be selected to host the farewell function for a departing colleague.

In fact, Africa Group was something of a political misnomer, since most of our small club of mission heads from the continent were North African, and were therefore strictly Arab rather than African, and the sub-Saharan resident ambassadors numbered precisely three (South Africa, Angola and Nigeria), with a chargé d'affaires from the Democratic Republic of Congo. The latter had by all accounts been forgotten in Buenos Aires by his government for more than twelve years and his very intermittent receipt of funds from Kinshasa meant he had to move offices and homes on a fairly frequent basis, to apparently cheaper accommodations.

## LUNCH WITH AN UNDIPLOMATIC FOREIGN MINISTER

On one occasion, however, the newly enthroned dean of our group after Dito's departure, Larbi Reffouh, ambassador of Morocco, announced with some excitement that our next meeting would be a working lunch with the newly appointed Argentine foreign minister, Héctor Timerman. This promised to be a welcome and substantive change from our normal and dull routine of picking menus or dealing with the complaints of the late arrival of duty-free goods. I much looked forward to this, my first up-close-and-personal meeting with the foreign minister, since it would provide me with direct access to the apex of the Argentine foreign ministry. And so it proved, although for thoroughly disagreeable reasons.

The Timerman name was famous in Argentina, and indeed throughout the world. This was entirely attributable to Héctor's father, Jacobo, a liberal journalist and publisher, who, at the height of the 1976–82 Dirty War conducted by the military junta in Argentina against its own citizens, fearlessly publicised their serial human rights violations and atrocities. In April 1977, he was arrested by the junta, severely tortured and kept for a long period in solitary confinement. It was only the result of sustained international pressure that secured his release and exile in Israel where he published a harrowing account of his ordeal, the international bestseller *Prisoner without a Name, Cell without a Number.* I read it at the time, while a law student at the University of the Witwatersrand, in about 1981. I developed a huge admiration for its courageous and pugnacious author, and was drawn to the similarity in his experience to that of thousands of detainees under the states of emergency then enforced in South Africa.

The son rose to prominence on the back of his father: a lengthy exile in New York was followed, after the restoration of democracy in Argentina, by a career back home as a journalist and TV talk show host, where he established a reputation as a fierce champion of human rights. He was initially a supporter of the liberal cause in Argentina but after the ascent of the Kirchners he became a fervent Peronist. This, in turn, led to diplomatic rewards, first as consul general in New York and latterly as ambassador of Argentina in Washington, D.C. It was from this perch that Cristina brought him home, in June 2010, after her fallout with the impressive Jorge Taiana. His lunch with our group was shortly after his surprise appointment.

It was a given that Spanish was the language of official communication in Argentina, although most of the top officials in the foreign ministry spoke and were happy to converse in English. Among our African group on the day of the Timerman lunch was the affable and jocular ambassador of Nigeria, who rejoiced in the splendid, if politically incorrect, name, Empire Kanu. Empire and his wife Tina were firm and popular fixtures on the Buenos Aires social circuit. He was always to hand with a ready quip and an expression of astonishment when I described to him some or other issue with which I was grappling. 'Tony, don't take life so seriously!' he would inevitably respond.

However, Empire resolutely refused to learn or ever speak Spanish, not even the most basic *hola!* would emanate from his lips. When I once asked him about his obduracy, especially since by then he had been in Buenos Aires upwards of four years, he responded somewhat tautologously. 'I am the representative here of Nigeria, and since English is the official language of my country, it is the language which I speak in order to represent my country.'

Many Argentines I had already encountered in high offices of state exuded an easy charm and affability, and expressed a genuine curiosity about the wider world, especially in the presence of foreign emissaries. I quickly gathered, during his rather stilted small talk over pre-lunch drinks, that the new foreign minister was not among their number. Or else he was having a bad hair day. However, the table conversation that followed was an eye-opener.

No sooner had the hors d'oeuvre been cleared at the lunch table than Minister Timerman peered around our table and announced that he would like to make some remarks. He then drew from his breast pocket a speech, which he delivered in Spanish to our group of just ten people. I made out from his rapid-fire delivery that he set a high premium on Argentina's relationship with Africa and then led into the inevitable monologue about how, since Africa itself had been a victim of colonialism, all Africans should stand in solidarity with Argentina as it confronted 'the last colonial anachronism', Britain's continued rule over the Malvinas.

'Ho hum,' I thought to myself, disappointed by the partisan and nationalistic remarks of the new foreign minister. Then Empire Kanu made bold to speak and addressed some or other question to Timerman, needless to say in English. Since the foreign minister had spent much of his life in the US, he hardly had any problem in comprehending my unilingual colleague. But he sneered at him and answered (in English): 'Why do you choose to speak the language of colonialism?' I could not believe this crass and undiplomatic response and felt impelled to interject. '*Perdón,*

*Señor Canciller, pero no es el idoma español también del colonialismo?'* (Excuse me, Mr Foreign Minister, is not Spanish also the language of colonialism?) Timerman gave a mirthless laugh, and a curt nod of forced agreement, probably thinking me to be something of a smart aleck. I marked him down as a boor, and his subsequent behaviour in various diplomatic spats fortified this initial impression.

CHAPTER 22

# DIPLOMATIC SILOS AND CHILL WINDS FROM SANTIAGO

Of the many wrong assumptions that I made initially about my new post in South America was the surmise that there would be frequent contact between my mission in Buenos Aires and our sister embassies spread across the Americas. While we were all joined at the administrative hip in the Branch Americas and the Caribbean in the DIRCO hierarchy, and our relatively ancient, unstable and erratic communications system operated out of a computer hub based in Brasilia, there was otherwise little direct contact between our embassies.

Part of the problem was that the branch head, Deputy Director General Ambassador Nozipho Mxakato-Diseko, had no sooner been appointed to take charge of our division than she was commandeered to lead the intricate preparations for South Africa's presidency of the United Nations Climate Change Conference in Durban in December 2011. But it was not simply that the boss was 'missing in action'; it was also structural – each embassy was effectively a self-contained silo. Despite the confluence of South African interests, which objectively existed among the embassies in Brasilia, Santiago, Lima and Caracas, with our station in Buenos Aires, contact between us was neither mandated nor particularly encouraged. The branch itself, which covered all South African diplomatic operations between Ottawa in the north and Buenos Aires in the far south, met exactly once in three years in a dedicated and rather desultory regional conference in São Paulo in Brazil.

I was, however, directly in charge of the small South African mission in Montevideo, Uruguay, headed by a chargé d'affaires, an amiable career diplomat of long-standing, Dawie Jacobs. Although I was his notional superior, he certainly did not require much supervision from me and we easily solved whatever issues needed attention by telephone and e-mail, interspersed with my semi-annual hops across the River Plate to Uruguay.

The major attraction of Uruguay, however, was leisure not work. The Atlantic coastal resort of Punta del Este resembled a combination of Plettenberg Bay and Monaco, with a touch of Las Vegas thrown in via the gaudy Conrad Punta del Este Resort & Casino that dominated the downtown beach area. Its gleaming seaside condominiums stood sentinel over seemingly endless golden beaches and were largely foreign-owned. Through a process of social serendipity I was amazed and delighted to discover that an early Durban childhood friend of mine, Mark Hackner, whom I had last sighted in my home town perhaps four or more decades before, was one such owner, in his case of one of the finest penthouse properties in 'Punta', as the resort town is universally known. Now a very successful real estate developer and resident of Atlanta, Georgia, we had a happy reunion in both Argentina and Uruguay with him and his wife Ruth and marvelled at how our triangulated lives, in South Africa, North and South America, should come together across an ocean of both distance and time.

My reunion with a far more recent and work-related acquaintance was to prove, however, a less happy affair. I had met my ambassadorial neighbour in Chile, Ms Dudu Moerane-Khoza at our regional conference. She had a departmental reputation for 'being difficult' and was apparently posted abroad, on a back-to-back basis, to keep her out of the hair of the paladins at head office. However, when in 2010 an earthquake shattered Santiago and severely damaged the South African Embassy there, I immediately agreed to dispatch our highly efficient corporate service manager, André Lizamore, across the Andes to lend a hand and assist with the loss assessment. I was to learn anew from this act of collegial solidarity the truth of the expression, 'no good deed goes unpunished'.

A year or so later, Michal and I were due to fly to Santiago to spend a long weekend with our friends Patrick and Siobhan Esnouf. Patrick, also a Durbanite of origin, had enjoyed a successful career at Anglo American and had spent the last several decades in South America where he had headed the mining giant's continental operations. Now he had his own independent mining venture company and Siobhan and he lived in some splendour in Santiago. We much anticipated spending a few days in their very agreeable and hospitable company. When we were planning the weekend, Patrick mentioned that he was chairman of a private luncheon club for expatriates and wondered whether during our stay with them I would consider giving the members an informal address about my career in South African politics and related matters. Once I had confirmed with Patrick that this would be indeed a private (no media) event, I accepted the invitation and thought nothing further of it until a few days before our departure.

Apparently, it is considered 'good form' or at least collegial etiquette to advise the resident ambassador of another country of your intended presence in their domain. I had no idea whether in fact such proprietaries were observed or strictly required, but decided, as a courtesy, to drop Dudu an e-mail of my pending visit to Santiago and added that I had been invited by Patrick to speak to some of his friends at the Chile Club and understood (as he had in fact advised me) that she would be present at the event, in which case I looked forward to seeing her there.

Instead of a polite acknowledgment or some other collegial greeting, I received back a barely contained fusillade of fury. It concluded with an admonition of bureaucratic gobbledegook and personal pique: In essence, she advised me that since I was undertaking a private visit, and as a serving South African ambassador in another country, featuring as a keynote speaker in a country where there was an accredited ambassador (namely herself), I would be well advised to clear my presence at this inconspicuous event with the chief of state protocol at head office in Pretoria.

Even more amazing than its bristling hostility was the fact that Dudu had copied the e-mail to no less than the director general, the minister and the chief of state protocol in Pretoria!

I was truly gobsmacked, and recalled the well-worn maxim, 'those who mind don't matter, those who matter don't mind'. Instead of repeating it to her, I wrote a response of icy politeness, which masked the disdain I now felt towards my diplomatic neighbour:

> With great respect, I believe this matter has been mischaracterised and indicates a predominance of form over substance. The invitation for me to address the club was private and there was no official imprimatur on the invitation and there was no public aspect to this event of which you complain. I can assure you that had the roles been reversed, I would have both welcomed and encouraged you to appear on a platform in Buenos Aires, since our Embassy here encourages and arranges a multiplicity of voices to advance the cause of South Africa.
>
> I also hardly think based on the facts in question that it was necessary to escalate my courtesy advisory to you to the Director General, the Minister and to Public Protocol. Doubtless these officials are preoccupied with more pressing matters of state … I certainly had no intention of involving the hierarchy in Pretoria in a matter of such insignificance.
>
> I do not think any useful purpose will be served by continuing the correspondence in this matter.
>
> Regards,
> Tony

Of course, I did press the 'copy all' icon ('Why not?' I thought, applying the 'misery likes company' principle). I cancelled my speaking engagement to the chagrin of Patrick, but we enjoyed a happy weekend in Santiago without sighting Dudu. I was later advised by a head office source that my experience with Dudu was nothing compared with the treatment to which her subordinates were subject. The embassy in Santiago was apparently not known, to understate matters considerably, as a centre of productive happiness and its head allegedly spent much of her time and effort fixating on and venting her furies on such trivia. South Africa certainly chose some strange vessels for its diplomatic accomplishment.

CHAPTER 23

# A GLORIFIED TRAVEL AGENCY AND POST OFFICE

The cold blasts across the Andes contrasted with the warmer vibrations that hummed down the wires with my direct point of departmental contact, the 'Mercosur Desk' or 'business unit' at head office, which was directed by Ben Joubert, assisted by Janet Kotze and Jonge Rabe. In a bureaucratic sea of often slow or indifferent and, sometimes, non-responsive units, our desk was something of an outlier, an island of resolute helpfulness and promptness.

Much of my working day was spent communicating with them and in clearing the messages that crowded my embassy inbox from the desk and elsewhere in the department. Of all the boring and banal tasks with which I was now seized, few exceeded the dreariness of having, every morning, to read the overnight 'cables' (in fact e-mails, since the 'official communicator' intended as a secure method for encrypted communications seldom, if ever, functioned) from Pretoria and beyond. While the occasional nugget (such as a useful trade report, a new policy initiative or a final response to a long outstanding request) shone out from the 50 or so messages awaiting my daily attention, most were of a far duller sheen.

I had much enjoyed Charles Dickens's masterful and mirthful take on nineteenth-century government bureaucracy with his creation of the Circumlocution Office in his fine novel, *Little Dorrit.* His satire on the absurdities, incompetencies and the strangulating effects of red tape was an act of creative and corrosive brilliance. I never imagined, when I first read it, that I would be starring in a twenty-first-century equivalent of the 'place of endless confusion'. But indeed such was it to be on the receiving end of the relentless demands of the DIRCO machine.

I usually managed to either meet or deflect Pretoria's endless requests for forms, filings and 'adjusted norms and prescripts' or whatever. But, just occasionally, I snapped. In one case, when our mission, severely incapacitated at the time due to the delays in transferring staff to fill our vacant posts and harried by other demands, received some ridiculous request for some or other adjustment for one or another audit, I decided to blast back and wrote to the requesting official:

> Frankly this is an intolerable situation. This Mission is without a Corporate Service Manager (CSM) as you and Ambassador ____ are very well aware, and we have been so since 01 July 2011 [the note was written in mid-October]. Despite our dire incapacity caused entirely by Head Office being unable to arrange for security clearances for transferred officials, this Mission has complied on time with every request and deadline. As you know our Attaché [I see today the post has been re-christened as 'Third Secretary'] has been doubling as both CSM and Attaché. She is currently finalising her preparation for her departure tomorrow to the Mid Term Budget Review in São Paulo where, without prior experience, she will have to defend our ever shrinking budget. Now you require certain further information on the budget by next Tuesday, and the only person who can provide it properly is going to be away from office on official business ... relating to the budget!

Just for once I received an empathetic response, which in its own masterful way indicated the Sisyphean nature of the bureaucratic beast:

> Dear Ambassador. Your frustration is quite understandable. The original request was formulated extremely vaguely, as you would recall, and seemed to drop out of the ether. In fact the format we attached is just a guess as to what they want. Who wants this? I have no idea. Why? I have no idea ...

Again, this was emblematic of diplomatic work and life the world over. Whereas in days of yore, the enciphering and deciphering of telegrams, typing and retyping of drafts was the daily mainstay of embassy activity, which, of necessity at least, were relatively few in number. In the words of one (British) ambassador, 'the painstakingly slow craftsmanship of old' where a diplomat could 'spend days (sometimes weeks) polishing a single dispatch' had given way to the advent of electronic mail, where 'faster communication means more communication'.[43]

A significant amount of our cable traffic reflected the fact that, in many ways, an embassy today is a sort of glorified combination of post office and travel agent. A South African candidacy for some or other international agency required Argentine support and our job was to lobby the foreign ministry (in truth this was less exacting a task than it might appear, since in essence it simply required a trip across the road by our counsellor clutching the formulaic 'Note Verbale' and the candidate's résumé and receiving the necessary assurance that the embassy would be notified in 'due course' of the Argentine determination).

'Political tourism', as I cynically dubbed the requests that we received to arrange the itineraries for one or other of the parliamentary/provincial/municipal delegation shortly to descend from home upon Buenos Aires, required more thought and effort, although the value of such visits to the unsuspecting taxpayers or ratepayers funding them ranged from the cost-effective to the questionable.

I now found myself on the other side of the fence: during my parliamentary career I had hardly been immune to the pleasures of overseas trips, although perhaps not to the extent of a senior colleague, a relentless foreign junketeer of whose disposition it was once observed, 'he's either irritable or overseas'. Sometimes, the South African contingent had a clear idea and specific purpose behind their mission. In late 2009, the somewhat obscure Amajuba District Municipality, from the far north of KwaZulu-Natal, for example, sent on a study tour a highly engaged group of councillors and officials among whose number were some serious agronomists. At our debriefing dinner I learnt far more from their extensive visit to the agri-rich areas of Argentina than I had hitherto known on the value and validity of technology transfers from Argentina to South Africa. The fact that some Argentine farmers were already at work in their municipality applying the famous 'no till' cultivation method on the soils of Zululand underlined the relevance of their tour.

At the other, and perhaps more typical, end of the scale was a note that the desk sent me toward the end of my tour of duty in July 2012. It was a request from the premier of the province of Limpopo, proposing a two-week visit to South America, including stopovers in Brazil and Venezuela (where President Hugo 'El Comandante' Chávez rendered Julius Malema a conservative reactionary by comparison) and a proposed two-day 'official visit' to the Argentine province of Salta. When I studied the suggested dates for the latter, I noted that it would occur over a weekend. I did not write back to the desk and suggest that given that the premier was presiding over a province that had been declared bankrupt and incapable of managing its own affairs and was embroiled in a scandal over the non-delivery and burning of school textbooks, it might be prudent for the premier to remain at his post in Polokwane. I did, however, tersely note that it would be impossible to arrange official meetings in sleepy Salta over a weekend and suggested the itinerary be reconsidered. We heard nothing further.

We were not always so fortunate and certain intrepid political junketeers would simply inform our embassy of their proposed visiting dates, outline an extremely vague *raison d'être* for the journey and then leave it to my hard-pressed embassy colleagues to fill in the blanks and arrange the meetings and the programme, which they always managed to accomplish with some aplomb.

Sandwiched between these petty tasks and urgencies was what I conceived to be the meat and potatoes of my work. In essence this meant explaining South Africa to South Americans and the reverse. It also entailed me becoming a maven, or temporary expert, in many matters from the issue of 'lumpy skin disease' in the Bonsmara cattle embryos we were trying to export to Argentina to (in this case unavailingly) obtaining tax relief for South African Airways, to offset the punitive landing costs levied in Buenos Aires.

I discovered, in my mid-fifties, that I was still capable of marshalling new information and, sometimes persuasively, arguing an intricate case to push the envelope for an investor or exporter. In their own way, these tasks could prove both absorbing and challenging. But the most intriguing, and maddening, aspect of my new work was to develop a coherent narrative on the long-running melodrama, or tragicomedy, of politics Argentine-style.

CHAPTER 24

# 'VOTE FOR A BETTER YESTERDAY'

'*El*' (Him), the president said in a quavering voice, her tear-filled eyes rolled heavenward, and the flag-waving crowd roared its approval. This was politics as grand opera, and Cristina Fernández de Kirchner, the black-draped widow for the past seven months, was the star, its leading diva, in the long-running power play, which stretched back eight years exactly to the day when her late husband and presidential predecessor, Nestor, first assumed power on 25 May 2003. In fact the 'Him' was not a reference to the Almighty, but to the late Nestor, although in the charged atmosphere of the stadium in the city of Resistencia, in the far northern province of Chaco, the distinction between the deities was evidently blurred.

Earlier that morning, 25 May 2011, the diplomatic corps had gathered at the local Buenos Aires airport to board a government-chartered jet and some two hours later had been delivered first to the local cathedral for the religious service (*Te Deum*) and now were in the stadium for the president's address to mark the 201st anniversary of the 'Day of the Revolution', which had set Argentina on the path to independence from the crumbling Spanish Empire of yore. That at least was the ostensible purpose of the commemorative events. But her speech and the banners in support of her governing Victory Front party (one of the several factions of the split Peronist movement), which draped the venue, had all the sounds and appearances of a partisan event in support of her yet-to-be declared presidential candidacy that she would announce a few weeks hence.

Meanwhile, as Cristina peppered her speech with references to the late Nestor with nuggets such as 'finally your dream of an inclusive Argentina has come true', some of my fellow ambassadors and I, seated a few rows behind, shifted somewhat uncomfortably. This was not simply because of the party-political capture of an official state event (something wearingly familiar for a South African, at least). More practically, we were enduring hours of endless speechifying from hard seats, facing an icy wind and other than a stale roll on the plane some hours before, had been entirely without refreshment. Deliverance came from my immediate neighbour at the event, Pakistani ambassador Naela Chohan, who had wisely anticipated just such an eventuality. She generously shared with me her roti bread and other eastern delicacies, which provided some much-needed fortification against the elements.

After the event, replete with brass bands, military parades and all the other panoplies of state power, we were rewarded with a brief presidential handshake, the exchange of meaningless pleasantries and then whisked to the airport for the flight back to the capital. Apart from marking my visit to my tenth province (out of 23) in Argentina, and about 90 seconds of presidential face time, I had not accomplished much in the nine hours since we had first assembled for the early morning departure. When later enveloped in the more familiar comforts of the Buenos Aires residence that evening and nursing my whisky, I glanced at the TV news, and saw, at least, the reason for our long journey northward with the president.

It was in the form of the most powerful Catholic in the country, the cardinal of Buenos Aires, Jorge Bergoglio, giving his *Te Deum* sermon from the pulpit of the splendid Buenos Aires Cathedral. But far from praising his president, he spoke against what he called the 'resentful vindications that seek to cover up their incapacity to offer creative and trust-inspiring alternatives'. Clearly, Cristina-loving Chaco had been a safer bet for the criticism-averse Kirchner (in the October election, she garnered more than 80 per cent of the Chaco vote, and while she won a majority in Buenos Aires it was by a decidedly more modest margin). I had heard on the rumour mill that when, a few years earlier, the cardinal had delivered a similar homily, interpreted as critical of the president's conflictual style of politics, she had vowed never to set foot in his cathedral again. In this matter, at least, she was a woman of her word.

## ENEMIES

But if my journey with the president had yielded modest results, it had given me further insight into what was termed locally 'the K. style of politics' (as in Kirchner). Right from their professional start in life, in the Patagonian province of Santa Cruz, where Nestor and Cristina made their first fortune as foreclosure lawyers buying up distressed (today we call them subprime) properties before seeking political office, the Kirchners had, in the words of one analyst, 'always taken a dim view of anyone rash enough to get in their way'.[44] And in the finest tradition of the movement, which they were eventually to lead, defining enemies and 'being nasty' became a matter of policy. A few months after her thumping re-election victory, ace local journalist James Neilson explained the practice of confrontation and its rewards rather well:

> Nestor Kirchner showed [Cristina] the way when, after moving into the Pink House back in May 2003, he quickly made himself highly popular by wading into military men, foreign investors, creditors, 'orthodox' economists, the IMF, and a great many others. Seeing the policy worked so well, ever since then Kirchnerite officials have continued to remind Argentines that wicked foreign 'neoliberals' and their treacherous local stooges are out to get them.[45]

Setting one sector of Argentine society against the other, or against shadowy external enemies, was a defining feature of Peronism in action, and one that had been practised to perfection and rewarded with electoral success by the movement's founders, Juan and Evita Peron. The illegitimate daughter of a wealthy rural landowner, Eva Duarte Peron had used her resentments against the circumstances of her birth and poverty-stricken upbringing as the rocket fuel for her husband and her own political ascendancy some 50 years before the Kirchners assumed centre stage and claimed the leadership of the movement. In her ghosted autobiography, *La Razón de Mi Vida* (which had been compulsorily prescribed to every schoolchild during the Peron government of 1946–55), Evita made her resentments about the causes of poverty plain: '... and the strange thing is that the existence of the poor did not cause me as much pain as the knowledge that at the same time there were people who were rich.'[46]

She died of cancer at the incredibly young age of 33 in 1952, an event that for Argentina was the occasion of a national outpouring of grief and rage, matched only perhaps elsewhere in the world by the reaction to the death of Princess Diana some half a century later. It also presaged the removal of her husband from power some four years later. But her political influence stretched from beyond the grave and across the generations and was certainly alive and well in the presidency of Cristina Kirchner, who clutched this mantle by constantly invoking the name, words and iconography of *Santa Evita*.

But as a detribalised politician myself, I was constantly amazed at the potency and longevity of Evita's appeal. Having led my own 'Fight Back' campaign in South Africa, I discovered that my brand of confrontational politics was, by comparison, distinctly mild and rankly amateurish. At the time of Juan Peron's return from eighteen years in exile to assume the presidency once again in 1973–74, Argentina was visited by the famous novelist and caustic essayist, V.S. Naipaul. He described the 'hate as hope' brand of Peronist politics as a form of redemptive, but destructive victimhood, which, in his view, chimed well with national sentiment. In 1974 he published his essay *The Return of Eva Peron*, and when I read it during my ambassadorship some 35 years later, it not only affirmed my own observations of modern-day Argentine politics but, more painfully and pointedly, I thought could have been penned about elements of the political discourse then ventilating back home in South Africa. Naipaul observed:

> Eva Peron devoted her short political life to mocking the rich, the four hundred families who among them owned most of what was valuable in the million square miles of Argentina. She mocked and wounded them as they had wounded her; and her later unofficial sainthood gave a touch of

> religion to her destructive cause … And in the end that was why Argentina (in 1973) virtually united in calling Peron back, though the first period of his rule had ended in repression and disaster, and though he was very old and close to death … He had become the quintessential Argentine: like Eva before him, like all Argentines, he was a victim, someone with enemies, someone with that pain about others.[47]

And I was not the only South African to be struck by the similarities. In April 2010, I arranged a visit to Argentina by three high-powered editors from back home: Mondli Makhanya (*Sunday Times*), Peter Bruce (*Business Day*) and Tim du Plessis (*Beeld*). We did some heavy interviews, but also had a lot of fun visiting leading technocrats, politicians, economists and journalists, enjoying a liquid lunch on the banks of the Tigre River delta and, of course, attending a tango show. But away from the programme, we had the chance to catch up, reflect and compare. After almost every session, one or other of the editors would say something along the lines of, 'it's just like home: a beautiful country and people, but the fantastic potential is being destroyed by foolish politicians'. In his 'home thoughts from abroad' piece, Tim reflected on the fact that in the 1930s Argentina was one of the top ten countries economically in the world, and a few decades later South Africa was amongst the top 20; whereas today Argentina and South Africa are stuck somewhere between number 40 and 50. 'We are both progressing backwards,' Tim wrote. He concluded, emphatically, that the cause of national malaise was identical in both cases:

> Argentina's current political leaders are just like the ANC: inherently corrupt, instinctive power abusers, with hardly any respect for democratic institutions like the courts, the media and the central bank … And nothing is ever their fault. They are masters of the art of handing out blame and finding excuses. Just like the ANC …[48]

Doubtless, the South African editorial trio was also struck by, and felt a frisson of identity with, the fact that their visit with us in Buenos Aires coincided with Kirchner's ongoing vilification of the Argentine press, particularly the mighty *Clarín* media empire, which the president blamed for many of her travails. Shooting the messenger was a popular presidential pastime. The newspapers (barring a few that supported the government) returned her dislike with interest: forests' worth of detail was devoted to one government scandal or another. It had no affect on her eventual election victory. Perhaps in this matter, as well, Argentina and South Africa were coupled on the tote. But in terms of chilling the public debate, along with its general misgovernance, Argentina was a considerably worse offender than South Africa: Cristina's party had pushed through congress a bill to regulate and control the newsprint industry, a considerably more anti-press measure than anything contemplated at the time by President Zuma's government.

And, like the ANC back home, the Peronist movement – more concerned with power than ideology – was not confronted by any serious electoral threat. Since 1945, and including eighteen years of proscription, it had won eight of ten presidential elections it had contested, and the two non-Peronists elected to power had been forced from office prematurely. And again I felt a deep sense of déjà vu for the politics of home when it was apparent that the most serious political divisions in Argentina were within the ruling party and its restless trade union allies, rather than anything on offer outside its powerful ranks. Perhaps the party founder, Juan Peron, had been factual more than cynical when he apparently noted on his return to power after his long exile in Spain, 'Argentines belong to different parties, but all of us are Peronists.'[49] Precisely because politics in Argentina fitted around the personality and whims of its president, and the checks on her authority were so flimsy, during my tenure Cristina – certainly after the death of Nestor – flew solo in the stratosphere of power. Her opponents never reached higher than the cumulus clouds far below her.

## FREEBIES FOR EVERYONE

Of course, the explanation for the Peronists' longevity in power did not lie simply in the cult of personality. Nor was it entirely attributable to the ability to fan the flames of class resentment and fuel the politics of envy, or to invoke ceaselessly past glories perhaps best left in one of the many of Evita's shrines and monuments that dotted Buenos Aires. 'Vote for a better yesterday' was a borrowed but, I thought apt, phrase, which fitted the president's pose as arch-custodian of the flame of Eva and Juan Peron. The truth was that Cristina and her government also delivered, big time, to her constituents, the poor, and particularly the lower middle-class sector of society, which meant the bulk of Argentines.

She faced re-election in 2011 backed by an economy that by then was firing on all cylinders. Global demand for Argentine food exports, coupled with a fairly weak currency and surging demand for its exports, particularly automobiles, from neighbouring Brazil, had seen growth surge to 9.9 per cent (more than triple South Africa's at that time) in the first quarter of the year, compared to the twelve months before. Eschewing the more orthodox economic approach, which suggested that good times are used to conserve resources for future bad times, she followed the precedent of her husband and ramped up public spending, subsidies and handouts (or *subtes*) on everything from cigarettes to public transport, petrol and even certain foodstuffs, and put in place what the *Financial Times* called a 'feel good consumer spending boom'.[50]

Kirchnerite economics (see Chapter 32) was 'addicted' (the newspaper's word of choice) to endlessly stimulating the economy, giving it shots in the arm by raiding the public purse (from private pension funds to central bank reserves) and splurging the proceeds on public sector pay hikes, raises for pensioners, bread and circus-type entertainment such as '*Fútbol Para Todos*' (Football for All), whereby the national government took over, at a cost of some 170 million dollars, the televising of local premier league soccer matches from the pay-TV channels.[51] In presidential election year, state spending rose by a scorching 34 per cent compared to a year before. Of course, such rampant spending fuelled inflation, which then touched around 25 per cent a year. You did not need to be an expert to realise the entire 'model', as Cristina proudly termed her version of 'voodoo economics', which the *Financial Times* labelled it,[52] was both unstable and clearly unsustainable. But that was a problem for tomorrow, in a land where yesterday and today mattered much more than anything as long-term as next year, or even next month.

Populist and expensive gestures were obviously tinged with cynicism and timed with electoral precision. This was best illustrated, I thought, in the tale of the notebook computer 'freebie' for schoolchildren. Next door Uruguay was far more economically fastidious than its free-spending neighbour, which doubtless accounted for the fact that most Argentines of my acquaintance kept a big bulk of their savings there, or further afield in the US. Its president also had a far more sober approach to the provision and purpose of public goods. He received high commendation when in 2009 he started to bridge the digital divide and boot up the skills set of the country by embarking on an ambitious scheme to provide every primary schoolchild with a basic laptop computer. The impeccable thinking behind the idea was not only to advantage the learners, but to introduce computers into the home environment and thus empower the parents as well.

A variant of the scheme arrived two years later, in presidential election year, in Argentina. But the twist in its tail, as the idea crossed the River Plate, was fascinating: instead of providing computers to young learners, the Argentine version gifted only school leavers with a notebook computer, on which each cover was thoughtfully emblazoned with the legend, 'A gift from the President of the Nation, Cristina Fernández de Kirchner'. I rather naively asked a local why the computers were only being provided to those about to leave school in July (when the educational year ends) rather than, like in Uruguay, to learners in the earlier stages of their education. 'Because they will all have votes in October,' he replied.

## 'CAPITALISM FOR HER FRIENDS, SOCIALISM FOR HER ENEMIES'

Cristina and her government found another way to deal with criticisms and pesky problems: deny their existence, as she did to F.W. de Klerk and I in our memorable interview with her (see Chapter 18), and harass the bearers of bad tidings. For example, it was illegal in Kirchner's Argentina for any economist to provide inflation statistics that contradicted the official and much-massaged figures churned out by the highly discredited national agency INDEC, which routinely understated inflation by about half. This was not just about winning elections – it was also about cheating the government's creditors holding inflation-linked bonds. But the truth was revealed in the annual wage negotiations, where both public and private sector workers received wage salary increases that were, in percentage terms on average, at least double the official inflation rate. Just for good measure, the International Monetary Fund was also banned from undertaking its annual country review of Argentina, which doubtless would have pointed all this out. All this was grist to Cristina's claim that she was an economic outlier, although her jiggery-pokery with conventional economics and splendid disregard for the country's bondholders placed the country more in the position of an international outlaw. Whatever characterisation one chose, the result was clear: Argentina was shunned by the international credit markets and became, increasingly, an extremely unattractive place for foreign investment, its resource treasure house of agricultural and minerals bounty notwithstanding; something I explore further in Chapter 31.

But in one area, the current president's operating style hewed to a tradition that had long served her predecessors. She was a keen practitioner of what has been termed the 'privatisation of power', the fusion of personal and state interests in the hands of the president's inner circle.[53] There were few, if any, major business deals that happened without the green light from and, government opponents suggested, backhanders to the Casa Rosada (the president's office). Political connectivity with the inner circle was the basis for much of the wealth of some of the current crop of Argentina's oligarchs. One commentator described Kirchner's methods as 'capitalism for her friends and socialism for her enemies'. The Kirchners were themselves extremely rich, by any standard, certainly for two professional politicians. Nestor Kirchner's estate for example, bequeathed to his wife and two children, included inheritances totalling over 25 million dollars. And that was just the portion of it that was publicised.

It also became increasingly apparent during my time in Argentina that the agencies of state would be wheeled out against the critics of the president and her policies: I mentioned the penalties levied against economists who dared to suggest that the government's inflation figures were false (ten of them were fined 123 000 dollars in 2011).[54] Another government weapon of choice was to unleash the national revenue service (AFIP) against enemies, real or imagined. In a country where, as noted in Chapter 31, tax evasion was rife and around 40 per cent of all economic activity was in the cash-only, tax-free informal sector, it was striking how the taxation authorities, generally so tolerant of widespread non-compliance, would very publicly go after government critics. The targets were impressively diverse: the usual suspects such as dissenting economists and the newspaper *Clarín* were fairly obvious choices for unwanted and visible attention by the taxman. More surprisingly, shortly after my arrival in the country in 2009, Argentine international tennis star, Juan Martin Del Potro, declined an invitation from Cristina to meet her after he won the US Open. The president was very unpopular in his home province. Ever since the snub, according to his manager, 'AFIP had been around the player, without finding anything.'[55]

Cristina's behaviour in office was perhaps no worse than some of her recent predecessors, especially the egregious Carlos Menem, whose zeal for free enterprise politics in the 1990s was matched only by the corrupt crony capitalism he practised in office. But her presidency coincided with the uptick of global transparency and international benchmarking. Unsurprisingly then, Argentina in the 2010s was sliding rapidly downward in the World Bank's Ease of Doing Business Survey (115th) and had positively cratered in the Heritage Foundation Index of Economic Freedom (138th). As Max Chafkin noted in a withering article following a visit to the country in June 2011: 'The rules change constantly, aren't enforced uniformly, and are forever subject to bending or breaking if a bribe is paid. And almost everybody pays: Transparency International ranks Argentina 105th (in the world) in terms of corruption, worse than famously corrupt countries such as Mexico, Egypt and Liberia.'[56]

CHAPTER 25

# OFF THE RAILS

February in Buenos Aires is not for those faint of heart or of delicate disposition: the normal frenetic energy of the place is literally sucked from the atmosphere by the stifling humidity. The wise and well-heeled are absent, and at play during this long summer break on the beaches of Uruguay and further afield. Government and congress are, likewise, on vacation. It is 2012 and I am relieved to escape the torpor of the streets and to be in the air-conditioned comfort of my office, bent over my computer screen and putting the finishing touches to what will be the final annual business plan of my ambassadorship. A dull, even agreeable, calmness envelops our embassy that morning. But as my mother used to say, 'everything changes in a moment'. A staff member suddenly rushes into my office and says, 'Ambassador, there's been a terrible train accident, and many people are dead.'

I immediately switch on the TV set in my office and view the live scenes of horror and carnage from nearby Once railway station. By the time the smoke had cleared from the wreckage, the bald and appalling facts were clear, even if the causes of the disaster remained shrouded in dispute and controversy: 51 commuters died that day and over 700 were injured when a packed commuter train entered the station and crashed into a retaining wall. Although the worst accident of its kind, it was not a single, freak occurrence. Less than six months before, on the same train line, a bus had crossed the tracks in front of an oncoming train that had crashed into it, causing the train to be derailed and to be hit by another train approaching from a different direction. That accident left 11 dead and 212 injured.

For my Argentine staff, it was a double trauma: as citizens they mourned the loss of lives, and as daily train commuters they lived and travelled now in dread. In addition to their complaints of overcrowding, lack of safety and lighting and a myriad other discomforts and indignities that plagued their journeys to and from the embassy, they now justifiably believed that the routine of the daily commute was, literally, a hazardous, even deadly, undertaking. I deeply empathised with their situation but could do little more than ensure that President Zuma issue a statement of condolence and sympathy, which Pretoria managed to dispatch with considerable speed.

But the horror accident brought to the surface the foul underground rivers of the sulphurous politics and toxic economics that lurked just below the landscape of contemporary Argentina. And there were almost as many villains as victims. In an accusatory commentary, under the headline 'Blood on the Tracks',[57] the *Buenos Aires Herald*, its editorial pen dipped in suitably condemnatory acid, noted how chronic underinvestment in infrastructure dated back over 50 years, across multiple presidencies. The military junta of 1976–83 had basically dismantled much of the rail network, while Carlos Menem's presidency in the late 1980s had used the smokescreen of 'privatisation' as an 'asset-stripping' exercise devised to enrich his friends. Cristina's contribution to this noxious brew had considerably worsened matters. Her obsession with providing short-term giveaways meant that the massive government subsidies of a whopping 750 million dollars a year, at the time of the Once accident, were exclusively used to keep train fares at ridiculously cheap levels (you could travel, for example, over 40 kilometres from the centre of Buenos Aires to Ezeiza Airport for the equivalent of a 5 rand train fare). This meant there were few funds left for the less visible, but far more necessary, investment in maintaining and overhauling the elderly, decaying and, as the accident tragically proved, life-threatening infrastructure. Evidence continued to surface of an army of middlemen and the network of insider cronies who skimmed off some of the funds as well.

An aspect of this gruesome event cast a harsh light on the sainted Nestor Kirchner, and also revealed the unholy trinity of politics, business and corruption, which were the governing pillars of contemporary Argentina, but by no means confined to it. There was a clear case of connivance between the official who headed the transportation ministry (put in place by Nestor and retained in office by Cristina) and the company running the concession on the Sarmiento line where these major accidents had occurred. At the time of his 'resignation purportedly for personal reasons' in late 2009, transport secretary Ricardo Jaime stood accused of multiple corruption charges, stemming from his alleged acceptance of many expensive gifts from the company whose management, safety standards and track and equipment maintenance he was meant to be overseeing. He had yet to be brought to trial at the time of the accident, but the company's concession was unaffected. It clearly had powerful connections right to the top of the political pile.

I spent a lot of my thinking time pondering why bad governance, corrupt politics and the longevity of Peronism, the latter in many ways an explanatory tool for the former, had become such entrenched features of Argentina. It was not the tough neighbourhood or even a distant hangover from the awful and rapacious nature of Spanish colonialism, which had ended, after all, more than two centuries before. Neighbouring Chile and Uruguay had identical colonial pasts, similar ethnic populations and far fewer resources, and yet they were, on the same international benchmarks, such as Transparency International, leagues ahead of much richer and much larger Argentina. I spent some time in the company of the impishly amusing and acutely intelligent Argentine political analyst Rosendo Fraga. He had a masterful ability to explain political puzzles with pithy one-liners. His most memorable observation was that Argentina was a 'perplexing combination' of two of its most famous sons, the literary giant Jorge Luis Borges, who walked with a limp, and the football legend, the decidedly non-intellectual Diego Maradona. 'But all too often,' he mischievously added, 'it is the foot of the former and the head of the latter.' Karl Marx provided a typically less humorous and more universal answer of sorts. In *The Eighteenth Brumaire of Louis Bonaparte* he observed: 'Men make their own history, but they do not make it as they please, they do not make it under self-selected circumstances, but under circumstances existing already, given and transmitted from the past.'

Although 'historical determinism' is often a treacherous quicksand of enquiry or explanation and frequently leads to question-begging rather than definitive explanations, there were some unique national events that provided a lens through which to view the contradictory nature of Argentina today. Three related items of the country's historical baggage, which weighed heavily on its present, are worth a brief elaboration: the fixation with a strong ruler; the military junta, which terrorised its own citizens after Peron; and the Falklands War. These were among the poisonous weeds that ruptured the country's socio-political ecosystem.

CHAPTER 26

# THE CURSE OF THE CAUDILLO

The image of the strutting, uniformed military strongman – unsmiling face offset by aviator sunglasses – has almost entirely disappeared from the presidential balconies and palaces of South America. The Argentine defence forces, once the ruling elite of the country, had in very reduced, even impoverished, circumstances returned to their barracks, more than two decades before my arrival in Buenos Aires.

But the shadow of the caudillo could be seen everywhere in the current politics of the country: the stunting of civilian institutions, the half-baked nature of its democracy and political formations, the instinct toward authoritarianism and, most keenly, in the almost messianic faith of the population that a strong man (or in the current case, an 'iron lady') could deliver national salvation. Most contemporary Argentine politicians, certainly the government but often the opposition as well, revered General Juan Peron and his second wife, Evita. But in Argentina's case, in contrast to the military dictatorships, which had held sway for much of the twentieth century in, for example, neighbouring Brazil and Paraguay, Peron and his party successors had for much of their rule enjoyed mass support in the country. The single best explanation for the ingredients of the cultural and ideological fruit salad of Peronism and its immensely long shelf life I came across was from the historian Jill Hedges. In her book *Argentina: A Modern History* she noted:

> Peron had a gift for saying what his audience wanted to hear and following rather than leading the desires of that audience. This allowed him to fill the vacuum between the working class and the country's rulers; a vacuum the working class had not filled with one of its own ... Peronism was a reflection rather than an imposition on (working class) culture, comprehensible because it reflected that cultural reality. That it mixed a range of concepts taken from nationalism, European fascism, socialism and (Spanish) falangism with Argentine paternalism, authoritarianism and sentiment was a benefit rather than a detriment. Argentina itself was a not entirely coherent mix of European, Latin and local customs and ideas and could well be represented by just such a mix as Peronism.[58]

Peron's shift from membership of the ruling military elite to workers' hero in 1946 not only gave him a ladder to ascend to power through the popular will, but also met a real need of the bulk of his supporters. Argentina's considerable wealth at the time was unevenly distributed, to put it at its mildest. The increasingly urbanising population enjoyed neither fundamental rights nor any basic social entitlements, beyond the charity of the rich and the church. This unsustainable and dangerous divergence between rulers and ruled led to revolutionary atmosphere in Buenos Aires after the arrest and brief imprisonment of Peron in October 1945 by his military colleagues, who, presciently, feared the popular appeal of then Colonel Peron and his strong-willed partner, soon-to-be-wife, Evita. The yawning chasm, and real antipathy, which separated the Argentine elite from the massed workers who thronged the streets of the capital demanding the release of Peron (in which they succeeded) was on full display on what Peronist folklore would describe as 'the revolution of 17 October 1945'. Even more interesting than Peron's speech to his supporters that day was the horror and fear that 'elegant Buenos Aires' expressed at the arrival in the city centre of the 'unwashed masses'. A conservative congressman dismissed the Peronistas or *descamisados* ('shirtless ones') as 'hordes' and a 'zoological deluge'.[59] In leading the movement Peron and his successors were certainly blessed by the prejudices and the tin ears of their opponents, whose ranks included the oligarchs, the resident US ambassador and, over time, the Roman Catholic Church.

After his election to the presidency the following year, Peron set right much that was then wrong with Argentina: public health care facilities and pensions were, for the first time, extended to all and, largely at the urging of Evita, women received the right to vote in 1947. Trade unions and workers – the backbone and spine of the movement – were extensively empowered with a raft of rights and entitlements, the consequences of which I was to grapple with in my embassy over 50 years later.

But if Peron himself was more a passenger in the vehicle that smashed through the gates of privilege and power, then there was little doubt that Evita was the driver of the movement. Neither forgetting her hardscrabble upbringing nor those she deemed responsible for it, she parlayed her first ladyship into an instrument of both revenge against the elite and restoration for the country's poor and neglected. Her harangues against the rich and her personal distribution of charity, from new houses to dentures, through her *fundación* where she laboured through the night to personally administer her deeds of mercy, left a powerful mark on Argentina and its most disadvantaged sectors. But it also came with a price tag. Whereas before Evita's ascent, rich society ladies inspected the recipients of their charity for clean nails and for lice, she never sought to humiliate but did demand of her beneficiaries unbounded loyalty to Peron whom she sometimes compared to Christ.[60] And even her many interventions were of limited effect. As Hedges notes: '[Evita] had a boundless and sincere desire to aid the poor but no strategy aimed at reducing poverty rather than sporadically alleviating it.'[61] But whatever her limitations in social reconstruction, her 'high-flying adored' tour of impoverished post-world war Europe, draped in Christian Dior's finest gowns and bedecked with shimmering jewellery, captivated everyone from Spain's dictator Francisco Franco to her adoring fans in Buenos Aires, who crammed the cinemas to watch newsreels of her triumphal progress abroad.

Peron, like his spiritual and political successor Cristina, could also take advantage of the favourable economic winds that were blowing in Argentina's direction at the time. Having sat out the Second World War until almost the end (Argentina, opportunistically, declared war against Germany only a month or so before its defeat), it was untouched by the ravages of conflict. Its food wealth placed it in a powerful position to transform its traditional, largely British-oriented, rural-based economy. General Peron, as he had become, proceeded to do so with gusto: he nationalised the railways from their British owners (paying full value for the expropriation) and set up a wall of tariffs to both stimulate and protect local industry. He added a heady dose of nationalism to this populist brew.

Some of these long-denied elements of social justice and a shared sense of national pride were clear and moral necessities. But there was a helter-skelter pace to the process, and an eccentric nature of some of Peron's assumptions. For example, he assumed, with a mysterious certainty, that a third world war was imminent and that Argentina could play a powerful role in the non-aligned world between the Soviets and Americans. Initially, indeed, the cold war boosted demand for Argentine resources, but it never led to the all-out conflict that the general imagined it would. But what was to do him in eventually, and to force him to leave the country in 1955 at the point of a gun, and in a Paraguayan gunboat, were the costs of his *justicialismo* (social justice). First, it essentially bankrupted the country. Greg Mills, for example, cites a figure of 1.7 billion dollars of reserves carefully accumulated during the war, the entire patrimony of the nation at the time, as being blown on public spending by Peron thereafter. An almost perfect economic storm followed: the public's appetite for public spending was aggravated by increased consumer demand for imports, which in turn worsened the terms of trade (i.e., imports surging over exports), and the inevitable exchange rate deterioration that followed (the peso declined seven-fold against the dollar in the period) led to a massive surge in consumer prices. Soon enough, the workers were again on the streets, but as often now baying for Peron's removal as expressing solidarity for him.[62]

The second cost, after bankruptcy, that Argentina paid for Peron was, sadly, neither new nor did it end with his initial ouster, or even with his death in 1974. But the country's historical and continuing flirtation with autocracy reached a tipping point with Peron. A creature of the army, he used his popular base outside it to close down or severely restrict most of the checks and balances, from the judiciary to the media, which incubate and flourish in mature democracies. There were clearly more bloody-minded figures in the country's past and, after his death, the military junta, which soon followed him, was infinitely worse and certainly more violent. But in many ways, he resembled science fiction's Darth Vader of the popular culture created a few years after his passing. In *Star Wars* he was the high priest of the Dark Side, which fuelled by anger and hatred conferred great power on the leader and his followers but at a steep price to their humanity.[63] He and Evita enjoyed considerable popularity, but they were also emblematic of the authoritarianism that was the dark undertow of the tides of history, both before, during and post-Peron. Of all aspects of the country's flirtation with the Dark Side, I suppose my own background led me to examine one chapter of it with a sort of horrified fascination: the arrival, by the boatload, of Nazi fugitives, including some high-echelon war criminals, in Peron's Argentina after the end of the Second World War.

CHAPTER 27

# THE NAZIS

A cynical Argentine friend of mine described a peculiarity of Buenos Aires in the mid-1950s: 'There were two elements of the German community in the capital; the larger section of it was Jewish and the smaller one Nazi. They obviously avoided each other, but would meet occasionally at the Thursday night concert at the Colon Opera House.' Only in Argentina, I thought, and not for the first time either.

Long before I arrived in Argentina, I had been reasonably familiar with the headline story of how Israel's Mossad (secret service) agents had kidnapped one of the chief organisers and implementers of the Nazi holocaust against European Jews, Adolf Eichmann, from his house in one of the outer suburbs of Buenos Aires, back in May 1960. (Eichmann had been working for more than a decade as a foreman at the local Mercedes-Benz factory.) He had then been drugged and smuggled out, some days later, disguised as an Israeli flight attendant, in a special El Al plane, which was parked at Ezeiza Airport ironically enough to ferry the Israeli delegation officiating at Argentina's 150th independence anniversary celebrations. Eichmann was later convicted by a court in Jerusalem, condemned to death and two years later was hanged, the only person in the 60-year-old history of the Jewish state to be judicially executed. What I only learnt when I was living in Argentina some 50 years after this cause célèbre was that Eichmann was only one of several major and lesser Nazi fugitives who had found refuge in Argentina after the Nazi Reich had been defeated.

Anecdotes and personal reminiscences from some of my Jewish Argentine friends had been the first source of information on this dark feature of the country's fairly recent past. It was actually when I was reading a rather riveting thriller, *A Quiet Flame* by Philip Kerr, which featured his fictional detective Bernie Gunther, a sort of German Philip Marlowe, that I realised the apparent extent and scale of Nazi fugitives who found a safe haven in Argentina, in both Buenos Aires and down south in Bariloche in Patagonia, whose lakes and mountains closely resembled the Austrian Tyrol and the German rural landscape. Suitably engrossed, I discovered that it was not simply geographic familiarity that attracted Eichmann, Josef Mengele (the infamous Nazi doctor, known as the 'Angel of Death' of Auschwitz, where he committed human experiments of indescribable cruelty on inmates and selected the less able for the gas chambers) and a clutch of others to the land of the gaucho. In fact, according to the book, it was Peron himself who rolled out the welcome mat for the war criminals. But, it was after all, a novel and therefore perhaps there was a degree of artistic licence in the tale. Or was it all based on what would now be termed 'an inconvenient truth'? In the author's note at the end of the novel, Kerr stated that 'the one indispensable source' of his information on the 'several thousand' Nazi war criminals who escaped to Argentina, most of them managing to live out their lives, unlike Eichmann, in post-war comfort and protection, was the work of an Argentine journalist, Uki Goni.[64]

I discovered that one of the advantages of being an ambassador was the ability to move quickly from fiction to first-hand sourcing. Immediately on finishing the novel, I enquired of our embassy's cultural supremo, Mony di Liscia, whether it would be possible to ascertain whether Mr Goni was still around the city and if I could meet him?

A few days later, Uki Goni and I duly sat down to lunch at an Italian restaurant in Recoleta. Uki, a quietly spoken, intensely well-informed Argentine journalist and writer, and, interestingly, the son and grandson of diplomats, recounted to me the essence of the 25 000 pages of official Argentine, Swiss and German records he had scoured to write his definitive account of how the Nazi escapees arrived in Argentina, *The Real Odessa*.[65] The fiction and films (such as *The Boys from Brazil*) was one thing, the real story was itself both dramatic and very disturbing.

Uki explained over the lunch that the Vatican – then headed by the Nazi-leaning pontiff, Pope Pius XII, who feted Evita during her European tour in 1947 – acting in collaboration with both Swiss and Argentine authorities, and with degrees of covert assistance from US agencies (then more concerned with the new cold war than the transgressions arising from the past conflict), established 'ratlines' of escape for the Nazi, especially SS, fugitives from Europe to bolt holes in Argentina, Paraguay and Brazil. However, as the author explained, although Eichmann changed his name (to Ricardo Klement), his wife and children did not bother to alter their surname. Of all the information he shared with me, the one aspect that I found most surprising was that the majority of the Nazis were not squirrelled away in Patagonia, but 'hid in plain sight' in the city and suburbs of Buenos Aires. The notorious Dr Mengele, for example, lived undisturbed for over fifteen years in the capital, and was only once briefly arrested by the local authorities (whom he bribed to release him) for performing an illegal abortion, apparently a far greater crime for them than the murder of hundreds of thousands of European Jews. Only the kidnapping of Eichmann spurred his move to Paraguay and later to Brazil where he eventually drowned while taking a swim off a beach near São Paulo. According to Uki, there was a natural affinity between the militaristic and fascist-sympathising Peron (schooled by Prussian offices at the Superior War School of Argentina and subsequently military attaché in Italy during the rule of Mussolini) and the Nazis. Indeed, Hitler's minister of food and agriculture, one of the leading Nazi race theorists, Richard Walther Darré, had been born and bred in Argentina where he had been known by the decidedly less Aryan first name of Ricardo.

Other historians suggest that Peron was never explicitly anti-Semitic (probably true given the significant number of Jews who lived, in often-flourishing circumstances, in the country) and that ever the ideological chameleon, he wished to ingratiate himself with the Vatican and to attract former Nazi professionals to help industrialise the country and possibly to placate the explicitly pro-German officer corps of his defence forces.[66] But whatever the explanation for Peron and Argentina's post-war behaviour, Uki told me that 'even today this is a painful subject for most Argentines – we don't like to have our dark underside examined'. Interestingly, despite the wide critical acclaim for his book in the English-speaking world and elsewhere outside his native country, Uki told me that he had never once, more than ten years after its publication, 'been invited to address a single university or literary event' about his research in Argentina.

CHAPTER 28

# DEATH FLIGHTS AND STOLEN BABIES

Applying the label 'Nazi' to other strains of authoritarianism is usually intellectually lazy and historically inaccurate shorthand, which negates the unique evil of the German Reich. But I could not keep the Nazi analogy far from my thoughts when one scorching hot summer morning in early 2011 I visited the white colonnaded set of buildings, just up the road from our residence, known as Escuela de Mecánica de la Armada (Naval Mechanical School). Its acronym ESMA became a byword for the brutality and perversions of the military junta, which held Argentina in its repressive grip between the years 1976 and 1983. Back then it had served as one of the main torture centres for the regime and had, even more ominously, operated simultaneously as a grotesque maternity home. Now a memorial museum, by the end of my harrowing tour of it I was convinced that, in this case at least, 'Nazi' was an apt analogy for the horror story that had unfolded behind its walls. At the time of my visit, one of the ringleaders of the torture centre, the strikingly blond-haired and blue-eyed former navy officer, Captain Alfredo Astiz, was on trial for numerous charges of torture, kidnapping and murder. He had been branded by his victims (or those who lived to tell the tale, at least) with Mengele's moniker the 'Angel of Death' (he was subsequently sentenced to multiple terms of life imprisonment).

Extraordinarily, after my visit, I discovered that this deeply repulsive but beguiling-looking character had served in Argentina's embassy in Pretoria as its deputy defence attaché between 1979 and 1981, appropriately perhaps as the number two to another major torturer of the regime, Rear Admiral

Rubén Jacinto Chamorro. The *Sunday Tribune* of Durban got it exactly right with its headline in its 18 October 1981 edition, 'Torture Camp Envoys in Pretoria.'[67] Since this duo of criminals would have arrived on diplomatic assignment directly after their involvement in the atrocities at ESMA and elsewhere in junta-ruled Argentina, they perhaps struck up some local relationships with those who went on to create the apartheid state's own death and torture squads. Whatever actually did or did not transpire during their South African sojourn, they doubtless found Pretoria and South Africa, then in the grip of the government's pro-military 'total strategy', a congenial place.

No one knows, with detailed accuracy, the number of 'dissidents' who were murdered in the six years that the clenched fist of the junta military held sway over Argentina – 9 000 is the verified figure, but some estimates suggest nearly 30 000. Many of the *los desaparecidos* (the disappeared), ranging from young students to militant guerrillas and even high-school kids, were apprehended in the same manner: picked up by plain-clothed policemen in dark glasses, who patrolled the streets of Buenos Aires in unmarked Ford Falcon motorcars. Our guide at ESMA that day explained how each new detainee, or batches of them, was systematically tortured in the basement and in various rooms on the third floor of the now stripped-down building. The majority of the ESMA inmates, some 5 000 according to our guide, were then 'transferred', one of the many sickening euphemisms engaged by the regime (which described itself as the 'process of national reorganisation'). This meant injecting the *los desaparecidos* with tranquilising drugs and then dumping the sleeping bodies on 'death flights', which departed from nearby Aeroparque domestic airport. Once the air force Dakotas and helicopters were overhead the River Plate or the Atlantic, the bodies would be thrown out of the aircraft, ensuring a traceless execution. I was privileged to meet, during my stay in Argentina, the brave editor of the *Buenos Aires Herald* at that terrible time, whose newspaper had helped unearth many of the hidden facts about the state-sponsored degeneracy of the day. Robert Cox had no coyness about labelling the regime 'Nazi'. He also provided a grisly footnote to the detail on the death flights: according to him, initially some of the bodies dumped into the River Plate started to wash up on its banks. 'So the military took to slitting open their stomachs beforehand, so that the corpses would fill with water and sink.'[68]

However horrifying the detail of this industrial-scale killing machine, the extremity of the regime and its limitless perversity revealed itself in the treatment of female detainees, who accounted for an estimated 30 per cent of the *los desaparecidos.* A recent account in *The New Yorker* described this perhaps grimmest chapter of Argentina's history vividly:

> Some were abducted with small children and some, perhaps three percent, were pregnant, or became so while in detention, usually through rape by guards and torturers. Pregnant prisoners were routinely kept alive until they'd given birth … One former detainee told Harvard Professor Marguerite Feitlowitz, 'Our bodies were a source of special fascination. They said my nipples invited the prod' – the electric cattle prod, which was used in torture.[69]

Professor Feitlowitz noted this as presenting 'a truly sickening combination – the curiosity of little boys, the intense arousal of twisted men'. Nazi-like might have been the methods used, but ideologically there was a distinct difference in the latter-day Argentine variant of fascism. In *Schindler's List*, movie audiences saw how the methodical Gestapo rooted out hidden children, applying stethoscopes to ceilings to detect breathing, to send them to the death camps. The Jewish race needed to be exterminated at root – that was the essence of Hitler's Final Solution. In Argentina, the children of the pregnant detainees – an estimated 500 of them – might in the professor's words have been 'seeds of the tree of evil' but purification of 'subversives' was the aim of the military rulers, not racial genocide. The children were thus handed over to childless military couples and others chosen by the junta. 'Perhaps through adoption, those seeds could be replanted in healthy soil,' *The New Yorker* piece speculated. Today, only the whereabouts of around one-fifth of the 500 are thought to be known.

It was the search for missing children and grandchildren in this most intensely family-oriented of countries that led to the flowering of two of the most poignant and, in their mutely eloquent way, most powerful symbols of protest against the regime: the Madres and the Abuelas de Plaza de Mayo (the mothers and grandmothers of the Plaza de Mayo, the square on which the famous pink presidential palace is situated, the very place where I presented my ambassadorial credentials so many years later). During the height of the military regime and the Dirty War it prosecuted against its citizens, the mothers, and later a group of grandmothers, whose children had disappeared, would gather every Thursday outside the palace and circle the area in silent protest, wearing white *doeks* embroidered with the missing children's names.

My time in Argentina was some 30 years after the junta held the country in its bloody grip. But its effects still loomed large over the politics of the country and the national psyche. Forensic science had advanced to the point where DNA samples could store the genetic profiles of families seeking missing offspring. But many children, now well into their thirties, suspected of being adopted by military and other families, could refuse to be tested. Extraordinarily, in 2009, congress enacted a law that allowed judges to order mandatory blood extractions in cases of children suspected of being the progeny of the disappeared. The timing of this legislation, which whatever else its intention seemed to negate the rights and interests of the children involved, was instructive. It was enacted at the height of the war being waged between President Kirchner and the mighty *Clarín* media empire, headed by Ernestina Herrera de Noble, whose two adopted children Marcela and Felipe, were suspected of being the biological children of *los desaparecidos*.

A year or so later, the children, now well into adulthood, were summoned by a judge and after refusing to submit voluntarily to a DNA test, had their clothing seized after a high-speed car chase with the police. The initial tests and subsequent voluntary one to which they submitted – in their words, to 'end the harassment' – proved to be inconclusive. But the suspicion abounded on all sides – that the Herrera de Noble children had indeed been adopted under false pretences and that the president would use the law as a battering ram against her opponents. But, by this time, the once universally admired Abuelas organisation had become an offshoot of the president's party, while the Madres were mired in a huge corruption scandal, its leaders and managers accused of skimming off millions of taxpayer-provided pesos for personal profit.

While the junta alone bears the responsibility for the unspeakable atrocities it visited on Argentina, it was Peron's death in 1974, and the tottering leadership of his widow and successor – his third wife Isabel – that provided the context for their ascent. Her twenty months at the helm of her country were disastrous: guerrillas, essentially a militant offshoot of Peronism, were pitted against 'death squads' sponsored by the government and determined to restore order. The splitting of Peron's movement into violently opposing factions was another typical outcome of his legendary prevarication. He had once said when confronted with making a hard choice, 'to define is to exclude'. By March 1976, some three weeks before the military executed its fifth coup since 1930, one newspaper estimated that a political killing was taking place every five hours, and a bomb attack every three; the corpses were often left where they fell on the streets.[70] Little wonder then that many hard-pressed citizens welcomed a 'firm hand' to arrest the anarchy engulfing the country. General Jorge Videla, the junta's head, announced a plan to rid the country of its subversives, in which category he included anyone 'who spreads ideas contrary to Western Christian civilisation'. And as to the methods to be employed, one of his underlings, General Ibérico Saint Jean, the governor of Buenos Aires province, put it starkly: 'First we shall kill the subversives, then we shall kill their collaborators, then their sympathisers; then those who remain indifferent; and finally we shall kill the timid.'[71]

In this morass, where the prime evil perpetrated by a military regime had never been fully expunged and where the current government's motives for pursuing collaborators were decidedly mixed, it was little wonder that South Africa's model of 'truth and reconciliation' was widely admired and was the topic on which I was frequently asked to address Argentine audiences. In Argentina's case, in contrast to South Africa's negotiated transition and constitutionally mandated Truth and Reconciliation Commission process, the military junta unilaterally 'withdrew' from power in late 1983, allowing elections and thoughtfully providing itself with a self-amnesty against prosecutions for its multiple crimes. This was later reversed by both the courts and Nestor Kirchner, leading to the prosecution of its ringleaders in trials, which were still continuing during my time in the country. The causes for the military's abandonment of power were multiple, chief among them being its disastrous decision to invade the Falkland Islands and lose the war in the South Atlantic against Britain in 1982. Three decades later, in a minor way, this conflict re-erupted across the dining-room table of our official residence in Buenos Aires.

CHAPTER 29

# 'DON'T MENTION THE F. WORD'

The British politician Richard Spring was one of the best friends I had made during my political career. South African-educated, he had gone on to a long career as a Tory MP. His languid, self-deprecating humour and easy charm had made him a firm favourite in our household. Richard, now ennobled as Lord Risby in the House of Lords, had sent word that he and his delightful daughter Sophia would be arriving in Buenos Aires in September 2011. I immediately invited them to stay with us and set about using his presence to arrange a dinner for local eminences and, for obvious reasons, included my diplomatic friend, British ambassador Shan Morgan, on the guest list.

The dinner party for some fifteen guests at the residence was proceeding smoothly enough. And then for some inexplicable reason, or perhaps all too explainable by my subconscious yearning to break occasionally the chains of diplomatic nicety and constraint, I forgot the first duty of an ambassador – 'to give no affront, to be pleasant in any company, to be conversable and easy' (a formulation penned by novelist Hilary Mantel about 1535 Tudor England, but still today a good shorthand description of the essence of diplomatic etiquette).[72]

During a conversational pause that evening, I turned to Marie-Jo Cardinal, seated on my right and one of our closest Argentina friends and asked her, in my booming voice, 'What is it about the Malvinas that makes all Argentines so agitated? After all you wouldn't go and live in that windswept archipelago?' I was tempted to add, but refrained from deepening the hole into which I was apparently digging myself, the acid description by Jorge Luis Borges of the extraordinary 1982 war there between Argentina and Britain as 'a fight between two bald men over a comb'. About the only nod in my remark to local sensibilities was to refer to the islands as the Malvinas, having been warned never to utter in Argentine company the 'F. word' as in Falklands, the British and resident islanders name for the contested territory, which lay some 500 kilometres off the Patagonian coast of Argentina.

Marie-Jo's response to my perceived provocation was immediate and indignant, her normal easy and sophisticated manner replaced by an uncharacteristic nationalistic zeal. 'How can you ask such a question, Ambassador?' she demanded. 'It is a fact that the Malvinas are Argentine, or as we say here Las Malvinas Son Argentinas. It has nothing to do with whether I would choose to go and live there.' In an attempt to calm the waters my question had churned, another Argentine guest, Jorge Mandelbaum, a major figure in Buenos Aires business and public policy circles, chimed in that Argentina's claim to the islands was one of the very few issues in the country around which there was almost universal agreement. I realised all too late in this uncomfortable discussion that I had placed Shan, seated opposite me, in a difficult situation. Aside from Richard, his daughter and a friend, she was the only British guest present and as the emissary of Her Majesty the Queen, whose diminished realm included the disputed territory, she could hardly remain silent. In her quiet but impeccably professional manner she simply said: 'Of course there is a dispute over the sovereignty of the islands between our countries, but there is a third party in the mix, the islanders themselves.' She hardly needed to add that the 3 000 residents of the islanders were fiercely attached to their British protectors. I quickly moved the discussion along to more neutral topics and later apologised to Marie-Jo for my faux pas, which she graciously accepted. Later on we would laugh about it.

But the Falkland–Malvinas issue was no laughing matter for Argentina, or for Britain. In a last throw of the dice, the increasingly unpopular military junta had invaded the thinly populated and lightly defended rocky islands back in April 1982. Their 74-day occupation ended in ignominy and defeat, as the highly efficient and professional British naval task force and marines stormed the islands after sailing 12 000 kilometres to recapture them. Six hundred and forty-nine Argentines, most of them ill-equipped raw conscripts from the poorer provinces of Argentina were killed, as were 252 members of the British armed forces.

The tidal wave unleashed from this conflict was immediately felt on both sides of the Atlantic. In Buenos Aires, the mass demonstrations that had gathered to support the invasion at its onset, soon enough turned into anti-government protests aimed at the junta and its head, General Leopoldo Galtieri. Not only had he vastly overestimated the competence of his military, but he had grossly underestimated British resolve and made the strategic miscalculation that the US would either support him or remain a neutral party.

A contemporary historian wrote that the shame inflicted on the country by its calamitous defeat was compounded by stories of abuse of the soldiers by their own officers – 'leading to the inevitable conclusion that Argentina's professional military officers were corrupt and incompetent even in their purportedly professional sphere'.[73] At the time, the conflict shone world attention on Argentina. Local journalist Andrew Graham-Yooll noted that over 500 foreign correspondents descended on Buenos Aires to cover the conflict, and required accommodation: 'Most of them had chosen the US-owned Sheraton Hotel. At US$100 a night it would be the only winner in the war. Oh yes, and the prostitutes who worked the Sheraton at a hundred dollars a night.'[74]

There was an objective winner of this war, British Prime Minister Margaret Thatcher. In her memoirs she recounts that she could not have survived as prime minister had the conflict been lost. Indeed, I recalled how at the time the satirical magazine *Private Eye* fashioned its own monument to the fallen from the conflict: a Corinthian column with Thatcher's head on a plinth bearing the legend: 'They died to save her face.' But she went on to win the 1983 general election and the result of the conflict, in her words, was to reverse the impression of British decline and international retreat: 'Everywhere I went after the war, Britain's name meant something more than it had.'[75]

The most unintended consequence of the conflict was to remove, probably forever, the military as a factor in Argentine politics. Within months of their defeat in the Falklands, they surrendered political power to a democratically elected president, Raúl Alfonsín.

The elemental force unleashed from the Falkland–Malvinas conflict so many decades before caused waves of activity in my current diplomatic work. The final year of my ambassadorship, 2012, marked the 30th anniversary of the conflict and the Argentines, having wisely abandoned any further military options, were determined to ramp up the diplomatic pressure against Britain and its 'colonial anachronism'. Deep-water drilling by British companies around the islands for commercially viable deposits of hydrocarbons inflamed domestic Argentine sentiment in an area that historically Argentina claimed to be in its exclusive economic sphere. Since Argentina used any international forum, from obscure United Nations committees to high-level meetings of the G-20, to press its claims, I was obliged to spend many hours researching the conflict in order to inform Pretoria and to suggest a response.

The Malvinas, so named by Spain in about 1765, had been claimed by Argentina as early as 1828, on the basis that as a former Spanish colony its territory automatically acceded to the newly independent republic of Argentina. However, since 1832, Britain had planted a Union Jack and a few settlers on the territory. Fast-forward through innumerable notes of protest, fitful negotiations and one major war and the essence of the dispute remained unresolved and, in my view, unresolvable some 180 years later. Argentina invoked the principle of decolonisation and demanded 'dialogue' with Britain to settle the matter of the sovereignty of the islands. Britain, in turn, held fast to the issue of 'self-determination' for the islanders, whose very presence Argentina regarded as a 'colonial imposition' and refused to recognise them as a party to the dispute, let alone countenance their presence at any discussion on the island's future, notwithstanding that some of the islanders were now ninth-generation descendants of the original settlers. My advice to head office, since South Africa claimed to support both principles in dispute, was to retain a position of 'strenuous neutrality' – advice that more or less was taken. I also added that since we would land up offending one of the parties if we backed the other we would do well to remember the injunction of former

US Secretary of State, James Baker, speaking in another context, that 'we did not have a dog in this fight'.

But for President Cristina Kirchner the strategic calculus was obviously very different. In highlighting her dispute with Britain, she was applying an old and trusty political rule: 'When you are in trouble, change the subject.' And by 2012 she desperately needed to distract her country's attention from the economic storm, which now threatened, once again, to engulf Argentina.

CHAPTER 30

# THE BIG MAC DISAPPEARS FROM THE MENU

Contrary to the advice of my cardiologist and my wife, I occasionally snuck around the corner of the embassy to the golden arches of McDonald's for a fast-food fix. The global home of the Big Mac had dozens of local outlets and endless queues of customers. When I first entered this hamburger heaven, I consulted the illuminated, and temptingly illustrated, menu with some puzzlement: on offer was everything from the McAngus to the McTasty, and even a few concessions to the new age, such as the chicken Caesar salad, widely ignored by the hungry carnivores. But nowhere in sight or apparently on offer was the universal food chain's basic signature burger, the Big Mac.

I thought nothing further of this matter, until one day a friend forwarded me a blog by a local writer, Daniel Politi.[76] He had intrepidly drilled down into the Big Mac's disappearance from Buenos Aires's menus. After visiting a number of McDonald's (the sacrifices made for the sake of investigative journalism, I mused), he arrived at a fascinating conclusion: apparently the Big Mac offer was hidden away and not advertised because of government pressure on businesses to keep prices frozen and 'manipulate economic statistics in its interest'. By forcing McDonald's to keep the Big Mac price down, the hamburger seller obliged by keeping the Big Mac more or less off the menu and thereby selling as few of the basic burgers as possible, since the government had less interest in the other, costlier items on offer. Of course, from the government's perspective, it had the added advantage of preventing *The*

*Economist* magazine, which used the global price differences between Big Macs, from determining whether a country's currency was over- or under-valued. Undeterred, however, the journal managed to ferret out the price of the Big Mac for its 2011 index, leading to Politi's conclusion:

> [T]he Argentine peso is 19 percent overvalued, a number that soars to 101 percent when adjusted to GDP per capita. Analyzing the data for the past ten years, *The Economist* concluded that 'burgernomics does support claims that Argentina's government is cooking the books' because 'the gap between its average annual rate of burger inflation (19%) and its official rate (10%) is far bigger than any other country'.

The search for the missing menu item revealed the Argentine economy in all its glory: fudged statistics, artificial propping up of the local currency and curbs on foreign exchange purchases (to keep dollars in the country), government pressure on businesses, suppression of inconvenient truths and discredited price controls to disguise the real rate of inflation, which accompanied the soaring growth spurred by a free-spending government. There were two other matters of some fascination flowing from this study of 'burgernomics'.

Argentina's gauchos are the living, macho symbol of the country's famed cattle herds, which had historically roamed the pampas and produced arguably the best beef in the world. Of course, the pressures of the competing soy product on the fertile grasslands had led to more whole-food-oriented feedlots, replacing the once more romantic and free-ranging livestock. Still, my friend, the gifted *Financial Times* correspondent, Jude Webber, hardly exaggerated when she observed 'most [Argentine] people consider a meat-free meal is the equivalent to not eating'.[77] In the same report, Jude noted that by late 2010, in the homeland of the famed, sizzling steak, beef production and exports had slumped to their lowest levels 'in a decade'.

The key reason here was similar in explanation to the missing Big Mac, which began life somewhere on the pampas as an innocent calf: government intervention. The authorities actively intervened in the market by restricting exports in an attempt to hold down domestic prices for meat-hungry Argentines. But, of course, given that the same manipulations also artificially suppressed the retail selling price of steaks (not apparently in our high-end supermarket, I noted, on consulting the monthly credit card statement), more and more cattle farmers simply switched to soy, which was in any event more profitable on a per hectare yield basis. The president of the Argentine Beef Promotion Institute was quoted in the same article as describing his country's price control policy as 'incomprehensible'. Meanwhile, in the same year tiny Uruguay, with a population a tenth the size of Argentina, had overtaken its neighbour as both an exporter of beef and 'as the world's top meat-eating nation'.

There was a second consequence to this triple combination of an overheated economy (through expansionary state spending), which, in turn, caused high inflation and which government attempted to offset via highly interventionist price controls. It was what *The Economist* termed 'an extraordinarily elaborate deception to conceal the rise' of inflation. As noted previously, they simply cooked the books, through manipulating data, criminalising independent economic reporting and crude protectionism. The magazine responded early in 2012 in kind: it refused to carry in its influential columns any official data provided by the Argentine government, noting acidly: 'Argentina has created a statistical labyrinth that might have been dreamed up by Jorge Luis Borges, the country's greatest writer. The story is unlikely to have a happy ending.'[78]

## ISOLATION AND THE RETURN OF *CACEROLAZO*

Indeed, by the time I left the country a few months after that report, Argentina was heading, and not for the first time in its turbulent history, over an economic cliff as the population raced to dump their pesos for dollars. A zealous and increasingly beleaguered government fought back through draconian exchange controls and import-suppression measures, which eerily began to resemble the antics of the apartheid government at its nadir in the 1980s.

In fact, having lived through South Africa's dark era of dual currencies, international economic and financial sanctions, currency round tripping and sky-high interest rates, I traced a direct connection between the besieged administrations of P.W. Botha and Cristina Kirchner. In South Africa's case, it was globally isolated as a result of its unacceptable domestic policies. Twenty years after the fall of apartheid, Argentina's government was increasingly detached from the world because of its eccentric economic course. But both had this in common: they were determined to defy the world for as long as possible, or sometimes literally give it the finger.

I uncomfortably noticed that in Cristina's endless state broadcasts, which the TV stations were obliged to air, she wagged her finger at the audience – just like the Groot Krokodil, I thought, the less-than-complimentary term of reference we once conferred on the apartheid strongman president. And, of course, both presidents lived in parallel universes, believing the whisperings of their closest and sycophantic advisers, rather than the howling gales of reality outside the cloistered walls of the presidential palaces.

It was the banging of pots and pans, rather than gusting winds, that signalled the rising discontent of Argentina's hard-pressed middle class. Michal and I were preparing ourselves on a Thursday night, some two weeks before our final return home in late September 2012, for one of the many farewell dinners friends were hosting in our honour. The quiet provided by the apartment's double glazing so many floors above busy Avenida Libertardor was pierced by the shrill sounds of banging steel and the honking of motorcar horns. Looking down, I saw dozens of people marching down the street carrying pots and pans and banging them loudly, with car drivers hooting in support. Many residents of neighbouring apartment blocks stood on their balconies eagerly banging pots in sympathy.

The cacophonic middle classes (for ours was a decidedly upper-income neighbourhood) were on the march, joining an estimated 60 000 demonstrators who gathered later that night, apparently mobilised by the ubiquitous social media, in Plaza de Mayo, directly opposite government house. Switching on the TV, I read the slogans on the banners and posters wielded by the decidedly well-dressed and peaceful protestors. They demanded an end to the dollar restrictions, a return of security to crime-ravaged suburbs and, most evident of all, opposition to the amendment of the constitution (then being energetically promoted by the president's supporters) to allow Cristina to run for a third term as president (like South Africa, the Argentine president is subject to a two-term limit).

It was not just the size of this demonstration, certainly the largest of its kind during my stay, and which simultaneously took place at other centres across the country, that commanded attention. It was the return of the *cacerolazo,* the Spanish shorthand for the banging of pots and saucepans to signify protest (it means literally 'casserole'), which sent a chill up the collective spine of the country. For this was the sound and the method that had symbolised and helped the overthrow of President Fernando de la Rúa from office during Argentina's financial meltdown of 2001. But that was midst the country posting the biggest sovereign debt default in a world economic country (okay, it was a decade before Greece!), and which ushered in no fewer than an incredible five presidents in a nightmarish three-week period from which, in conditions of deep recession and rising poverty, the country took five or more years to recover and stabilise.

'Was history repeating itself?' was a question many asked at our dinner party later that night. This led me to recall, somewhat flippantly, Mao Zedong's famous aphorism that 'a revolution is not the same as inviting people to dinner'; nor presumably could it be predicted by our table talk. But if there was not a direct parallel between the 2001 crisis and the current situation, there were certainly some uneasy similarities.

CHAPTER 31

# A CONSTANT FEELING OF CRISIS

By 2012, the once mighty greenback might have declined somewhat across the world as the premium reserve currency of choice, but in Argentina the US dollar remained king. This had everything to do with the keen local memory of a recent history of financial turbulence and the sliding real (as opposed to government fairy-tale figures) value of the local peso. The more uncertain the economic outlook, the greater the rush into foreign currencies. But herein lay the rub: by the time of the September 2012 protests, permission to purchase dollars had pretty much evaporated and, like apartheid South Africa, severe criminal penalties awaited transgressors. Such local habits as pricing property sales in dollars were banned and the tax inspectors began to scour credit card statements for illicit transactions abroad (the empty suitcase syndrome of wealthier Argentines decamping to Miami to do the family shopping becoming commensurately more difficult).

The key reason behind the government move was simple enough: the controls were meant to combat both widespread tax evasion and, more crucially, stem capital flight, which crested in 2011 at an estimated 23 billion dollars. This way the state hoped to keep enough dollars in the reserves to pay Argentina's debts and tamp down runaway inflation. The country's extremely shallow credit markets, aggravated by its effective exclusion from international sources of finance (for not settling its debts), worsened matters and made the government's fiscal space very tight indeed.

But these measures often attracted the opposite results from those intended. The black market defied the clampdown and appeared to be roaring into life as traders (including hole-in-the-wall operations off busy Calle Florida) arbitraged the difference between the official rate of the peso and the so-called 'blue market' one that was nearly 40 per cent higher. As a local expatriate journalist explained: 'If you are lucky enough to have dollars, you must change them on the black (or blue) market – who wants to lose so much money by doing it legally?'[79]

The option of recycling dollars into pesos for their real worth was hardly available to South Africa's ambassador to Argentina: although my US dollar foreign allowance was paid into an offshore account, quite legally by our government, I received the peso equivalent at the highly unattractive official rate. But our South African diplomats were far better off than the Argentines in our embassy: they were paid in pesos and despite vigorous efforts on my part to adjust their salaries to account for the realities of local inflation, their pay packets never matched the ever-steepening rise in local prices.

The other option for currency hoarders of keeping the money at home stuffed under the proverbial mattress was also decidedly risky. At the time of our departure, it was reported that someone was killed in a home invasion robbery every second day – another matter that fuelled the angry anti-government protests, and that also, not for the first time, chimed with the South African experience. But even the deepest pit of South Africa's economic decline in the late 1980s, one of the under-appreciated factors that forced the pace of change there, was positively shallow compared with the Argentine financial crisis that began a few years after apartheid's demise – the strong and searing memory of which was so embedded in the national psyche during my ambassadorship a decade later.

## 'CONVERTIBILITY', *CORRALITO* AND CHAOS

In 1991, inflation in Argentina was hitting around 95 per cent, and vivid scenes in supermarkets of prices having zeros added to items before shoppers ever reached the checkout till were commonplace.[80] To arrest the chaos and restore confidence, President Carlos Menem and his economy minister, Domingo Cavallo, introduced a radical so-called 'convertibility plan' or currency peg by replacing the currency with the peso and pegging its value, on a one-for-one basis with the US dollar, with which it was legally convertible. Simply put, this meant that the supply of pesos in the country could never exceed the dollar reserves of Argentina, effectively outsourcing Argentina's monetary policy to the Federal Reserve in Washington. Virtually overnight, confidence and a measure of stability returned as the fears of hyperinflation disappeared. But there was a price tag, in fact several of them, attached to this bold move: local industry became less competitive (since the currency could not be devalued) and unless the now over-valued currency could be offset by gains in worker productivity (a faint hope in a country with such militant trade unions), Argentina's export edge would be reduced, which is precisely what occurred.

The plan also depended on the goodwill of the International Monetary Fund to provide much-needed injections of international lines of credit and loan facilities, and it in turn demanded that Menem's administration exercise flinty discipline over its hitherto free-spending ways. All went swimmingly for a few years, especially as Argentine embraced the framework (or appeared to do so) of the so-called Washington Consensus – privatising state assets, shrinking the size and the role of the state and other elements of the neo-liberal economic agenda.

Since the peso was now directly linked to the dollar, Argentines' appetite for imports surged and travel abroad became relatively inexpensive. Many years later, on a visit to Buenos Aires, well-known Cape Town hotelier Otto Stehlik reminisced about this time when planeloads of Argentine taxi drivers would fly across the South Atlantic for a long weekend at his five-star emporium, the Heerengracht Hotel – now, like those tourists, a memory of yesteryear.

In fact, many of the reforms were illusory. The privatisation process was mired in corruption and the yield for government coffers were much more modest than targeted. The curbing of government expenditure, which had impressively targeted a 'zero deficit' in the budget, spun out of control. At the same time, Menem increased payments to the provinces and their political overlords in an attempt to firstly win re-election (in which he succeeded) and thereafter to amend the constitution to extend his term of office (in this case, the spending splurge did not help him). By the time his presidency ended in December 1999, the 'convertibility plan' he bequeathed to his successor was in tatters. Ambitious growth targets had been missed and the appetite of the International Monetary Fund to continue its hitherto generous lending patterns, which had helped balance Argentina's books, was fast fading.

Many years later, Barack Obama also inherited a financial mess from his predecessor George W. Bush. But Menem's replacement, the colourless Fernando de la Rúa, lacked Obama's skilful intelligence to at least stop digging the ditch deeper. Whatever De la Rúa's personal attributes or limitations, the structural situation of Argentina was far more precarious than in the mighty US a decade later, or even the position of hapless Greece and other teetering southern European economies on the edge of sovereign bankruptcy in current times.

The US president, or more precisely his Federal Reserve, has almost limitless powers to print their own currency and borrow in it. Greece, and other endangered and default-threatening members of the Eurozone have, until their patience expires, 'counterparty support and institutional safety nets' in the form of the European Central Bank and other mechanisms of the European Union.[81] Argentina was, at the time of the looming crisis in 2001, more or less on its own. 'Convertibility' had been its own unilateral invention, and when De la Rúa surveyed his inherited mess he decided the only remedy was to recall to office the architect of the plan, Domingo Cavallo.

In order to keep the faith of the International Monetary Fund and Argentina's international bondholders, and also defend the increasingly unsustainable dollar peg, Cavallo was forced into a series of desperate measures: parallel exchange rates (to boost exports), debt swaps and, finally, savage cuts in public spending, including reductions in civil servants' pay packages and social pensions. It had little effect: Argentina's exports remained expensive and uncompetitive (since convertibility prevented currency devaluation), tax revenues fell and the interest rate paid by government on its then 141 billion dollar debt burden absorbed much of its revenue base. Critically, it became apparent that unless the International Monetary Fund in Washington continued to advance more loans and rollover Argentine debt, then the policy of pegging the peso to the dollar would collapse, and probably the government along with it. The one thing he never contemplated, as few politicians in a tight corner often cannot, was to abandon his signature policy of holding the peso's value fast to the US greenback.

More or less, and in conditions of high drama, exactly this scenario unfolded in the final months of 2001. The International Monetary Fund, soon to enter local popular folklore as the villain of the piece, demanded that government spending remain within the limits of the ever-shrinking revenue base of the state. Meanwhile, as nervous bank account holders anticipated that their savings might be at risk, and a run on the banks saw 20 billion dollars removed from the system during 2001, as alternative safe havens, ranging from Uruguay to the bedroom mattress, were sought. This flight consumed two thirds of the country's foreign exchange reserves, the very funds needed to maintain peso parity with the dollar.

In desperation and in order to halt the continuing haemorrhaging of the financial system, Cavallo introduced *corralito* (or containment). This froze any removal from any dollar-denominated accounts and limited the withdrawal from any other account to a maximum of 300 pesos per week. Into the bargain and in a final measure to meet government expenditure needs, he effectively confiscated funds from the private pension funds, forcing their administrators to accept 'almost certainly unpayable government bonds' in exchange for their long-term deposits.[82] But still Cavallo and his president clung onto the wreckage of their policy of convertibility, when all the evidence suggested its abandonment, and the widely anticipated devaluation of the peso had in fact triggered the bank run in the first place. The Argentine financial system froze up: there was simply no credit and liquidity left in the system.

The public reaction was swift and furious: people banged their pots and pans and marched on the banks, which soon resembled besieged fortresses, and on government buildings, demanding the president's resignation. Widespread looting was met by police fire and scores of people were shot dead by security forces across the country as unrest spread. Finally, the International Monetary Fund, the last line of defence for the government, lost its faith in the government's credibility and creditworthiness. It suspended the disbursement of a loan tranche due in December and with the money running out, the game was up. Cavallo resigned, and De la Rúa quit office, departing the Casa Rosada in a helicopter. After the revolving door of three interim presidents in as many weeks, Eduardo Duhalde, governor of Buenos Aires, was installed as interim head of state to serve out the remainder of De la Rúa's term in early 2002.

Argentina could not pay its then 160 billion dollars in debt due to its international creditors, and so it effectively went into bankruptcy and defaulted. At that stage, this was the largest sovereign default in world economic history. Duhalde immediately moved to stabilise the economy, abandoning the convertibility policy and sharply devaluing the peso, and oversaw a painful process of national and financial reconstruction. This saw the economy contract by over 16 per cent in the first year or two of his presidency, while unemployment hit over 20 per cent. Many comfortably well-off Argentines found themselves in conditions of virtual penury – their dollar wealth extinguished and their pensions placed at risk.

Three factors rode to Argentina's rescue in the years that followed this national trauma: the country soon noted a record trade surplus (since it could no longer afford so many imports and devaluation cheapened the price and thus the competiveness of its exports); a world commodity boom for the next decade took off creating a mighty tailwind for Argentine agriculture and its famed food-production economy; and most, although not all, of the country's international creditors accepted in 2005 a discount ('haircut') on the country's debt. In fact, by the time Duhalde made way for his hand-picked successor, Nestor Kirchner, in April 2003, the economic situation was already returning to a degree of normalcy.

CHAPTER 32

# 'WE MUST NOT IMPORT A SINGLE NAIL'

My ambassadorship, which occurred nearly a decade after the drama of 2001, coincided with the rule (often appearing more as a reign) of Nestor Kirchner's successor and widow, the famed Cristina, whose own brand of economic management has already occupied considerable space in this narrative. As both a diplomat and as a resident in her country, I was to feel, and battle first-hand, the full effects of what I came to call 'Cristinanomics'. It proved a distinctly bumpy journey.

For example, for my 55th birthday in December 2011, my good friend Brian Doctor in London, always eager to improve my access to new technology, decided to send me a Kindle, the electronic book-reader. In the era of the twenty-first century globalised and accelerated supply chain, it seemed a very basic transaction. But neither of us had reckoned on the eighteenth-century mercantilism that now governed Argentina. The package arrived by DHL courier in Buenos Aires, a few days after Brian advised that he had sent it. My office received a call from the company advising that in order to receive it, I would be obliged to pay the equivalent of nearly 200 dollars in order to 'nationalise' it. This, in fact, amounted to more than double the price of the item. We then explained that as a diplomat I did not, in fact, have to pay duties and imposts. The courier announced that it would require 'authentication' of this proposition. My office then unavailingly sought a note from the relevant section of the foreign ministry.

Meanwhile, wherever in cyberspace the package originated, a five-day limit for collection had been placed on the order. If it was not collected in that time, it would be automatically sent back to the supplier. A very perplexed Brian called a few days later, advising that Amazon had credited his account and had cancelled the order. I explained the delays and the difficulties and he then decided to simply slip the Kindle in his suitcase, and deliver it to me personally, after my birthday but on his forthcoming visit to Argentina. I should have saved him the initial bother. A few days before my birthday, I had attended Cristina's inauguration for her second presidential term. During her lengthy address that day, she had thundered: 'Argentina must be self-sufficient – we must not import a single nail.' Or an iPad or Kindle or any other convenience from the modern world for that matter, as I had already discovered.

Kirchner's administration was battling many of the same ghosts (and indeed had helped to conjure them up) that had felled her predecessors: high inflation, runaway public expenditure, thin credit lines and dollar flight – each being fed by the other and most of them attributable to her stoking of consumer demand and her championing of public giveaways highlighted in Chapter 25. One of her government's attempts to exorcise these economic demons was to simply stamp out imports as far and as crudely as possible. This highly inefficient and outrageously protectionist strategy had the advantage of promoting local industry, but in turn drove up prices, which subsequently fed the inflationary fires. But for consumers it was hell: in short, no quality imported goods were available, except at exorbitant prices. For example, the iPad and the BlackBerry, to the extent you could find them at all, were about 400 per cent more expensive in Buenos Aires than they were in Hong Kong. According to the September 2011 edition of Global Trade Alert, a database of restrictions on international commerce, Argentina imposed 'more trade limitations deemed "harmful" (to world trade) than any country save Russia.'[83]

My irritations as a consumer were, comparatively speaking, minor. It was in my day job as ambassador that the real problems manifested themselves. There I began to encounter major difficulties in growing our trade volumes and protecting the interests of South African investors in Cristina's republic, the two essential pillars, as I conceived them, of my diplomatic work. Early on in my tour of duty, I stumbled upon the core of the problem for South African companies operating in this part of the world. Our embassy was hosting a pavilion at a Buenos Aires trade fair, and I was on hand to open it and utter the formulaic words of welcome to the assembled South African exhibitors and local dignitaries.

Shortly after my address, I was approached by a visiting South African exhibitor. He represented one of our country's leading fruit juice exporters. Much to our trade section's delight, and with their energetic assistance, this company had recently secured a potentially lucrative contract to export and display, in a high-profile promotion, South African juices on the shelves of a leading chain of Argentine supermarkets. The South African was, however, far from happy. He explained to me that indeed the first container of juices had recently arrived in Buenos Aires, and been unpacked and displayed on the shelves. However, he had just had a meeting with the supermarket's sales director and had been told that they were to be removed from display. The following explanation was given, which was so incredible that I had difficulty believing it.

After the display commenced, he told me, the sales director received a telephone call from one of the most powerful ministers in Cristina's circle, the domestic trade secretary, Señor Guillermo Moreno. I had read much about this hard-driven ideologue, her all-purpose enforcer, but we had never met, for the simple reason that he refused to meet with foreign emissaries. As the tale unfolded, I understood why. Apparently Moreno asked the supermarket director: 'Why are you selling those cheap South African juices?' When it was explained to him that they were being sold on the basis of their landed costs and as part of a trade promotion strategy, the minister allegedly issued a blunt warning to the effect: 'I suggest that you get them off your shelves, or else I will send my inspectors round to your warehouse and I will find many things wrong with your operations.'

In mafia terms, this would be termed a 'shakedown', an impression bolstered by the fact that Moreno (who was seen in the 2011 elections strong-arming an opposition supporter) looked like an extra from *The Sopranos* TV series. But, I wondered, could a government minister be really so crude and act in such flagrant violation of Argentina's, at least theoretical, commitments to free trade under the rules of the World Trade Organization? As it transpired, my South African interlocutor was dismayed by the turn of events and told me that there was really no point in continuing with the promotion – the first container would also be the last. I was also to discover, soon enough, that the story was neither far-fetched nor unusual.

Thus began my learning curve into the morass and murky swamp of doing business in this climate. The fruit juice story was repeated many times over in the future, and Señor Moreno usually, although not always, emerged, in the lurid accounts fed to me by exasperated Argentine importers of South African goods and their counterparties back home, as the prime villain. The sagas, in which I was to intervene with varying degrees of both success and failure, ranged from the serious to the comic.

In the former category, the Argentine representative of a South African investor of some standing and weight came to see me with a dismal, and by the time I met with him not unusual, tale of woe. When it had invested in Argentina some years before, his company had received, under the prevailing law, a 30-year waiver from the payment of royalties on their exports. Shortly before our meeting, this exemption had been revoked unilaterally by government decree. During our consultation, I referred him to the relevant section of the bilateral investment protection agreement, signed by no less an eminence than Nelson Mandela during his state visit with Carlos Menem in Argentina in 1998. It explicitly forbade such an act and allowed the injured party, in such an event, to appeal such a decree to the World Bank body, the International Centre for the Settlement of Investment Disputes in Washington, D.C., that conducts arbitrations between businesses and governments. But Menem, who signed a flurry of such agreements in his time to attract investment to his country, had been long replaced by Cristina, who had very different ideas. Still, I pointed out to my visitor, the treaty remained valid and he should invoke it, and the embassy, of course, stood ready to assist.

Suitably relieved, my visitor went off and arranged and duly served a strongly worded letter of protest to the Argentine government (with a copy to me), threatening to refer the action to Washington, unless relief was afforded. A few weeks later, my visitor returned, in a far less buoyant mood. After receipt of the letter, he had been 'called in' by the relevant minister (not Moreno in this case) and given the shakedown. He was told, in blunt terms, that if the company proceeded with its proposed action, then the Argentine authorities would simply refuse to allow the company to 'import a single item' to ensure the continuous running of their local operations. 'What choice did we have,' my guest asked, 'except to withdraw the letter and accept the decree?' Actually, the Argentine government probably saved the company a whack of future legal fees. I later read that Argentina refused to honour awards made against it in Washington unless 'brought to a local court for collection', which meant years of protracted litigation and a hazardous outcome. And where it did pay over awards against it in the past, it usually did so by way of government bonds (of doubtful value) rather than in hard cash.[84]

On the lighter side of the ledger, the South African resident representative of one of our multinationals finally secured a meeting with the fabled Moreno. He had a simple and, from Argentina's perspective, hugely attractive proposition. The company wanted to expand their local operations and thus increase the capacity and the jobs in their Argentine factory. But the specialised equipment required for the purpose had been imported from Europe and was currently stuck in the customs house due to an automatic ban that Moreno had placed on all imported items (a so-called 'non-automatic licence', which the World Trade Organization allows to be placed for 60 days on imported items, and which in Argentina was often extended, sometimes into infinity). Moreno, as the account was retold to me, thundered at the South African and his Argentine colleague. But this was not because of the merits of their request, but as a result of the state of their business cards. They were emblazoned with the name and the logo of the South African-originating multinational (in terms of the corporation's global branding strategy), with the name of the Argentine subsidiary beneath it. 'Come back and see me when your cards reflect that you are an Argentine company,' the trade secretary dismissively advised them. The cards were duly reprinted, and in the interim my trade officer and I managed to release the goods through contact with one of Moreno's underlings.

Soon enough, I heard from my diplomatic colleagues, and then read in the local press, of quirky and bizarre bartering deals, which seemed to have no place in a twenty-first-century trading nation but which had become, in this retro-economy, a matter of routine. For example, mighty BMW, the luxury car manufacturer, agreed to sell Argentine rice abroad in exchange for permission to import its vehicles. Porsche's barter struck me as more appropriately upmarket: they bought a wine estate to satisfy the government demand that for every dollar of imports there should be a dollar of exports. Even the famous Barbie dolls fell afoul of local authorities. Officials reportedly blocked their release until the importing company agreed to export Argentina's version of Lego toys as well.[85] But such deals often lacked transparency, protected failing and uncompetitive local enterprises and usually, since they were essentially book entries purchased via a local middle person from an existing enterprise, did not add a peso of additional growth to the economy.

Into this import-hostile environment, ruled by personal whim and often with caprice, amazingly enough we did in fact managed to increase South African exports to record levels in 2011 largely due to world demand for Argentine soy production. This, in turn, required value-added fertiliser, which South Arica produced in great quality and quantity and at hugely competitive prices. So, in the decidedly unsexy realm of manure (in addition to our traditional coal and plastics exports), we somehow improved our trade balances by 80 per cent and into the bargain fulfilled one of the very few direct instructions I ever received from the minister of international relations, Maite Nkoana-Mashabane.

CHAPTER 33

# CRISTINA'S BIG BAZOOKA

Back in South Africa, Julius Malema (the recently dethroned king of the ANC Youth League, who was finally expelled from the ruling party in early 2012) was enflaming local opinion and terrifying foreign investors. He was demanding the nationalising of the country's resource wealth without compensation. At around this time, the president of Argentina did, more or less, precisely that.

In the span of just two decades, since 1990, Argentina had gyrated wildly between a burst of privatisation (accompanied by rapacious personal enrichment by the politically favoured – a process widely seen as 'a corrupt fire sale of the state's crown jewels', to quote the august *Economist*)[86] to a zealous and Kirchnerite-inspired nationalisation, which was also accompanied by insider favouritism. State-owned enterprises became bloated patronage machines for the ruling party faithful, especially members of the president's youth movement, La Cámpora.

My direct involvement in one of these money-guzzling monuments of inefficient uncompetitiveness was when I accompanied South African Airways to a meeting at the Ezeiza Airport. South African Airways and all other airlines arriving in Argentina had to contend with the fact (and the cost) that it was more expensive to land a plane in Buenos Aires than at New York's JFK airport! The reason? The state-owned ramp services company, which handled everything on the ground from baggage clearance to aircraft maintenance, had a monopoly at the airport and set their own charges, untouched by the remotest whiff of market forces. We did not succeed in getting a discount on our landing costs. But this had nothing on the benighted national carrier, Aerolíneas Argentinas. It, too, had been taken over by the state from its private owners. And with no compensating gains in either service or efficiency, it was, by 2011, losing more than 2 million dollars *per day* in its operations. However, commercial considerations appeared to be absent from its operating agenda or narrative. Its boss, a labour lawyer turned airline executive (whose father, unsurprisingly, was a ruling party congressman) enthused on the airline website: 'The Argentine colours rise with every take-off of an Aerolíneas flight.'[87] And so did the losses.

But none of these state-takeovers reached the scale, or inspired the international backlash, of Cristina's radical move in April 2012, when she seized a majority 51 per cent control, from the Spanish-owned Repsol Energy group, of Argentina's largest oil company and energy producer, Yacimientos Petroliferos Fiscales (YPF). YPF had been privatised in 1992, and its government ownership before then had led to the company being described by one Latin American economist as 'the most badly run enterprise in the history of the world'.[88] This time around it looked no more propitious.

The move on YPF, claimed the president in a public address to her adoring and cheering supporters, was a consequence of the company's 'failure to invest' in the country, which she noted was now stuck with a nearly 10 billion dollar fuel import bill, compared to the 6 billion dollar fuel surplus it had recorded in 2006. But the reasons for the 'investment strike' were, in fact, largely of the president and her late husband's own making. Firstly (and here Argentina bore an eerie resemblance to the South African government's botched attempt to involve the private sector in rolling out electricity power stations in the 1990s), the Argentine government artificially held down the price of petrol and gas, which led, simultaneously, both to an underinvestment in the sector and an overconsumption of its products. This was, of course, hugely popular with consumers, but unsustainable.

The second factor in YPF's underinvestment in tapping and developing Argentina's huge shale oil and gas reserves, the third biggest in the world, also had an echo back home in South Africa. In 2007, when the micro-managing president Nestor Kirchner put together the Repsol acquisition of YPF, he decided that one of his powerful business allies, Enrique Eskenazi, and his son Sebastian, would be the minority shareholders in the new company. In an only-in-Argentina twist, Nestor and Enrique first apparently met in the reception rooms of the psychotherapist they both consulted in Santa Cruz, the Kirchners' provincial political base.[89] The Eskenazis, in the tradition of many of South Africa's black economic empowerment barons, had neither a background in the oil business and, more materially, lacked the cash to pay the 3.4 billon dollars to acquire 25 per cent of the newly privatised (and Repsol majority-owned) YPF. Thus, at Kirchner's insistence, the family acquisition was entirely debt-financed. This obliged YPF in the years that followed to pay high dividends, in part, to allow the Eskenazis to pay back their debt. It was strongly rumoured that following Nestor's death in 2010, there had been a fallout between the widow-president and the family. It was being darkly suggested that the Eskenazis had 'reneged on whatever (private) arrangement they had with Nestor following his death'.[90]

It all smelt distinctly Russian, with oligarchs moving in and out of favour and riches, although in Argentina they did not land up in a prison in Siberia. South Africa's politically connected business elite had also suffered, although not so steeply, when Thabo Mbeki lost his presidency in 2008. Although the nationalisation of YPF by Cristina did not theoretically affect the Argentine shareholders, the inevitable decline, if not complete halt, in dividend payments going forward suggested the highly leveraged Eskenazis might be left with very little indeed, as they would be unable to meet their debt repayments. But the Repsol company in Spain had been expropriated outright and there was no certainty as to how their shareholding would be valued, and by whom, and whether they would ever receive any reasonable compensation. A furious Spanish government immediately arranged for the European Union to formalise yet another complaint against the Argentines and threaten retaliations. However, much closer to home, the words of outgoing Mexican President Felipe Calderón put his finger on the real consequence of this step: 'No one in their right mind would now invest in Argentina,' he said.[91] And given that it would cost an estimated 25 billion dollars a year to exploit properly the oil and energy reserves of her country, the flight and fright of foreign investors suggested Cristina had, not for the first time, dug herself and her country into a deep hole.

Cristina's populist exercise in resource nationalisation was, however, welcomed in another part of Latin America, by her ally, Venezuela's self-proclaimed Bolivarian socialist 'El Comandante' president, Hugo Chávez. He took time out from his cancer treatment to signal support. And, of course, he had made precisely the same grab against oil companies in his own country. Doubtless, Cristina was too busy counting the short-term dollar saving her nationalisation would provide for her emptying state coffers and basking in the sugar rush from the adulation of her supporters at her 'boldness' to study the Venezuela model too closely: for there, in a decade of such asset grabs, output had declined steeply.

A few months after this dramatic event, I arranged a lightning visit to Argentina by South Africa's widely admired and economically prudent finance minister, Pravin Gordhan. The centrepiece of his engagements was an address to our Argentine–South Africa Chamber of Commerce, headed by a staunch ally of South Africa's in Buenos Aires, Oscar Hansen. The good and the great of the Argentine business community packed the lunchtime talk, which Pravin delivered in his customarily sensible and no-frills style. To the battered locals, still reeling from the YPF saga and now hemmed in by new dollar restrictions and other delights from Cristinanomics, his balanced economic prescriptions were like balm on an open wound. I had told the audience in my introduction that, appropriately, Pravin was a trained pharmacist. I had omitted to add that he was also a leading light in the local Communist Party. I do not know if they would have believed this or even much cared. He was a pragmatic and thoughtful steward of his country's finances and had no opposite number in the current set-up in Argentina.

Happily, other aspects of my work delivered me, for a while at least, from the depressing realities of bad politics and odd economics. It was in my journeys into the vast hinterland and along the relatively untamed coastlines of Argentina and other parts of South America that I witnessed worlds of wonder about which I had only previously read or seen on TV. And in the first such venture I would meet the most remote Boer community on earth, appropriately in a place dubbed 'the end of the world', Patagonia.

CHAPTER 34

# JOURNEYS

Napoleon apparently observed: 'Look at a country's geography if you want to know its foreign policy.' Shortly after arriving in Buenos Aires in November 2009, I noted that a key pillar of South Africa's and my new department's international outreach was cut from this cloth, to wit 'the advancement of the African agenda'. Particular emphasis was placed on our embassies forging ties with what the business plan termed the 'African diaspora'. Doubtless, the remnants of a Boer enclave, settled more than a century before in the desolate, windswept, southern vastness of Argentina's Patagonia region, was the last community that the politically correct paladins of Pretoria had in mind when articulating this objective. But they were, in fact, certainly the largest South African, and probably even the biggest African-originating group, settled and still living in the country. Inspired by their story, retold in somewhat romanticised form by everyone from the famous travel writer Bruce Chatwin[92] to amateur historian-bloggers, I decided to pay them a visit.

Actually, to be perfectly accurate, I piggybacked on a journey that the embassy was busy arranging for South African journalist Richard Davies of the South African Press Association. A thoughtful and considered member of the media fraternity, Richard had expressed a desire to go down south some 2 000 kilometres from Buenos Aires to the oil town of Comodoro Rivadavia, in the province of Chubut, and report first-hand on the world's most remotely settled Afrikaners.[93]

In my imaginings, fed by the travel literature,[94] Patagonia conjured up images of glacial ice, majestic mountains and unspoiled wildernesses framed by the raging seas of the Atlantic and the Antarctic. In truth, as I would discover on many future visits, all these elements, plus others, abound in a sprawling landmass, which constitutes roughly the bottom third of Chile and Argentina and stretches over three of the latter's under-populated provinces. Throw in a necklace of magnificent lakes, alpine scenery and vast deserts and you get a snapshot of the scale and incredible diversity of an area where, to borrow the cliché, 'nature is writ large, and man stands very small'.

Our arrival in the south commenced with an amazing day of whale, orca and sea lion watching, with thousands of penguins added in for good measure, off the Península Valdéz, near the Atlantic Patagonian town of Puerto Madryn. The profusion of sea life was a visual feat: famed southern right whales and endless schools of dolphins emerged alongside our small dinghy, and swam shotgun with us, to our delighted gasps and a few nervous twitches. It was almost as though our tour guide had summonsed their presence, and the vast bulk of the whales and the flopping mass of the elephant seals became, after a few hours, almost commonplace. The peninsula more than deserved its status as a UNESCO World Heritage Site. The taxpayers back home in South Africa were not, however, paying me for a vacation in this maritime wonderland; the pleasures of tourism yielded to the obligations of diplomacy.

Given the relative indifference of the central government in Buenos Aires towards resident diplomats (the sub-Saharan desk at the Argentine foreign ministry being an exception), this, my first visit to an Argentine province, was an exercise in status enhancement. At the airport, aides of the governor bustled our group (which comprised Richard, Michal and the embassy's effervescent Mony di Liscia) into a VIP waiting area and whisked us to our hotel, before the peninsula tour. An eager local press contingent noted down my banal boilerplate observations, and, after the peninsula visit, I was taken by high-speed motorcade to a meeting with the provincial governor, Mario das Neves. He expressed great appreciation for the contribution of the Boer community to the development of his province, and, after an exchange of further pleasantries, he presented me with a handsome *mate* tea set. I regretted that our very modest embassy gift budget only afforded a coffee-table book of *Beautiful South Africa* in return.

The town of Puerto Madryn was also the base of operations for the South African fishing giant Irvin & Johnson's (I&J) Argentine company, Al Pesca, which trawled the surrounding waters and beyond for hake, prawns and other abundant harvests from the seas. But the operation was a far from happy one at the time of my visit. In the nine years of I&J ownership, the company had ground to a halt for an incredible cumulative total of six months, while militant and factionalised unions went on strike and terrorised both management and non-striking workers in the process. In fact, an uneasy peace of sorts prevailed at the time of my tour of its factory headquarters, but at great cost: the company was apparently paying the captain of one of its trawlers more than an airline jumbo jet pilot received. I would subsequently accompany I&J to meetings in Buenos Aires with the minister of labour and others in a partially successful attempt to obtain some redress. But a very relieved I&J was happy to find a buyer for Al Pesca a year or two later. Doubtless the problems they experienced would only be replicated for the new owners given the anarchic labour situation in the local fishing industry. Fortunately, South Africa no longer had a dog in that fight, nor had to fish in those waters.

These viewings and visits were essentially sideshows. The main attraction, our rendezvous with the Boers, lay in wait for us more than 400 kilometres south, in Comodoro Rivadavia.

## BOERS AT 'THE END OF THE WORLD'

The barren hills and desert scrubland, dotted around with grazing sheep, framed the empty road between Puerto Madryn and Comodoro, and brought to mind the vast landscape of South Africa's Karoo region. Perhaps, I thought to myself as we motored along it on an appropriately windswept Saturday morning, this was the attraction of the region for its improbable early Boer settlers. The facts, I would later learn, were less romantic and starker: the 800 or so South African refugee families, who arrived on these shores between 1902 and 1909, were in fact driven by a desire to escape from the heel of British rule, following the defeat of the

Boers in the second Boer or South African War, which ended in 1902. This, far more than any real idea of the inhospitable land 'at the end of the world', as southern Patagonia is often called, informed and motivated their sea trek across the South Atlantic, more than a century before our meeting with their descendants.[95]

In truth, there is no shortage of fascinating facts in the background story to this settlement. Certainly the most exotic personality who drove the founding of this colony of exiled Afrikaners was Camillo Ricchiardi.[96] This apparently dashing and gallant Italian military officer fought in the South African War alongside the Boers. Among his achievements were his role in guarding the imprisoned Winston Churchill and marrying one of the grandchildren of President Paul Kruger, whom he met while convalescing from his war wounds in a Pretoria hospital. Equally amazing was the fact that in 1900 Kruger apparently had no fewer than 156 living children, grandchildren and great-grandchildren, considerably shortening the odds that one of them, at least, would wed an *uitlander* (or foreigner). Ricchiardi, together with a Ladybrand farmer, travelled to Argentina before the war's conclusion and negotiated directly with President Julio Roca to establish Boer settlements in the province of Chubut, in Comodoro Rivadavia and inland at Sarmiento. The first ship carrying the new settlers sailed from Cape Town a year or so later.

It was easy enough to understand the factors that willed their journeys. Many of the settlers had emerged at war's end from Lord Kitchener's 'scorched earth' tactics, which destroyed their farms, and from the cruel conditions of British concentration camps in which many Boer families were imprisoned during the war. One of the young Boer children who accompanied her family flight from South Africa to Argentina and helped found the early settlement in Chubut was Petronella Niemann. Hers was a family of *bittereinders* (Boers who refused to yield to British rule), understandable in the context of their own privation and loss. In her remarkable memoir of both the war and the following years in Argentina, she describes in unadorned prose (written later from memory when she was 90 years old!) the harsh conditions in the Bethulie concentration camp in the Free State. Epidemics of whooping cough and measles were commonplace and many children, including her brother, died from disease.[97] But the world she and the Boers left behind was to be matched, in different ways, by the extremity and severity of their new environment. One of the first Boers to settle in Patagonia, on farmland unadorned by trees, housing or even accessible water and only the screaming wind as constant companion, Francis Behr, was moved to observe: 'God forgive me for bringing my wife and children to this place.'[98]

I could empathise with this sentiment, even more than 100 years later, when I surveyed the bleak landscape in and around Comodoro Rivadavia, shortly after our arrival there. Optimistically dubbed 'Argentina's answer to Houston', other than the ubiquitous and ugly presence of oil derricks and other features marking it as the headquarters of Argentina's petroleum industry, I could see no similarity between the two cities. Perhaps the tourist book's considerable understatement that the place was 'frayed around the edges, having little of the old world charm found in colonial Latin American cities' rang more true.[99]

The early Boer settlers more or less made a go of it, setting up sheep and cattle farms of up to 3 500 hectares. Although local legend suggested it was their drilling for water that led to the first oil find in the area, it was the infamous YPF company (see Chapter 33) and not the Boer families who profited from this discovery. By the time of the centenary of the Great Trek in 1936, more than two thirds of the original families were repatriated to South Africa. Of the remainder, many married into local families, and the community, which until 1953 had enjoyed the services of an Afrikaans *dominee* (minister) at the local Nederduitse Gereformeerde Kerk, was now far more Spanish- than Afrikaans-speaking. And, like their Great Trek forebears, they were also divided into various, apparently often quarrelsome, factions.

On the afternoon of our arrival in Comodoro, we set out to have tea with a group of them at a nearby teahouse. I suppose that along with the *melktert* served to me with old world charm and courtesy by Graciela Hammond, from a recipe she acquired from her mother, an original Boer settler, the most memorable take-away from the encounter was to meet a Van der Merwe (this is not a joke, incidentally) who could not speak a word of Afrikaans, or English for that matter, only Spanish! But Juan van der Merwe was hardly alone in this deficiency: a community of

Afrikaans surnames without the language of their forebears was a common feature and the subject of bitter complaint from the dozen or so in the group who could speak a form of Afrikaans, probably closer to the High Dutch spoken to them by their grandparents. However, as Richard would note in his report on our tea party, 'the surnames of those present at the event could be found in any South African telephone directory: De Lange, Botha, Kruger, Norval and Schlebusch, among others'. And, of course, Van der Merwe.

The realities of the community conditions were explained to our group by Danie Botha, one of the senior members, about 65 years old, who actually spoke Afrikaans. He told me: 'You'll see no Afrikaners here who are well off. Other people who came here, such as the Portuguese and the Italians, they are wealthy. But the Afrikaners did not come here to make money; they came here to escape the English.' Given the hostility then prevailing between the British and Argentine governments over the Falkland Islands and other matters, they probably came to the right address. But the group was not much interested in the South African ambassador's take on geo-politics; they wanted assistance in acquiring an Afrikaans teacher and some other help to ensure that the language and heritage of the Boers could, in some or other form, be passed down the generations. In realistic terms and speaking modern Afrikaans, 65-year-old Carlos de Lange, whose father was a young child when his grandparents arrived in Argentina in 1905 – two years after the British had destroyed their farmstead – lamented that he and a few others were the end of the line: '*Na my geslag is daar nie meer Afrikaans nie*' (After my generation there will be no more Afrikaans).

Listening to these rather heartfelt accounts and pleas for assistance, I felt like the proverbial eunuch in the harem: I had the desire to please, but lacked the power to act. Before journeying to meet them, I had carefully researched their position and the embassy means, or lack of them, to assist. We had until a few years before maintained one of the community members as a South African honorary consul. But the position had been closed; among other reasons being that the person appointed processed no consular work since, despite the familiar surnames, none of the community members were in fact South African citizens. Our ever-shrinking budget also meant we could hardly justify and fund an Afrikaans teacher to maintain the language in this far-flung outpost. With a sense of hope over expectation, I wrote in the commemorative book presented to me at the end of our visit: '*Ek hoop dat hierdie gemeenskap, met sy erfenis en taal, sal in Argentinië oorleef*' (I hope that this community, and its heritage and language, will survive in Argentina).

On my return to Buenos Aires, I set about trying to mobilise interest and funds from Afrikaans institutions back home – from the language and cultural organisation, the ATKV, to media houses. But three years after my visit and despite constant prodding by the embassy and corresponding expressions of interest in South Africa, there was little of substance, or concrete aid, to show for the effort. Like a fading footnote in the book of history, I fear that Carlos de Lange's prediction will be realised, as the Argentine Boers and their language die out in Patagonia. But their remarkable story of settlement and endurance will doubtless be kept alive in the recounting of it to future generations, even if it is told to them in Spanish.

## JUDGING BEAUTY QUEENS, SWIMMING WITH SEA LIONS AND OTHER ADVENTURES

Back home in the Cape, few weekend pleasures can exceed the delight of tasting wine and enjoying a long lunch in one of the many splendid vineyards in the Stellenbosch and Franschhoek area, less than an hour's drive from Cape Town. The agreeable combination of cutting-edge food and new world nectars in such a heavenly sweep of countryside marks the area for me as a world-beater; and my journeys into the winelands of northern California, southern France, Australia and Chile did not alter this opinion. But now I was resident in another wine country of note – Argentina's signature Malbec cultivar had propelled its viticulture into the front rank of global producers. And here I was in receipt of an invitation from the governor of Mendoza, its best wine-producing province, to attend as his personal guest (well, actually alongside about 50 other ambassadors, give or take) the annual Fiesta Nacional de la Vendimia (Grape Harvest Festival). Could there be a better diplomatic assignment,

I wondered? After an exhausting and, at times, bewildering weekend, the short answer would be, indeed, yes, there can.

Mendoza – both the name of the province and its tree-lined capital city – is some 1 000 kilometres south-west of Buenos Aires and sits flush alongside the mighty Andes mountain range, which borders Argentina and Chile. I was to discover on future visits that the city had fine hotels and restaurants and a profusion of parks and nearby wine estates. However, on my first visit there, the governor chose to house the diplomats invited to the Vendimia in a hostelry, which rejoiced in the name of Hotel Modern, but, other than the fact that it had recently been constructed, appeared, with malfunctioning showers, collapsing cupboard doors and eccentric service, to be the Latin equivalent of Fawlty Towers. Its situation in the grim motor town district of the city – about as attractive as Malvern in Johannesburg or Paardeneiland in Cape Town – did not bolster first impressions.

In its own weird way, the festival provided one of my more unforgettable Argentine experiences, specifically due to the role assigned to the visiting ambassadors in it. It became soon apparent enough that the contemporary winds of gender equity and of political correctness had never blown in the direction of Mendoza or its Vendimia. As we were herded into a bus for the opening cocktail function, our guide breathlessly informed us that we were about to meet 'the prettiest women from each wine district in Mendoza'. And lo, when we arrived at the venue – like a scene from a 1950s Miss Margate pageant or a slightly down-at-heel matric dance, in shiny ball gowns and with imitation tiaras to match – dozens of local beauty queens awaited our inspection. Each of them wore a sash proclaiming which of the wine areas – Godoy Cruz, Maipú, Lujan de Cuyo and several others – they had been, like state winners in a Miss America contest, chosen to represent. It was then explained to us that the diplomats' specific tasks this weekend would be to help choose the winning queen of the Vendimia (or the Reina Nacional de la Vendimia to give the full title), apparently more an aesthetic than an intellectual contest. The cocktail function was simply an initial meet-and-greet exercise, during which I wryly remembered that my department back home had a deputy director general for gender matters. I never did find out what she actually did with her time or in her position, but doubtless a South African ambassador judging a beauty contest in Argentina would not have incurred her approval. Nor in fact did it much appeal to Michal or me, and after a few obligatory moments with the aspiring queens we escaped back to the city in a taxi. But no such speedy exit was possible the following evening, the crowning glory, as it were, of the weekend festival, when – thrillingly or not – we would crown the new queen.

The next night, our bus duly trundled up a steep hill outside the city where the travelling diplomats were deposited in small plastic chairs arranged in a vast terraced amphitheatre. Below and behind us thousands of excited locals were seated, cheering the sound and light show, featuring literally a cast of hundreds, which seemed to cover – at exhaustive length – the entire history of Argentina since before the arrival of the Spanish conquistadores some 400 years before. Finally, and it seemed like forever, the midnight hour approached and the *pièce de résistance* of the evening was at hand. We were handed out voting paper, and were asked to place our X next to the name of a preferred candidate. I had no significant opinions on the merits of any of the aspiring queens parading below us on the vast stage; in fact the only preference I had at that stage was to return to the hotel and go to sleep, but this option was not available on the ballot. This was one election in which I had no strong, or in fact any, views. I recall that Michal and I voted for the candidate whose district had the same name as the cross street of our Buenos Aires residence, Miss Godoy Cruz. After the ballots were collected from the ambassadors and other notables who enjoyed voting rights, they were rushed down to the stage. Then what followed defied belief: the master of ceremonies, a man of many words and rolling cadences, proceeded to shout out every one of the 100 or so votes, as in the manner of 'S-e-n-or-i-n-a Maaaaaaaaaaaaaipppppppppuuuuuuuuuuu!'. 'Oh no,' I said to Michal, 'at this rate we will be here for another two hours or so.' With a small box of fruit and a bottle of water to sustain us, and absent of any alternatives, we toughed it out, as the winner was, in this excruciating manner, finally proclaimed (Miss Rivadavia, I vaguely now recall). At around 2 a.m., we were shepherded back to the bus, and the guide excitedly announced that we were to proceed for dinner at the local golf club!

The announcement resulted in a low-level diplomatic rebellion, in which I was happy to join. At our insistence, we skipped the dinner and in an advanced state of grumpy fatigue finally reached the hotel, and with it the promise of much-delayed sleep.

Strangely enough, I managed to decline, somehow, the invitations to the Mendoza Vendimia in the years that followed my initial and sole attendance at it. But one of the huge advantages of being posted to Argentina, and living in the southern tip of South America, was the access it afforded to a treasure trove of scenic and natural wonders, none of which entailed adjudicating late-night beauty contests. Just as at university, where I found the books not on the reading list far more compelling than the works prescribed, I found the journeys we undertook on leave and paid for ourselves far more interesting and, freed from the shackles and rituals of protocol, much more liberating than many I undertook officially around South America as an ambassador.

In the very top tier of these excursions was our Easter visit in 2012 to the Galapagos Islands, some 1 000 kilometres off the coast of Ecuador, which, as its name suggests, straddles the equator. During our five-day cruise to several of these islands of infinite wonder and enchantment, I kept thinking I was starring in my own National Geographic movie, except I was, in fact, simply a dazzled observer. The leading players were the sea lions, stingrays and sea turtles we swam with most afternoons and the lava rock we gingerly walked on one morning. We watched a booby bird pinpointing its hapless sea prey with the precision, and with the killer efficiency, of a stealth bomber. The far-flung basalt islands we visited, while staying in the comfort of our efficient catamaran, were of course never attached to any mainland, hence the unique nature of the plant and animal life on them. Situated on the confluence of three of the earth's tectonic plates, the islands arose literally from the sea as volcanic tips or 'hot spots' where the weakness in the earth's crust at least 700 000 years ago (in the case of the 'newest' of the islands) caused the eruption, which in turn created the land surfaces we were now exploring.

The islands entered history, and severely challenged the church-ordained theory of 'divine selection', when Charles Darwin visited them for five weeks in 1835. Some 25 years later (probably delayed by the revolutionary nature of his findings), he published one of the most famous and consequential books in human history, *On the Origins of the Species by Means of Natural Selection*. The excellently well-informed naturalist and tour guide who accompanied our catamaran explained the theory not by reference to the humble and differentially specied finch birds, which abound on the Galapagos and which Darwin studied to explain so much about biology and its intersection with geology. They certainly received an honourable mention. But it was the unique flightless cormorant (in fact the name of our catamaran), which was at the core of his lecture. It possesses only tattered and vestigial wings and, in fact, cannot fly at all, for the excellent reason that it does not need to, not in these islands at least. The abundant food available in the waters around the islands, and the absence of land predators, means the bird's wings adapted to swimming rather than flight and developed muscles appropriate for the purpose. Natural selection, in refutation to millennia of clerical dogma, which instructed that animal life was immutable, was the explanation for the emergence of new species that adapt and diverge from the original population from which they arose.

Other travels were perhaps not as dramatic or as instructive as this visit to the gold standard of the natural world, but there is only one of those and one such archipelago. But I would certainly rate highly and recommend the trip we undertook to Brazil's Bahia region and the city of Salvador. This melting pot of Afro-Brazilian culture and rhythms, and especially its coriander- and coconut-infused spicy food, was a welcome contrast to the European bias and blandness of Argentine cuisine. Our exploration of the far-flung northern beaches of the Natal region of Brazil was equally exciting and revealing, especially riding in a buggy across and over its epic sand dunes.

We also found a world of contrasts within the vast and varied sweep of Argentina itself, from visiting the Jesuit estancias of Córdoba in the Argentina heartland to watching down in the far south, very dramatically and from the comfort of our hotel bedroom, the blue ice of the epic Perito Moreno glacier crack and fall into the lake at El Calafate. In the splendid company of my political comrade Mike Ellis and his wife Phillida we journeyed to the tri-border area of Paraguay, Brazil and

Argentina to watch the thunderous waterfalls, in fact nearly 300 of them, crash over the dense jungle land of Iguassu. It reminded us of the opening sequences of Jeremy Irons's and Robert de Niro's famous movie *The Mission*, which was not exactly a surprise since it had been set and filmed there! This visit came with a sting at its end. As our airplane was about to land back in Buenos Aires, it was announced that Ezeiza Airport was closed due to volcanic ash sweeping in from Chile. We were obliged to fly on to Córdoba, where some four or five hours later, and amidst scenes of quite spectacular disorganisation, we were eventually boarded onto buses and then had to travel 10 hours overnight to reach Buenos Aires at around 4 a.m. the following morning, some twenty hours after departing Iguassu. It was an extreme refutation of Robert Louis Stevenson's adage that 'to travel hopefully is a better thing than to arrive'.

We wasted many pesos searching for the perfect estancia, or authentic Argentine ranch, and had almost given up the search after enduring expensive evenings in mosquito-ridden and crumbling manor houses, which gave new meaning to the term tourist trap. Then in the last year of our stay, we hit a somewhat pricey jackpot. We were introduced to Massimo Ianni, 49-year-old Italian-French-Argentine who cut his teeth developing hotels with Giorgio Armani. We heard a lot of hype about his acquisition, La Fortuna, which was situated nearly 200 kilometres south-west of Buenos Aires in the pampas. Just for once, and in the company of my hyper-critical brother, we were not disappointed when we gazed at a small French palace that nestled at the end of the tree-lined driveway and signalled our arrival at perhaps the most perfect estancia in the pampas. This jewel of French architecture, plonked in 1860 seemingly in the middle of nowhere and surrounded by grazing llamas and a pristine gaucho village, was, in every sense, a delight to the senses. We watched the amazing gait of Peruvian show horses, and rode the sturdy Argentine breed, and enjoyed über-gourmet cuisine served from a designer kitchen. While the only authentically Argentine artefact inside the magnificent estancia was the art – the furniture was French and Italian – we marvelled at this corner of excellence set in the dusty back area of the province of Buenos Aires.

But I actually got to see more of Argentina by following and hosting various South African sports teams around the country than via traditional tourism. And since the 'business plan' placed a heavy emphasis on 'sports diplomacy', as the resident diplomat I was to follow the flag and the teams.

CHAPTER 35

# SPORTS DIPLOMACY

Football is the civil religion of Argentina. La Bombonera (literally, 'chocolate box', a nod to its shape), home stadium of the famed local Boca Juniors soccer team, and situated in the down-at-heel and garishly coloured La Boca southern neighbourhood of Buenos Aires, is its most important shrine. The often deadly rivalry embedded in Argentine football is played out among many top tier teams, but two of them, Boca and River Plate, enjoy the support of a whopping 70 per cent of all fans. 'If you want to understand Argentina and its passions and underlying psyche, you had best attend a football match,' a local friend had suggested.

## LA BOMBONERA AND THE CULT OF MARADONA

So advised, one humid Sunday evening early in 2012 found me and a visiting friend, Cecil Bass (our close friendship had been forged on the backbenches of the Johannesburg City Council some 25 years ago and he now lived in Australia), heading toward the Bombonera in the expert company of Jorge. I was pretty agnostic on supporting local teams but River, whose stadium was far closer to our residence, had enjoyed a reversal of fortune. In fact, one Sunday the previous June, an explosion of angry sounds had wafted across from its stadium to our residence. I discovered earlier that evening River's dismal draw in the match had ensured its relegation from the first division premier league for the first time in 110 years. Their fervent supporters were less than pleased and had rioted, resulting in injuries to more than 70 of them. Violence was the constant companion of Argentine football and its frenzied fans, and I guess we had a few nervous frissons as we now approached the Bombonera. And just to add to my inner tension that evening, I recalled a recent story in the press about how a gang of 30 football hooligans, aligned to a faction of another team, had invaded a Buenos Aires hospital, trashed the waiting room, and then moved into the emergency room and stabbed a rival gang member who was being treated for injuries he had received earlier the same evening. Football Argentine-style was, clearly, not for the faint of heart.

Both reinforcing and relieving any anxiety that Cecil and I felt was the massive police presence on both the perimeter and inside the stadium. We had to pass through several security checks before being admitted to the fabled home ground of Diego Maradona, arguably the best and most controversial player of his time (and, some experts suggest, of all time), whose legendary on-field skills and lifestyle excesses off it had helped globalise the Boca brand.

I barely noticed the general dilapidation of the packed-to-capacity 50 000-seater stadium: rickety seats, mean Soviet-style concrete tiers and overflowing toilets. Cecil, something of a football aficionado, was surprised by its poor condition. After nearly three years' residence, little about the infrastructural deficits of my host country now surprised me. What was striking, however, was the 5-metre glass wall that surrounded the stadium, clearly intended to keep the spectators off the pitch, and the massive fences erected behind the goals: visible barriers against the passionate furies that football unleashed among its followers.

But even I, by then something of a veteran attendee at presidential and political rallies and so many other public displays of Argentine passionate exuberance, was staggered by the ferocity and fervour of the fans that night. I had once read about American hillbillies handling wild rattlesnakes in a frenzy of religious exaltation. This came to mind as I watched, agog, as Boca supporters whipped themselves into a froth of ecstasy around us in the stands: they hollered and sang, took off their shirts and waved them about and then cheered as some younger ones scaled the stadium roof, with a splendid disregard for safety, to place their homemade banners alongside the giant blue and yellow Boca signs that adorned the Bombonera. And all this cacophony of sound and visual feast was before the match even started!

Lusty anthems, somewhat ageing cheerleaders and an explosion of fireworks heralded the commencement of the on-field combat, which pitted mighty Boca against the less-fancied team of Independiente, from across town. The fast-moving play was, to my inexpert eyes, a sight to behold. In something under 90 minutes, a staggering nine goals were scored, which must rank close to a record for a first division football match anywhere in the world. Cecil, who had witnessed an FA Cup Final at Wembley and a few 2010 World Cup matches in South Africa, observed, 'It's not a night I will easily forget.' And he was not just referring to the high score in a match, which contra form and expectation, the visiting side won. Off the field, the red-shirted Independiente supporters were corralled, for safety purposes presumably, into the worst seats on the ground, high above the goals, and separated from their seething and chanting rivals seated in the stands alongside us. This did not prevent a few of the visiting supporters scaling the massive fence to seek a confrontation with their enemies, which some robust policing managed to interdict. Policemen in full riot-squad gear were much in evidence around the touchlines as well. When Independiente was awarded its first corner, I turned to Jorge, whose expertise behind the wheel extended to all matters football as well, and asked him why two riot policemen appeared to be interfering with the player taking the corner. He laughed and explained that far from interfering, the policemen, who were standing right behind the kicker with raised riot shields, were in fact protecting him, the glass wall notwithstanding, from the missiles and projectiles, which the Boca fans were raining down on him. How the player managed to take the corner in such circumstances, which he accomplished with some aplomb, was a miracle to behold.

After the match, the entire stadium was placed in lockdown mode, with only the ecstatic visiting fans allowed to leave it. The rest of us were released some twenty minutes later. We emerged unscathed but far better versed in the anthropology of the most significant football tribe in Argentina, and probably in all of Latin America.

And what of the leader and moving spirit of the Boca tribe, Maradona? Maradona, who grew up dirt poor in a shanty town (or *villa miseria*) outside Buenos Aires, was outsized in everything he did both on and off the football pitch, except in his compact physical frame, although by the time of my arrival in Argentina, his one-time svelteness had given way to obesity. Maradona's life matched peerless football accomplishment and skill in sport as a ladder from poverty to global fame with reckless excesses, ranging from cocaine to alcohol abuse, in almost equal measure. He was held in god-like adoration by many Argentines, and not just those who dreamt of emulating his leap from obscure origins to international stardom. Shortly before the 2010 World Cup, we were at a movie house in upmarket Recoleta and Maradona appeared on screen starring in, of all things, a commercial punting an insurance company. The entire audience broke into sustained applause and whistles of approval.

His place as a secular deity (in fact it went beyond this since in certain rural areas a religious cult had formed around his image) was cemented (perhaps canonised) during the 1986 World Cup with the two goals he scored against mortal enemy England (just four years after the defeat of Argentina in the ill-starred Falklands War) in the quarter-finals. The first of them was notorious, since his clear handball went unnoticed and was allowed, leading him to declare it 'the hand of God'. But it was the second goal that revealed him to be the footballer of the century, the very title that FIFA went on to co-award him alongside the legendary Brazilian player, Pele. He dribbled past no fewer than five English players in a 60-metre run to score one of the most amazing goals of all time.

Fame did not improve or humble him: he was eventually bundled out of international football for failing drug tests, and his battles with addiction (on which he appeared mostly to be on the losing side) were epic. But his huge popularity and totemic status and – no small matter in such a politicised society – unflinching support for the Peronists and all causes of the populist left ensured his selection as Argentina's national coach for the 2010 FIFA World Cup in South Africa. His prodigious gifts as a player did not transfer to the technical rigours of team management, selection and training. Notwithstanding the presence of such international stars as Lionel Messi and Carlos Tevéz, the team had a calamitous campaign in South Africa and were pushed out of the tournament by the methodical Germans 4–1 in the quarter-finals in Cape Town. In probably another country and with any other coach, the return home of the vanquished hopes of the nation would have been met with either indifference or hostility. But this was Argentina and this was Maradona. An estimated 20 000 cheering supporters went to the Ezeiza Airport to greet him in a manner befitting a hero, although a journalist waspishly noted, 'They were there to thank him for his disastrous performance.' However, for the rising chorus of media disapproval of his training tactics (which apparently did not go much beyond hugging and kissing his players and performing cartwheels on the sidelines of the stadiums when they scored), he seethed with contempt. 'Go and suck it, and keep on sucking it,' he advised a hostile questioner. Although he was later relieved of his duties as national coach, I could not help but wonder whether there was something in the Maradona story – the life, the legend, the talent and the squandering of such prodigious ability and giving the finger to the critics that did not at many levels mirror the country for whom he remained, even in the embers of defeat, an iconic symbol. I was not alone in my wonderment, either.

A few weeks after the team's homecoming, my friend John Carlin, of *Invictus* fame, co-authored a piece in the influential Spanish newspaper, *El Pais,* for whom he was a columnist. It was entitled 'Maradona as a Metaphor for Argentina'. Soon enough it was published in the staunchly anti-government Argentine broadsheet *La Nacíon*, and it caused no end of local controversy.[100] Among the other nuggets, broadly translated, from this pyrogenic piece were the following:

> Maradona embodies the [Argentine] problem: idolatry to redeeming leaders, the worship of ticks and, its twin brother, the disdain for work ethics; narcissism, faith in magic solutions, the drive to exonerate oneself by blaming others and pigheadedness … The starting pointing is the denial of reality. That is the ground on which Maradona operates and that is also the ground on which his legion of supporters go on worshiping him.
>
> The failure of Maradona in the World Cup mirrors the failure of Argentina as a country … There is a lack of discipline and humility in

> planning and a waste of available resources [a reference to Maradona's odd team selection process, which left some talented players on the bench] … Only in the Maradonean system illusion shines. When out of fantasy, coaches or presidents or systems with populist, authoritarian and anti-democratic features are chosen, which are not well grounded in reality, the inevitable outcome is failure.

Appropriately perhaps, shortly after Maradona's return from South Africa, Nestor Kirchner telephoned him to 'congratulate' him on the World Cup campaign.

## THE (SOFT) POWER OF SPORT

In an aviary of wise owls I met during my sojourn at Harvard in 2007, few were wiser than the John F. Kennedy School of Government professor, Joseph Nye. He coined the influential concept of 'soft power', which became a massively utilised tool of international statecraft. As I understood it, 'making power soft' at root is the use of an international actor's values, cultures and institutions as a primary currency to attract or repel other players on the international stage. The 'hard power' stuff refers to military and trade relationships, but it was sport as an exemplar of soft power that was to fuel many of my public projects in Argentina.

South Africa's hosting of the 2010 FIFA World Cup provided our embassy with no end of opportunities to showcase our country to the world, and it had a special resonance in soccer-mad Argentina and surrounding countries. In fact, with the other two neighbouring countries of Uruguay and Paraguay also booking a place in the finals in South Africa, I was one of the few South African ambassadors who scored, as it were, the perfect trifecta: all three of my countries of accreditation were in the mix back in South Africa, and our embassy was spoilt for choice in arranging events around the football festival to leverage our tourism and public diplomacy offers.

For once the budget for these events was fairly, by the parsimonious standards of the department at least, generous, and soon after my arrival, we hosted various visiting South African soccer stars, such as Lucas

Radebe (a real gentleman, who oozed professional charm in his retirement just as he dazzled on field when he was on the pitch) and 'Doctor' Khumalo (who was pleasant but indolent and much more fixated on enjoying his champagne than meeting the local teams and schools we had arranged for his visit). For the opening match of the tournament between South Africa and Mexico on 11 June, we hired the massive ballroom of the downtown Panamericano Hotel and hosted, in conjunction with my good friend the Mexican ambassador, Francisco del Rio, some 500 locals and a contingent of South African and Mexican supporters, replete in soccer shirts and blowing vuvuzelas and Mexican trumpets, respectively, backed by a thumping Mariachi ensemble. The cacophony in the ballroom was complemented by the exquisitely diplomatic match that we watched on giant screens, as the two teams drew 1–1.

The real result of the month-long festival of football, which showed the rainbow nation at its best and most unified, was to be seen in the huge increase of Argentine visitors to South Africa, including the infamous football hooligans (see Chapter 16). During the event, some 20 000 Argentines made their way to the Republic, a massive 300 per cent increase, in just 30 days, from the total figure of arrivals in 2009. With energetic marketing off the back of the event, we managed to maintain this surge, in somewhat reduced but still significant form, in the years that followed. Back home in my previous capacity as opposition leader, I had been deeply sceptical about the profitability or longevity of hosting these global sports events. Aside from the 'feel good' factor and upgrading of infrastructure, I was doubtful about the balance sheet for the country. After all, FIFA would walk away from the tournament with about 3 billion dollars in profit, and South Africa would spend about 5 billion dollars to meet its requirements. The soon-to-be mothballed football stadia would be a baleful reminder of the costs to the country's hard-pressed bottom line. But my ambassadorial stint and the huge interest and hard numbers that the tournament generated made me rethink my initial cynicism. If not now a complete convert to the cause and cost of global sporting events, I was a diplomatic beneficiary of this golden moment for South Africa's projection in the world.

## THE RUGBY AFFAIR

For someone who never made it out of the Kearsney College 7th XV (okay, there was even an 8th team!), it was quite extraordinary how central rugby became to my diplomatic mission in Argentina, and how successful we were in using the game, and the linkages it had forged between the two countries, to advance our work.[101]

Linking South Africa and Argentina was, among other things, the British influence. It was precisely the reach of empire that had led to the standardisation of sport across the world, including cricket, rugby and football. Even the modern Olympics originated in the 'home country'. For all the reflected fame that football stars such as Maradona and Messi had shone on their home country, it was the game of rugby that remained for me a matter of unresolved contemplation in Argentina: why was it that in all the countries of North, Central and South America, only Argentina played internationally competitive rugby of world standard?

The first and obvious answer, sunny skies aside, was the English influence. Once dubbed the 'forgotten colony', it was easy enough with all the Anglo-Argentine animosity kicked up by the Falkands to forget just how pervasive and permanent the influence of elite private schools – veritable little Etons – has been here in the land of the gaucho and Evita. In fact, I would speak at many events at schools that rejoiced in names such as St Andrew's, Cardinal Newman and St George's, and could happily and fluently do so since, here at least, English was the language of instruction. These institutions provided the foundations for the 40 000 rugby players in the country. I would also host some of the Argentine and South African school teams, at least 100 of whom crossed the South Atlantic in both directions every year to play rugby against each other.

But as I delved further into the background of our bilateral rugby relationship I came across another, more politically incorrect, factor that had drawn our countries rugby ties ever closer. During the 1960s and 1970s, the sports isolation forced on South Africa by apartheid had, forgive the pun, a knock-on effect down here in the southern cone of South America. South Africa's shrewd and far-sighted rugby supremo, Dr Danie Craven, had realised, I gathered, that the development and modernisation of rugby in Argentina was a way out of the increasingly fraught and frozen ties with our usual rugby partners in Australasia and the United Kingdom. And so he dispatched Natal coach Izak van Heerden to help train the Argentines. Even the team moniker, 'Los Pumas', was a South African contribution; some Springbok fans confused the jaguar badge worn by the Argentines with the puma, but the latter name was adopted.

I was to be the happy inheritor of this involvement many years later. I mentioned early on in this narrative how the premier of *Invictus* was a launch pad of a slew of public events I would host involving rugby in Argentina. Joost van der Westhuizen starred in them all. He was a big hit in the Argentine, whose rugby fraternity well remembered his splendid pass to Joel Stransky, which led to our heart-stopping victory in extra time in the 1995 World Cup against New Zealand. Through my childhood friendship with the South African Rugby Legends president, Gavin Varejes, we arranged his attendance as guest speaker at the *Invictus* event. His arrival in Argentina in January 2010 was also a good excuse to organise a dinner for him with the Puma legend, Hugo Porta. I had long admired this rugby giant of small frame and outsized ability. But I had also noted, back in the 1990s, how effective a diplomat he had been when President Carlos Menem shrewdly (in view of his acclaim among the legions of rugby-loving South Africans) appointed him as ambassador to South Africa. At dinner that night in our residence, Hugo revealed himself to be the most rare of human beings: arguably the greatest fly half of his generation (no one of my generation could forget his demolition job of the Springboks in Bloemfontein in 1982, when he scored every winning point himself) and yet a person of incredible modesty and gentility. We were to become good friends. And I also discovered that night that he was exceptionally quick-witted. Sizing up the towering Joost in our dining room, he observed, 'In my time, scrum halves were about half your size, but then they were only about half as good as you!'

Joost returned to Argentina later in the year, at the invitation of Standard Bank and the embassy to lead the South African Rugby Legends against a team of former Pumas. But within weeks of that event he was stricken with a deadly form of motor neuron illness (or amyotrophic lateral sclerosis), known as Lou Gehrig's disease. This devastating and debilitating disorder apparently was known to afflict high-performance sportsmen, and in Joost's case being struck with it before he had reached the age of 40 seemed especially cruel. By the time he returned to Argentina for a third visit, this time in August 2012, when we invited him to Mendoza to join our celebration of the Springbok test against the Pumas and to host a fund-raiser for his medical foundation, we had become good friends. But he spoke in a slurred voice and could not cut his own food or hold a glass unless he was using both hands. He very matter of factly told me that he had 'around two years to live'. Yet he faced his mortality with the same courageous determination as he had once confronted the All Blacks. I was delighted that the Standard Bank-arranged fund-raiser for his J9 Foundation, which reaches out to motor neuron sufferers, netted a cool 400 000 rand. Joost made a speech of special grace, despite his impediment, and the auctioneer of the memorabilia donated by Gavin Varejes was the Puma great, Augustin Pichot, who told the audience how his own stellar career as an acclaimed international scrum half had been largely inspired by the now stricken South African.

Fittingly perhaps, the last public events that I arranged at the end of my ambassadorship in spring 2012 involved the accession of Argentina to the reconfigured tri-nations rugby tournament, christened 'The Rugby Championship', which became the most important annual southern hemisphere rugby event.

Like a military or political campaign, our embassy planning of a series of events involving the first Puma–Springbok test in Mendoza commenced many months before the kick-off in late August. As always, Standard Bank was front and centre of our collaboration, and we also inspanned the sponsorship of other South African rugby partners, including BMW and South African Airways. We hosted everything from trade seminars to team breakfasts to official receptions in the leafy city of Mendoza, and every event proceeded with clockwork efficiency and according to a meticulously prepared script. The only contingency we could not anticipate was the performance of the Springbok team. I much enjoyed meeting the coach, Heyneke Meyer, and the captain, Jean de Villiers, and other stars from home. But the match itself at the packed Malvinas Stadium was, for South Africa, a disappointing draw, as the fired-up Pumas put in their best performance against South Africa in a generation.

## BEST IN THE WORLD

The frequent presence of so many South African sports teams in Argentina, and these included both senior national hockey teams, in addition to the rugby and football visitors, meant that a lot of my time was spent out of office cheering them on, and hosting receptions in their honour, often in outlying areas, far away from the capital. This not only allowed me to see more of the vast and under-populated Argentine hinterland but also to interact with the provincial governors, who certainly were more welcoming of diplomats than the largely indifferent central government.

I could not help but notice during one such early away match of the men's hockey side in far-flung Salta, which sits on the Argentine border with Bolivia and where lashing rain did not improve the performance of the visiting Proteas, the complexion of our team. I rather incautiously observed to the manager of the South African hockey team seated next to me, 'Our team looks a little like that old Herstigte Nasionale Party poster, "*bly blank my volk*" [stay white, my people]! Aren't you subject to all manner of pressure back home to "transform" the team?' I enquired further, given the lily-white nature of the team then going down to a big defeat in front of us. 'Except when it comes to deciding berths for the Olympics, we are left quite alone,' he responded, and went on to explain that 'there is no money in hockey, and every player on the field tonight had to pay or fund-raise for his own air ticket'. Apparently the ANC chairperson of the parliamentary sports committee could not get his head around the absence of money in hockey, and the entirely voluntary commitment of the management to the sport, and left them alone.

But while South Africa could compete, often on the losing side against Argentina in hockey and football and more on the winning side, Mendoza excepted, in rugby, we were never able to play officially against the Argentines in polo. They were simply too powerful and too skilled for any South African side to compete against, and that went for the rest of the world as well. The Argentines are overpoweringly good at this sport, another globalised collaboration that originated in Persia, was modernised in India by the British Army and then, via English emigration, reached the rest of today's polo-playing countries, including

Argentina. It had been discontinued as an Olympic sport in the 1930s, since Argentina scooped most of the gold medals since the inception of the modern games. Today, Argentina, where the powerful combination of skilled gaucho riders, ample outdoor fields and honed polo-pony breeding techniques is regarded as the 'Mecca of Polo', has produced the greatest number of ten-handicap (the highest level of accomplishment) players in the world.

I glimpsed this prowess when with the expert assistance of my friend Johan Roets (himself a keen player) I attended the premier polo event in the country, the Argentine Open, played just across the road from our residence at the national polo grounds. Theoretically open to the top polo teams in the world, it is contested in the finals only by Argentine teams!

As we watched the incredibly skilled horsemen and equines manoeuvre for advantage at great speed and with daring skill, Johan explained that each of the eight players (four per team) had about ten horses, that they would interchange frequently in the course of the two-hour match. 'Each horse at this level is worth about 100 000 dollars; so that is eight guys, ten horses each, a total of around 8 million dollars worth of horseflesh!' he usefully tutored me in this most obviously elite and expensive of sports.

But sport was simply a powerful add-on to my diplomatic tasks, the most essential of which was to provide an answer to an essential question: 'Where in the world is South Africa and what informs its foreign policy?'

CHAPTER 36

# CRACKING THE CODE

My diplomatic friend, US Ambassador Vilma Martínez, amused her guests one evening around her dinner table at her palatial Buenos Aires residence by telling us that in state department-speak 'OBE' meant 'overtaken by events'.

After three years of trying to decode South Africa's foreign imperatives and make sense of its often erratic implementation, I thought it a fair description of our own policy-making process. I also thought that Abba Eban's famous aphorism about the Palestinians – 'they never miss an opportunity to miss an opportunity' – applied to South Africa's external projection.

Once again, on paper, our objectives were clear enough, if not hugely ambitious and very generalised. When I read my department's 2010–13 Strategic Plan, which covered the period of my ambassadorship, I also discovered that it covered the world without admitting, on paper at least, the need to make tough choices or fix priorities. Were we to place a premium on our African hinterland? What about our ties with the developed economies of North America and Europe, our traditional and current major economic partners? Did the rise of China afford it primacy in our international partnerships? And what of 'the South' (a polite update of the term 'third world')? Our accession into the grouping of the BRICS (Brazil, Russia, India, China and South Africa) presumably meant that this quartet was where our heart and national interest lay.

In fact, the strategic plan simply listed the lot of them without distinction and suggested a box-ticking 'all of the above' approach. When the plan was redefined into a much-anticipated White Paper, Dr Mzukisi Qobo, senior lecturer in political science at the University of Pretoria, described the exercise and its outcome as 'old wine in new bottles … it includes almost everything under the sun'.[102]

Policy analyst, Greg Mills, was crisper and harsher. He described our foreign policy as a 'bit of this and a bit of that'.[103] In the same article, he also dismissed our diplomatic techniques as 'largely analogue for the digital world, and leadership anodyne, rather than dynamic'. This rather painfully chimed with my lived experience as an ambassador.

In fact, in the run-up to the publication of the department's White Paper, which Minister Maite Nkoana-Mashabane had been trumpeting since her first budget speech in March 2010, I rather naively accepted at face value her invitation to all embassies to prepare a response from our mission to the draft document.

My colleagues and I laboured away against a tight deadline, and produced, I thought, a crisp seven-page critique and sent it back to head office. We addressed a range of problems and inconsistencies of foreign policy in practice, which the White Paper, far from resolving, did not even admit existed! Our response, with detailed referencing, pointed out that the 1993 claim of Nelson Mandela, on the eve of his presidency, that 'human rights will be the light which guides our foreign policy' had been largely observed in the breach. We cited numerous examples of our rights delinquencies, particularly during our first term, and ill-starred role in the United Nations Security Council, which ended in 2008, and which had seen South Africa turn a blind eye to violations of fundamental rights – from Belarus to Zimbabwe. Our posturing there appeared to be animated by an anti-Western, struggle-solidarity that I termed (to my colleagues but omitted from the response) 'gesture politics'. Needless to note, there was no acknowledgement from head office to our carefully crafted views and not a word of them appeared in the revised document.

One of my ambassadorial colleagues, at another of our foreign outposts, expressed surprise that our embassy had even engaged in the exercise. 'It's just a form of occupational therapy, to which no one back home will pay the slightest attention,' he snorted dismissively at what I had assumed to be an effort of collegial participation.

I did not, however, confine my concerns about our various lapses and inconsistencies on the international stage to a joint embassy response to a White Paper. On two occasions, I wrote directly to the minister and the director general to express serious and personal concern at acts and omissions that I thought seriously diminished our moral capital in the world, as I will recount shortly.

In certain areas, for example, condemning the Burmese junta in 2009 for detaining opposition leader Aung San Suu Kyi (who was subsequently released and participated in its restored parliament) and taking a tougher line against Zimbabwean President Robert Mugabe (to little discernible effect as he enters his 33rd uninterrupted year in power in 2013), South Africa under President Zuma appeared to have noticed and even acted on some of the criticisms.

## THE WRONG SIDE OF HUMAN RIGHTS

But, as we used to say during my time in legal practice, 'hard cases make bad law'. Nothing perhaps exposed the glaring contradictions and the somersaults of our foreign policy than the Arab Spring, which started to burn in December 2010 and soon spread across much of North Africa and the Middle East. Long-repressed citizens under the heel of various fiefdoms and tyrannies began to demand and demonstrate for basic democratic and economic rights, just as their compatriots in South Africa had done some two or even three decades before.

Libya and Syria tested the limits of South Africa's 'new approach'. To my intense and pleasant surprise, one night in early March 2011, I was watching the CNN live feed from the United Nations Security Council debate on the situation in Libya and witnessed South Africa cast a historic vote in favour of Resolution 1973 (uncharacteristically parting company with Russia and China on the Council, which abstained). The resolution called for 'all necessary measures to be taken to protect Libyan civilians under threat [from dictator Muammar Qaddafi] including the imposition of a so-called no-fly zone'.[104] 'At last,' I shouted out to a somewhat startled Michal, then in another room in the vast residence, 'we are on the right side!'

Subsequent developments on this front severely tempered my initial enthusiasm. South Africa rapidly backtracked on this vote, often performing such contortions of logic or illogicality that our reversals of position undermined our initial posture. Zuma soon enough denounced the air strikes that NATO commenced against the Qaddafi forces, which was entirely on all fours with the no-fly provision (this essentially meant that Libyan ground and air forces could not operate in the area of exclusion). South Africa had entered the big league of 'having your cake and eating it'. Days after the historic United Nations vote, Zuma denounced the 'killing of civilians' and 'the foreign occupation of Libya' to a local crowd at home. This led *The Economist* to question whether Zuma was naive enough to believe that the 'all necessary measures' he was in favour of to protect Libyan civilians could be 'done without recourse to force'. Appropriately, this critique on our foreign policy was headlined 'All Over the Place' – a good shorthand description of our zigzagging pronouncements.[105]

Of course, behind these lurches was a severe dose of what George Orwell famously called 'double think' – holding two contrasting views in your head and firmly and simultaneously believing in both of them. Many political leaders suffer from this affliction, but South Africa's foreign entanglements seemed to represent this ailment in extreme form. There was, at least in the case of Libya, a backstory. South Africa's desire, stronger under Zuma than under his predecessor, to be 'on the right side of history' and to – at least on occasion – stand on the side of the oppressed, collided with the debts his movement owed to Qaddafi, both of the literal and political sorts. Qaddafi had been a big bankroller of the ANC (this nugget I was told first-hand by Nelson Mandela in 1994). In return, Mandela showered the Libyan dictator with state honours in 1997, and it was widely rumoured that the Libyan dictator had then funded Zuma's wilderness years after his ousting by Mbeki as deputy president in June 2005.[106] Doubtless, this constituted an explanation for our subsequent gyrations over Libya: a ridiculous call for a 'negotiated settlement' between the imperilled Qaddafi and the rebels, who were closing in on him, and then, when it was clear that the rebels were effectively in power in Libya, a refusal for quite some time to recognise – in contrast to most

Arab and Western states – Libya's National Transitional Council as the government of that country.

In late August 2011, my colleagues in the Africa Group of ambassadors in Buenos Aires (which included North African Arab representatives) expressed to me considerable surprise at South Africa's stance over Libya. I muttered some banal explanation, but was vehemently embarrassed by our posture. On return to office that day, I wrote a note to the director general, Jerry Matjila, who had replaced Ayanda Ntsaluba in the top departmental position the year before. In my missive of 31 August I told him:

> There is a perception that we have a policy of either support for Qaddafi or have placed such a premium on avoiding regime change that other foreign policy commitments (support for human rights and the democratic aspirations of subjugated people) are subordinated to this end. Whatever the merits or demerits of the NATO campaign against his regime, it seems to me infinitely less bad than the suffering he has inflicted on his own people and the apparent lack of support and legitimacy which his 42-year-old rule has enjoyed.

Matjila was usually a very slow and indifferent communicator (in contrast to his very able and efficient predecessor). But there was an almost immediate response from him to this note. He advised that one of the issues confronting all ambassadors 'from time to time' was the need to advance positions with which they personally disagreed. But this, of course, was not the point at all: no Argentine authority had asked me for a brief on our Libyan stance and since it was difficult to fathom any consistency in it, I would have been stymied to advance one of any coherence. He simply evaded my central contention.

The slippery slide down the road to inconsistency gathered pace as the Arab Spring lit the fires of resistance in Syria. I had been quite stunned when, during a heads of mission gathering in Pretoria in mid-2011, 'our man in Damascus', the South African ambassador to Syria, had taken to the floor to denounce the abuse of social media by Syrian pro-democracy activists for presenting, in his myopic view, the world with 'a distorted view of the position on the ground'. No doubt our emissary was a keen supporter of the besieged regime of President Bashar al-Assad, who at that stage was energetically slaughtering his civilian population as they rose up against his dictatorship and rule of fear. By late 2012, it was estimated that over 60 000 Syrians had been killed, largely by government forces.

While a direct military option was not on the table, it was clear that most democratic countries and the bulk of the Arab world and neighbouring Turkey were of one mind to apply coercive diplomacy, from sanctions to asset freezes and even arming the rebels in order to express revulsion against Assad's savagery. South Africa was not among them.

Instead, my department issued a mealy-mouthed statement of spectacularly misguided even-handedness, as though there was a moral equivalence between a brutal regime and its opponents. One paragraph from the department's 'expression of concern about the situation in Syria' was truly remarkable. The DIRCO statement noted that 'South Africa condemns all forms of violence, including the use of force against unarmed civilians, *as well as hostility against security forces* and sectarian violence' (my emphasis).[107]

Elsewhere in the Middle East, however, South Africa found one arena in which to proclaim its solidarity with the rights of oppressed and marginalised people: in every forum and statement, it energetically stood up for the beleaguered people of Palestine. But since their adversary was (for the ANC) the easy target of Israel, this selectivity simply drew attention to our silence on far worse rights violators in the same neighbourhood.

Unsurprisingly, when the United Nations Security Council later voted to condemn the human rights abuses by the government of Syria against its own civilians, South Africa abstained.

I thought this was appalling enough. But our straining every sinew to stay neutral, at best, between oppressor and oppressed or, more balefully, to provide succour to the Assads and Qaddafis of the world impelled me to take advantage of the invitation of Minister Nkoana-Mashabane, offered at the outset of my mission, to express to her 'any concerns'. So, on 12 October 2011, I sent her a letter indicating that our posture on Syria and our refusal to grant the 14th Dalai Lama a visa to visit South Africa 'undermined our commitment to advancing a principled foreign policy, based on human rights and democracy'.

My politely worded rebuke received no response, but it did (I noticed from the ensuing timeline) lead to the department enthusiastically endorsing my decision to return a year early from my posting and even trying to advance the date. As Britain's great jurist, Lord Denning, once noted: 'The arm of coincidence is long, but it does not stretch unto infinity.'

After my return home, the South African Institute of International Affairs invited me to address a meeting at the University of the Witwatersrand on my view of foreign policy. I concluded my remarks by noting: 'I think the point is plain: whatever else might be said for our foreign policy, and there are in fact some significant accomplishments, the promise of Nelson Mandela in 1993 that "human rights will be the light which guides our foreign policy" is not among them.' I had obviously become very diplomatic by then, since this was something of an understatement.

## 'HOME THOUGHTS FROM ABROAD'

The gifted and now deceased *New York Times* columnist (who had migrated to journalism from Richard Nixon's White House, where he served as a speech-writer), Bill Safire, once coined the acronym MEGO (mine eyes glaze over) to describe the point of exhaustion one reaches after reading about too many scandals, acts of corruption and serial instances of misgovernance.

Following events back home from Buenos Aires was similar to watching a movie with the soundtrack switched off. We could read everything, without the background noise and context in which it was happening. Every morning, my embassy colleagues and I would scour the Internet and departmental media digests to track the news and developments in the homeland. It was easy enough to succumb to MEGO – given the mushroom clouds of venality and stupendous breaches of constitutional faith detonated by those in the highest reaches of government.

In 1995, a year or so after the democratic parliament was first elected, a single departmental scandal – the misuse by the minister of health of European Union donor funds intended to combat the spread of HIV/AIDS, but splurged instead on a play, *Sarafina 2* – had mesmerised the legislature and the press. Those were, in retrospect, halcyon days. Seventeen years later, in 2012, I noted a report by my old parliamentary colleague, Willie Hofmeyr, an honest and decent public servant now heading the anti-corruption Special Investigation Unit. He told parliament that he believed that 20 per cent of the entire state procurement budget, equivalent to a staggering 30 billion rand, 'was being lost to corruption, mismanagement and incompetence'.[108]

Our small outpost of the public service – the embassy in Buenos Aires – was in my three years at its helm subject to no fewer than three audits (one from National Security, another from the departmental internal auditors and then the big cheese, in the form of the Auditor General's office, descended upon us to inspect our books). Tiny items of expenditure and minor discrepancies in such esoterica as the 'asset disposal register' were ruthlessly and appropriately – given we were spending taxpayer funds – examined. Fortunately, and after several anxious days for my staff and me, we were given 'clean audits' by each of them.

During one such audit being undertaken at our embassy, I happened to read, with feelings that ranged between wry amusement and contempt – that 'my' minister, Maite Nkoana-Mashabane, had incurred expenditure of 235 000 rand for a single flight from Norway to Bulgaria, when she refused to have her handbag searched at the Oslo airport and having missed her commercial flight had insisted on chartering a private jet. The departmental spokesman invoked a hitherto unknown 'principle' to justify this pillaging of the taxpayer's pocket. He claimed the Vienna Convention exempted diplomats from having their luggage searched – an entirely different matter from scanning her handbag, which is in fact what happened at the airport.[109] I also noted that the cost of this one junket was equivalent to my embassy's entire annual budget for public diplomacy projects to promote South Africa.

Still, I kept reminding myself that for all the bad news pouring across the wires, South Africa had enjoyed some golden moments during my three years in its service abroad. The opening bracket for my ambassadorship commenced on the eve of one of the finest pinnacles of our national achievement and international acclamation, the global football fest, known as the 2010 FIFA World Cup, our flawless hosting of which did so much to advance our image-building, tourism and trade in soccer-mad South America.

And even the worst events back home seemed to suggest that some buds of a new spring were sprouting in even the harshest of political winters. The judiciary, for example, was under assault by the government and some very dubious characters were promoted to the bench while some excellent candidates, for reasons of race or intellectual independence, and usually for both factors, were passed over. Yet, the highest courts of the land still continued, in some very significant judgments, to find against the government. It had all been preordained before in the old South Africa. In the 1930s, the National Party minister of justice, Oswald Pirow, noted with disgust: 'The problem with political appointments to the bench is that six months after their appointment, they presume they were appointed on merit!'

I had told Michal as we set off on our foreign adventure that there was unlikely to be – in the context of the uncontroversial diplomatic relationship with my countries of accreditation – any issues on which I would be obliged to advance a policy proposition that conflicted with my political principles. Fortunately, my optimism was justified by my real-time experience. However, I added as an afterthought to her: 'If the Protection of Information Bill [which had been introduced into parliament shortly before my departure and later renamed the Protection of State Information Bill] is enacted, I will have to reconsider my position here.'

This spectacular piece of legislative mischief in the opinion of many was designed to inhibit severely, if not totally interdict, the media and prevent the exposure of corruption by giving ministers of state sweeping powers to classify information as secret and imposing sentences of up to 25 years in prison on those convicted of violating its muzzling provisions.

Yet, amazingly, the bill remained a work in progress even at the time of my return in late 2012. Actually, its slow passage and some significant amendments offered by government to ameliorate some, although not all, of its more extreme provisions were not just due to executive lethargy. It was occasioned by an energetic pushback by a range of political and civil society actors, from across the racial and partisan divides. In fact, a decade or so before, I had strongly warned against the cronyism and constitutionally damaging acts embedded in ANC-sponsored concepts and practices such as the 'national democratic revolution', 'cadre deployment' and 'black economic empowerment'. I was dismissed at the time (often, I noted with an amused irony, by the most stringent critics of ANC excesses today) as, variously, 'anti-transformation', 'the voice of white privilege' and 'the fight-back king'. Now, an entire chorus, including some significant black intellectuals, media editors and trade unionists, was singing from the same hymn sheet, often in far more strident and less polite notes than any I had sounded from my perch as leader of the opposition.

## OPPOSITION STIRRINGS

On the subject of the opposition leadership, I noted with some approval the strides made by my successors in title to expand the reach and widen the diversity on the other side of South Africa's political aisle, particularly in the party that I had devoted most of my life to serving, building and leading, now incarnated as the Democratic Alliance.

I did, however, get slightly irritated when I noted anonymous 'top leadership sources in the Democratic Alliance' stating that the party's new repositioning was a conscious effort to move away from the 'conservative liberalism of former party leader Tony Leon with his fight b(l)ack campaign', to quote from one media story. Oh yeah, I thought, and who do they think created the platform on which the party now stands? I had done what had needed to be done, in a very difficult set of circumstances, to create a viable and larger opposition. The very beneficiaries of the 'fight-back' era had entered the portals of power, in the Western Cape at least, through the platform that I, and at the time very few other colleagues, had built.

But I was enough of a political realist to know and to recognise that creating critical distance from your own past was part of the terms of the political trade, however ahistoric and unfair it might be. However, irritation gave way to extreme anger when, in October 2011, Lindiwe Mazibuko, who had been a junior media officer in our parliamentary office when I had left South Africa three years before, challenged the incumbent parliamentary leader Athol Trollip for my old job. This had nothing to do with the merits of the candidates: Athol was a good friend, who had performed yeoman service to the party over many years; Lindiwe, whom at the time I knew very slightly, appeared to have all the right stuff – bar experience – to take the party forward. Anyway, I had no vote in the matter and, being far away in Buenos Aires, a declining interest in the outcome. Yet, I was dragged into the contest. First, press reports back home stated, 'it is understood that former DA leader Tony Leon backs Trollip'.[110] But this public outing, inaccurate as it was, was trivial compared to what was going on behind the scenes. I was sent correspondence that misstated my role in the leadership election in 2007, after I had stood down as party leader. One of the consequences of this placed my relationship with Helen Zille in cold storage for the remainder of my time away. However, shortly after our return to South Africa, we patched our quarrel and reset our relationship to its previous warm basis. As she would acknowledge, and I certainly knew to be true of my own time at the helm, every leader has their blind spots. But Helen's unerring gaze on the future and her stellar stewardship of the Western Cape offer real hope for South Africa.

## LESSONS FROM 'THE SOUTH'

My departure from home had also coincided with the rise of the egregious Julius Malema, whose role as an ANC kingmaker of Zuma and the political assassin of Mbeki had given him a prime position in the political spotlight, which, along with high-living courtesy of apparently corrupt and tax-avoiding tenders, he clearly relished. But while his economically illiterate ranting in favour of wholesale nationalisation of mining assets and 'economic liberation' scared foreign investors and delighted the mass of unemployed youths, he, too, had been, via the ANC disciplinary machine, removed from office before my return (as ANC Youth League president and he was later expelled from the party). But for all the hypocrisy and populism of Malema, he had given voice to a rising and justifiable discontent among many, some 50 per cent, of the youth, who had never enjoyed a formal job and had little prospect of obtaining one. For all the things that South Africa had got right in the past two decades, the failure of both our system and leaders to address meaningfully this burning issue remains the greatest danger for the country going forward.

South America offered no end of lessons on how to address this central failure: copying Argentina, through raiding the public purse to buy off discontented voters and fuel inflation and scare off investors was one path; but it was, at the time of my departure from Buenos Aires, leading to a cul-de-sac of evermore desperate short-term measures that crippled its future prospects. The other and smarter course was the tougher road hewed by neighbouring Chile and Brazil and further away Colombia, which was on the verge of overtaking Argentina as the second largest economy in South America by October 2012. This required the creation of a virtuous cycle of addressing unemployment through boosting and building the platform for sustainable growth and incentivising responsible behaviour in exchange for subsidies (for example, in Brazil, child support grants were only obtainable on proof of school attendance and vaccinations). And, of course, this necessitated subjugating short-term considerations for long-term pay-offs.

South Africa gave voice to both options and the government itself, in another display of 'double think', often seemed to embrace rather than resolve the contradiction. One winter morning in August 2012 in Buenos Aires, during my last stretch in ambassadorial office, freed from so many of the real and often petty urgencies that usually made up my working day, I decided to finally sit down and read a document that had been gathering dust in my in tray. It was the 'diagnostic overview' of the National Planning Commission, which had been released in November 2011. It was authored by a powerful committee, appointed by President Zuma, to chart a national course into 2030. It was chaired by Minister Trevor Manuel and included weighty luminaries such as Cyril Ramaphosa, Bobby Godsell and Vincent Maphai, to mention just four of its commissioners whom I knew and respected.

On its last page, a paragraph perfectly encapsulated the sort of winning and inclusive state that South Africa, with the right admixture of far-sighted politics, bold leadership and an engaged citizenry, could become. The commission stated:

> Successful countries have what is called a 'future orientation'. Their policy bias is to take decisions that lead to long-term benefits, as opposed to short-run solutions that could have negative effects later on. Such countries generally prefer investment over consumption, have high saving rates, sound fiscal policy, high levels of fixed investment, a high degree of policy certainty and clear rules of engagement for the private sector. A clear and predictable policy environment enables business to take a long-term perspective on growth and development. Countries with a future orientation generally spend more on education, and value it more in communities and households.[111]

I had barely said to myself 'amen to that' when a colleague rushed in with news that a police massacre of striking miners had occurred at a platinum mine I had never heard of near Rustenburg in the North West province. Marikana was a name that would soon echo across the world as a synonym for everything that was wrong and ugly in today's South Africa. For on that bleak winter's day, police shot and killed 34 miners engaged in an illegal wildcat strike. More than a dozen others, including policemen, also lost their lives at the hands of violent strikers. It was the single most lethal use of force by state security forces against civilians since the end of apartheid and even well before that. Between the fine prospectus for a better South Africa, offered by the National Planning Commission, and the dismal events at the Lonmin mine at Marikana, lay a gulf. Whether we cross it, in safety and in time, remains the essential challenge for the future.

## LEAVING

Zach de Beer, my kindly predecessor as leader of the Democratic Party, had once observed that I 'suffered from divine discontent' – a very accurate diagnosis of my great impatience and striving for, in John Lennon's phrase, 'the next big thing'. Throughout my life, I have always been more keenly aware of what no longer enthralls, rather than having a clear road map of the way ahead. And so it proved in my role as an ambassador.

I had ticked every box in my performance agreement, and created a few new ones outside the modest benchmarks set by my department. I had also been true to my school motto *carpe diem* (seize the day), but there were also real limits in being the South African ambassador to three South American countries. Professionally, once I had worked out what the job entailed, I began to find the daily routines of it somewhat humdrum. I loved working with the team in the embassy and derived enormous satisfaction from watching its members flourish with the enhanced responsibility I tried to give each of them. I was very proud of the metrics that we had achieved, in a challenging environment, in terms of trade flows, exports, tourism, and political, cultural and sporting contacts. In fact, I reckoned the successful accession of the Puma rugby team alongside the Springboks in the new four nations championship in Mendoza in late August 2012 would be a suitable bracket on which to close my ambassadorship.

But other factors also contributed to my decision to return a year or so before my contract expired: I found the bureaucracies on both sides of the South Atlantic, in South Africa and Argentina, unresponsive and slow-footed. Often the most trivial of matters would take hours of exasperated phone calls and innumerable e-mails to resolve. Then there was the question of language and lifestyle: living in Spanish was alienating, to put matters at their mildest, and our family was now triangulated across three continents – in South Africa (my ageing father and brother and the children) and in Israel (Michal's mother and sisters) while we were in South America. After a while, as well, the constant chaos of Buenos Aires, with its bad traffic, dilapidated infrastructure and negative energy levels (the constant feeling of economic and political crises has been well canvassed in these pages) began to pall.

There was also a great deal happening in South Africa, some of it profoundly troubling. But for all its challenges, it was my country and I had been privileged in helping to shape some of its democratic and constitutional contours. I had no desire to re-enter the party political fray (the wise ancient Greek philosopher Heraclitus was onto something when he opined, 'never step in the same river twice, everything flows, and nothing stands still'). But at the age of 55, I still felt I had some energy and thoughts to add my voice and views to the country's forward projection. I had also learnt a great deal about the dynamic markets in South America, which I felt I could put to good account on my return.

And three years away had seen distance lend enchantment to the homeland. I kept thinking of the unknown (to me at least) French philosopher who had wisely noted, 'If you want to appreciate your own country, go and live in another.'

During his tenure at the helm, I raised some of these issues with the director general, Ayanda Ntsaluba. He thought there was some merit in me being posted somewhere else in the world, where my ability to communicate clearly in English and my possible engagement with a larger group of South African corporates and citizens would be useful. Nothing came of this, and in any event my increasing alienation from elements of our foreign policy probably would have made another post an uncomfortable fit. His replacement, Jerry Matjila, was nothing if not doggedly loyal to his minister. And when I had a conversation with him along these lines, it was made perfectly clear that she, the minister, at least, would be perfectly happy for me to return from my mission at an earlier date. Since I had no desire to simply count down the clock to the expiration of my contract, I set the return date for 30 September 2012, exactly three years, to the day, since our arrival in Buenos Aires.

When news of our return seeped out, some four months before the date of departure, there was consternation and dismay from my staff, deep regret among our friends and effusive outpourings of kind remarks from some of my diplomatic colleagues, who were appropriately too diplomatic to comment about my often unconventional and sometimes impatient approach to statecraft.

Our last weeks in Buenos Aires were characterised by a whirl of packing up the residence and farewell functions. I stopped counting after about ten of them, only observing that it was the Latin equivalent of

*Monsoon Wedding*. Appropriately, on the night before our departure, Johan Roets, my firmest friend and greatest champion in Argentina, put on a 'Standard Bank special' to honour our leaving. Some 200 of our friends, colleagues, fellow diplomats and a significant swathe of people from the contacts I had established among the good and the great of Buenos Aires and beyond, pitched up at the high-end museum that overlooked the shimmering lights and gleaming structures of the waterfront area of Puerto Madero. It was in every sense a grand affair – overflowing with fine food, the best wines and the good vibrations from both the band and especially the guests, whose warmth and affection were, far and away, the most wonderful and positive feature of Argentina.

Hardest of all was to say goodbye to our staff and the many friends we had made during this short, but all-enveloping, phase of our lives. I then rose to deliver the very last speech I would ever have to give in Spanish ('Thank God for that,' muttered Michal). I said in an uncharacteristically quiet, even shaky, voice: 'You have come here this evening to honour Michal and me; but in fact it is you who have honoured us by letting us into your lives and making us so much part of them.' And my drop from my usual booming tone to a bare whisper was not just due to the issue of language.

# POSTSCRIPT

Pretoria, the seat of South Africa's government, in November is a riot of colour and noise – the jacaranda trees are in full flower and the traffic snarls across its busy streets. Dusk envelops the city in that wonderful and lingering Highveld twilight, which I had so missed during my time away. But I was headed to a much quieter part of the bustling capital, into the very heart of the state, whose service I had left only a few weeks before.

Mahlamba Ndlopfu is the residence of the president. It stands as a magnificent Cape Dutch sentinel on the highest point of the Bryntirion Estate, with sweeping views of the majestic Magaliesberg Mountains to the north. What history must have been witnessed within its grand salons, I thought as I drove into its precincts, remembering that I had first visited it as a callow backbench MP when F.W. de Klerk's consequential presidency was at its height in 1990. Back then it was named Libertas. The change of name was certainly justified and apt, Mahlamba Ndlopfu, is Shangaan for 'the new dawn'.

A single steward ushered me into a vast sitting room. Within minutes of my arrival, President Zuma entered alone. Of the stresses and strains of his office, and some of the extreme criticisms of his conduct in it, he showed no outward sign. He chuckled on greeting me and enveloped me in a hug.

'Welcome back,' he said.

APPENDIX

# MICHAL'S MUST-SEE LIST

It is impossible to include all the thousands of good restaurants, wonderful coffee shops, museums, galleries, neighbourhoods, buildings, parks and other interesting places on offer in Buenos Aires.

More information is obviously available in guidebooks and brochures, so this is just 'The List', our private and informal guide, which we happily shared with all our visitors in Argentina, from high-level officials to the Springbok rugby team and our personal friends. We hope that you enjoy using it, too.

If we were forced to choose a few 'not-to-be-missed' gems, we would recommend the following:

## SIGHTS

The **Recoleta Cemetery** – combine this iconic mausoleum with a walk through the elegant Recoleta streets, especially Avenida Alvear (pop in for tea or a drink at the famed Alvear Palace Hotel, and visit Patio Bullrich for high-end shopping).

**San Telmo** – a suburb worth visiting for its architecture, history and antique shops. At the markets, which are open only on Sundays (any time after 11 a.m.), you can browse antiques, bric-a-brac and crafts, and rub shoulders with locals and tourists alike.

**La Boca** – because it is where the city began, despite it being so touristified. Visit Caminito (the main street with tango dancers, shops and tourist-trap eateries) and Bombonera, the fabled home stadium of Boca Juniors football team and Diego Maradona's club. If you like soccer, visit the museum next door.

**Casa Rosada** – the President's Palace, Plaza de Mayo and Avenida de Mayo (you must visit Café Tortoni on adjacent Avenida de Mayo 825).

**Malba Museum** – the one we would choose if all you can fit in is one gallery visit. But if you can do two, do not miss the Museo de Bellas Artes: it is pink and central and houses some real gems.

**Palermo Soho** – old neighbourhood that has been gentrified and made into a centre of fashion designers, galleries, cafés and restaurants. The buzz starts only at around noon.

If you wish to understand Argentina, we also recommend visiting the Evita Museum (Lafinur 2988, Palermo. Tel: 011-4807-0306)[1] and taking a stroll in Palermo Park on a weekend morning. See the families spending the day sharing a picnic together and sunbathing, and the incredible variety of outdoor sports practised everywhere. The rose garden is beautiful, too.

## CULTURE

Buenos Aires oozes culture. And it is really not just about tango. Go to a tango show (touristic affair, always) if you must, but there are dozens of bookshops (although very few sell any English titles), music cafés, jazz joints, music halls and theatres. The famous Colon Opera House (newly re-opened after brilliant renovations) is a delight and ranks as one of the best in the world. Take a tour if you can, and try to attend a concert, ballet or opera. It is beautiful. See the programme in English at http://www.teatrocolon.org.ar/en/.

Every single night people flock to the dozens of venues to listen to music and eat with friends (usually mediocre food at most music places). Going out is BIG and sharing time with friends is equally BIG. They even have a Friendship Day on 20 July.

1 This is a landline number. If phoning from outside Argentina, dial +54 (Argentina), then 11 (drop the zero), and then the eight-digit landline number.

Some of our favourite places include the following:

**Clasica y Moderna**, Callao 892, is a lovely space with better food than similar places, and it features various shows, http://www.clasicaymoderna.com/.

**Notorius**, Callao 966, offers a variety of jazz and other musical shows with average food offerings, http://www.notorious.com.ar/.

**Torquato Tasso**, Defensa 1575, San Telmo, is charming, with mainly locals and jazz or tango music and average food, http://www.torquatotasso.com.ar/.

**Teatro San Martin**, Corrientes 1530, is a very important public theatre (run by the city government) showing excellent dance, music and theatre shows.

## TANGO

Taste the 'real deal' by going to a *milonga* (dance hall). It is not staged and is attended by people who just love tango and make it part of their lives.

Some examples: Confitería Ideal, Suipacha 383, 1st floor. Tel: 15-5006-4102.[2] Hrs: 11 p.m. to 4 a.m. every Monday and Friday. Or combine your trip on Sunday to San Telmo with a visit to Plaza Dorrego, Humberto 1449. Tel: 15-5061-3215. Hrs: 8 p.m. to 12 p.m. A very popular option is La Catedral, Sarmiento 4006 (close to the corner of Medrano Street), http://www.lacatedralclub.com. Tel: 15-5325-1630. It is open every night from 8 p.m. to 4 a.m., and offers both tango classes and just *milonga* (anyone can just dance).

Alternatively, you can get a free tango magazine called *B.A. Tango* (monthly), bilingual Spanish/English, which has listings and is available at tourist information centres, tango shoe stores and at *milongas*.

A good way to find out what is going on is check the online magazine (in English), *Argentina Independent*, http://www.argentinaindependent.com/events-listings/.

2 Telephone numbers starting with 15 are cellphone numbers, which are dialed this way in Argentina. If phoning from outside Argentina, dial +54 (Argentina), 911 replaces the 15, and then the eight-digit number as above.

## FOOD

It is amazing that *porteños* (residents of Buenos Aires) are not much heavier in weight as a result of the thousands of eateries (and *kioscos* or spaza shops) that abound. Add to that the fact that they eat their main meal after 9 p.m., often at 11 p.m. or later.

At 5 p.m. to 7 p.m. people here have *mirienda*, which is a snack eaten between lunch and dinner. For example, coffee and some toasted bread with dulce de leche (a very popular, sweet condensed-milk spread).

*Empanadas* are like samosas but often baked and not fried, with various fillings such as minced meat, chicken, spinach, cheese and onion.

A *parilla* (grill house) is the best option for meat dishes. Try chorizos, the local boerewors, which is usually eaten as a starter. Then try the tastiest *bife de chorizo* (which is a steak – confusing name) – always a safe choice just about anywhere. *Lomo* is fillet (but different to the variety we are used to in South Africa). If you want to try the short ribs, order *asado de tira*. More exotic choices include *vacío*, *entraña* or – one of our favourites – *ojo de bife* (ribeye, but not like the one we know from home).

*Provoleta*, which is grilled cheese, is a very typical starter at any *parilla*.

Try some of the artisanal ice cream (*helado*). The brands Freddo, Volta and Persico are very popular, as is the Patagonian brand, Jauja. The first two have lots of outlets everywhere.

*Alfajores*, which are shortbread biscuits joined by a layer of dulce de leche and then covered in chocolate or powdered sugar, are very sweet and popular. Locals claim Havana is the best. There are many coffee shops all over town and you can buy *alfajores* in boxes, or in singles, wrapped individually.

*Locro* is the local hearty stew that comes from the north and north-west parts, and is made up of legumes, meat and vegetables.

Argentines often drink *mate* at various hours of the day. *Mate* is an infused beverage that is also common in Brazil, Paraguay and Uruguay. It is made from the dried leaves of the *yerba mate* plant, which are placed in a small hollow gourd (also called *mate*). Hot water (but not boiling) is poured into the gourd, left for a minute to infuse, and then sipped through a metal straw called a *bombilla*. Some take it bitter (*amargo*) and some sweeten it. It is an acquired taste! But if offered to share a *mate* (as it is a social drink), give it a try.

## CAFÉS

At all hours of the day and night, people drink coffee here. Do not expect Italian espresso-based coffee at its best, but the vibe is great.

*Cappuccino* here is not what we know – in most places Argentinians serve it with cream, foamed milk and cinnamon, in a large cup. *Cortado* is similar to *macchiato* (strong, small coffee with very little foamed milk). For the closest to our *cappuccino* ask for *café con leche en jarrito* (small coffee mug as opposed to a small espresso cup, it is usually half coffee, half warm and slightly foamed milk).

*Lagrima* has a wonderful translation: it literally means 'teardrop' – for a lot of milk and a mere 'drop' of coffee.

*Café Doble* is when the order is a double serving of any coffee on the menu. For example, *café con leche doble* or *lagrima doble.*

*Submarino* is a tall glass of hot milk, served with a chocolate bar.

*Recommended places*:

For historic reasons – **Café Tortoni** (a few blocks from Casa Rosada).

For a taste of trendy Palermo Soho – **Mark's Deli**, El Salvador 4701, Palermo Soho, which opens at 8.30 a.m. (10.30 a.m. on Sunday).

**Boutique del Libro** (books and coffee shop in one), Thames 1762, Palermo Soho. Tel: 011-4833-6637. Hrs: 10 a.m. but Saturday from 11 a.m. and Sunday from 2 p.m.

*For a taste of Palermo Hollywood and of the French influence on this city*:

**Oui Oui**, Nicaragua 6068 (but it is often full). There is another branch at the corner of the next block that we did not like as much. Try **Pani** (brand new and charming), Nicaragua 6044.

RESTAURANTS

The earliest you can eat dinner is 8 p.m. The places start filling up at 9.30 p.m. El Mirasol will serve you anytime. A word of warning: inflation has made dining here an expensive experience so be prepared to pay higher prices than at home (for example, about 90 pesos for a steak with no side dishes, which in July 2012 was about R180).

*For the meat, and other typical Argentine food*:

Reliable, consistently good, some say it serves the best meat in town – **El Mirasol de La Recova**, Posadas 1032, Recoleta. Tel: 011-4326-7322/23.

Elegant and decent – **Fervor** (also serves very good fish), Posadas 1519 y Callao, Recoleta. Tel: 011-4804-4944. Next door to it there is a very traditional eatery serving *empanadas* and *locro* (local stew) in a very simple and old-fashioned place – **Sanjuanino**, Posadas 1515. Some claim they offer the best *empanadas* in Argentina.

Vibey, crowded, chaotic, huge portions (share the *bife de chorizo*, it is inhumanely huge) – **La Cabrera**, Cabrera 5099, Palermo Viejo. Tel: 011-4831-7002. It has another branch in the same street, in case it is overflowing (usually it is). Try to book early.

To sample the restaurant-strip at Puerto Madero – **Happening** is a safe bet with great meat and competent service at saner prices than famed neighbour-restaurant Las Cabañas De Las Lilas. Alicia Moreau de Justo 310, Puerto Madero. Tel: 011-4319-8712/5.

Another great old establishment, which is always reliable – **Don Julio**, Guatemala 4691 and Gurruchaga, Palermo Soho. Tel: 011-4831-9564/4832-6058.

Our neighbourhood eatery (literally a few blocks from our residence) and Tony's favourite is a very traditional *parilla*, which seems like it came right out of the 1950s, complete with male-only waiters who pride themselves on never writing your order down and getting it 100 per cent correct. The meat is also great at **Rio Alba**, corner of Oro and Cerviño 4499. Tel: 011-4773-5748/9508.

At the lovely San Telmo barrio, **La Brigada** has lots of ambience and very good local fare, bedecked with football memorabilia. Estados Unidos 465, San Telmo. Tel: 011-4361-5557/4685. We entertained F.W. and Elita de Klerk, Mac Maharaj and Pravin Gordhan here, and they all enjoyed the experience.

*Higher-end porteño gourmet cuisine*:

**Tomo 1**, Carlos Pellegrini 521, Mezzanine Floor, South Tower, Panamericano Hotel & Resort – some say this is the best one in Argentina. Tel: 011-4326-6698.

**Crizia**, Goritti 5143, Palermo. Wonderful atmosphere and great food. English website: http://www.crizia.com.ar/crizia/homeingles.html.

**Chila**, Alicia Moreau de Justo 1160. *Porteños* and foodies rate it very highly. It is creative, but very Argentine, in the hub of restaurantland, Puerto Madero, the city waterfront area, which is worth seeing at night. Tel: 011-4343-6067.

**Oviedo**, Beruti 2602, Recoleta. A classic. Wonderful food and service. Tel: 011-4821-3741.

**Leopoldo**, Cerviño 3732. A relative newcomer, chef-authored as they call it here. Not-too-large dishes, creative and delicious, great décor, ambience and good service. Tel: 011-4805-5576.

**Unik**, Soler 5132. A recently opened hip place, in Palermo Soho, which boasts retro 1960s style, gourmet, small selection of food options, all by the young talented chef. Tel: 011-4772-2230.

**Casa Cruz**, Uriarte 1658. For the design and ambience, it is very hip but the service is slow. The food is good and it is a great neighbourhood at night. It also has a very cool bar next door. Tel: 011-4822-1112.

*Other flavours/ethnic options:*

### PERUVIAN FOOD

Excellent and elegant but expensive – **Astrid & Gaston**, Lafinur 3222, Palermo. Tel: 011-4802-2991.

In a very indifferent location but the food is wonderful – **Sipan**, Paraguay 624, Retiro (Centro). Tel: 011-4315-0763. A new location for Sipan was recently opened in Palermo Soho, which is much more elegant – Uriarte 1648. Tel: 011-4833-9383.

For some fusion with a lot of Peruvian-Asian flavours an excellent choice is **Osaka**, Soler 5608, Palermo. Tel: 011-4775-6964, http://www.osaka.com.pe/.

### ARMENIAN FOOD (MIDDLE EASTERN/ARAB INFLUENCES)

Delicious food, reasonably priced – **Sarkis** (cash only!), Thames 1101, Palermo Viejo. Tel: 011-4772-4911. Opens at 8 p.m.

### SHOPPING

The specialities include leather, silver (which is often alpaca), ladies' handbags, wallets, belts and men's shoes. Leather jackets are best when they are made of sheepskin rather than cow leather. You can find those softer ones in most good leather shops.

**The Calle Florida** pedestrianised street has known better days, but it remains an easily accessible and vast warren of shops, with a few nice leather boutiques (and many terrible ones, too). The concentration of shops, though, makes it a good choice if you have limited time.

**Plata Nativa** – typical and original silver and other local jewellery. Galeria Del Sol (Galeria is a mini strip of shops; Plata Nativa is on the right-hand side) on Florida 860 (the number sign seems to be missing), close to Avenida Cordoba.

**Galerías Pacifico** – a high-end and large shopping mall on Florida Street, housed in a renowned and impressively renovated old building. It has just about everything, all major Argentine fashion designers, the lovely and very Argentine country-style shop Cardon and some decent leather emporia (handbags, coats, belts and shoes).

*Top-notch leather*:

**Casa Lopez** – for classic, top-quality leather goods. Large shop on Plaza San Martin very close to where Florida pedestrian starts (diagonally across from the Marriott Plaza Hotel). There are outlets in some of the city's malls, too.

**Peter Kent** – the verdict of many of our local friends is that this is the country's top handbag designer. He has a few shops – Arenales 1210 and Alvear 1820 in Recoleta, and in the Paseo Alcorta shopping centre close to the Malba Museum. http://www.peterkent.com.ar.

*More comfortably priced leather*:

**Prune** – a huge chain with shops in every shopping centre and a few on Calle Florida (the pedestrian).

Sometimes you can find nice bags at **XL** shops (http://www.xl.com.ar) or at **Lazaro** (http://lazarocuero.com.ar). Both chains are available in most shopping centres and streets, selling fashion shoes as well.

**Cardon** – a proud Argentine gaucho-inspired, sophisticated chain selling country-style clothes and accessories, including silver-buckled belts, chunky leather bags and riding boots. Shops are beautiful, prices are high, but it is quintessentially Argentine and the quality is very good. http://www.cardon.com.ar/.

Otherwise, the city has a few well-known malls, which are very similar. The most upmarket one, offering many international brands as well as the top local ones, is **Patio Bullrich** in Recoleta.

A very large, lively and popular mall is **Alto Palermo** on Santa Fe in Palermo.

A smaller mall, with a good selection of local designers, as well as some international brands (Zara, for instance) is **Paseo Alcorta**, also in Palermo, close to the parks and to Malba Museum.

For the trendiest, Soho-style, more creative and young fashion items, hit the streets of Palermo Soho, especially Malabia, Armenia, El Salvador streets and surrounds.

If you are after big bargains, well, Argentina is not the right place. Yet, there is an area full of outlets of all the chain stores, including Lacoste and Prune. It is located on Gurruchaga and Cordoba and the streets around it (especially around Aguero). For leather finds, head to the Murillo area (any taxi driver will know about it) in Villa Crespo.

## HIGHLIGHTS OF ARGENTINA

Argentina is a huge country (the eighth-largest in the world) with a variety of landscapes and climates. It offers varied and memorable tourist experiences, which are impossible to cover in a few paragraphs. If you have to choose the absolute best, we would suggest the list below. One catch is that because of the vast distances, flights are the easiest and fastest, but the connections are usually only to and from Buenos Aires, making 'hopping' from one place to the next challenging. There are very good English-speaking travel agents who can help check what is possible within the time (and budget) limit at your disposal.

**Iguassu Falls** (*Las Cataratas*) is a two-hour flight (or a fourteen-hour bus trip) from Buenos Aires, in the province of Misiones, on the border with Brazil and Paraguay. The falls make our own Victoria Falls look small scale. A great system of walkways enables spectacular views from myriad vantage points, with some lovely forest walks and great birdlife, funny coatis (similar to raccoons) and many butterflies. Take the boat ride in a powerful speedboat close under the falls (you will get soaked!), or splash out on a helicopter flight. We preferred staying at the Sheraton Hotel simply because it is the only hotel inside the national park, enabling a stroll down the lawn straight into the falls, plus the bonus of a great view from the top floor. Do not miss visiting both the Brazilian and Argentine sides. The shortest trip would include one night, but try to stay for two. Arrive at midday, walk the Argentine side, and go to the Brazilian side (guided tours are readily available) for half a day the next morning. In the afternoon take the boat ride. On your final morning do not miss the Devil's Throat, a truly wonderful walk (to get there, take the inside train in the park) and leave that afternoon. The area is hot and humid all year round.

**Parque Nacional Los Glaciares** (National Glacier Park) is approximately a three-and-a-half-hour flight from Buenos Aires to the nearest town, El Calafate, in the far south of Patagonia, in the province of Santa Cruz (the Kirchners' home and political stronghold). The park includes the Upsala (largest glacier in the world), O'Neil, Spegazzini and Perito Moreno glaciers. Astoundingly beautiful in ice-blue, complete with spectacular crashing sounds, we would recommend spending at least two nights and three days, and more if you wish to venture to see El Chalten, famous for its trekking, and perhaps travel across the border to Chile to visit the magnificent Torres Del Paine. We splurged and stayed in the most exquisite location, Los Notros, right across from Perito Moreno. But it is very expensive, and many of our friends were happy using the little touristic town of El Calafate as their base. Do not miss trekking on the ice, and taking a cruise amongst the glaciers. For a better experience, opt for the VIP special upstairs in an enclosed cabin, and get spoilt with snacks and drinks with a comfortable escape from the very cold air outside. This trip can take place only between December and March due to the cold weather.

**Peninsula Valdez** is located in the province of Chubut in Atlantic Patagonia and is spectacular for watching whales, sea elephants, seals and penguins. The best time to travel is September through to November to catch the whales. A nice side trip in this area is a visit to Trelew or

Gaiman for high tea to learn about the history of the Welsh immigrants' settlement. Especially interesting for many South Africans would be a visit to the local Boer community, descendants of the *bittereinders* from the South African War, who arrived at the beginning of the twentieth century. The community lives around the rather bleak oil town of Comodoro Rivadavia. Their touristic excursion arrangements are less accessible than the Welsh community's. The Peninsula Valdez trip takes a full day, and your base would be the town of Puerto Madryn next door. A minimum stay would be one night and two days. Flight time from Buenos Aires is about two hours.

**San Carlos de Bariloche** is the main town in the province of Río Negro, at the foothills of the Andes, surrounded by magnificent lakes and mountains. Nahuel Huapi National Park is the oldest in Argentina and the mountains include Tronador, Cerro Catedral and Cerro López. It is famous for skiing but also great for summer sightseeing, water sports, fishing, golf, trekking and climbing. The more charming Swiss-like nearby Villa La Angostura, as well as Bariloche itself, offer many chocolate boutiques, restaurants, ice-cream factories and breweries. We loved Blest, a local institution that brewed beer and served bistro-type food but there are also dozens of brilliant foodie places around the town and the lakes. In fact, some of the most fantastic restaurants in Argentina are here. We also loved Il Gabbiano (Italian), Cassis and everything about the Correntoso Hotel in Villa La Angostura. The best thing to do is rent a car and embark on the Circuito Chico, a picturesque 60-kilometre route, but you can opt to take a bus (line 10), bike or hike. If you cannot bring yourself to pay the steep prices at the stunningly situated Llao Llao Hotel, treat yourself to tea or lunch there, at least. Another recommended tour is to go by car or bus to the Los Siete Lagos (the seven lakes). This is an all-day tour to see the seven picturesque lakes between Bariloche and San Martín de los Andes. If time allows, spend a minimum of one night in Bariloche, another in Villa La Angostura and another in San Martín de Los Andes to experience the different vistas and atmosphere each town offers. One could easily spend a week in this area, exploring, hiking, tasting the foods and relaxing in these Tyrol-like peaceful mountains and lakes. There are also lovely boat trips (from simple to luxurious) on offer to the El Bosque de Arrayanes (a forest of rare, orange-coloured trees that only grow on a little local island; but apparently there is also one in Japan). Again, if you have enough time, you can actually cross to Chile via the lakes on a trip renowned for its beauty.

## URUGUAY

The last recommendation might sound odd to some, since technically it is actually in another country. Uruguay is so similar to Argentina and the only other place in the Spanish world that uses the Argentine version of Castellano. Across the River Plate, a short ride on the Buquebus ferry gets you to the charming historic town of Colonia del Sacramento. Founded in 1680 by Portugal, this colony was later disputed by the Spanish, who settled on the opposite bank of the river in Buenos Aires. It kept changing hands from crown to crown due to treaties and alliances, until Uruguay gained independence. This history left a fascinating little place featuring colonial influences from both empires. Colonia offers you a small half-day to a day escape from the bustle of Buenos Aires. You can also splash out and stay at the nearby Carmelo Four Seasons Spa. But more interesting is another part of Uruguay, which could well be part of Buenos Aires as whole chunks of the city move en bloc to populate its luxurious apartment blocks, villas and beaches, crowding the fancy bars and restaurants and shopping in the boutiques that are filled with imported goods. Punta del Este is Plettenberg Bay on steroids. Its season lasts from late December to early March. Its best part, in our view, is the lovely little fishing village of José Ignacio, a few kilometres up the coast from the town, where one of the best restaurants in the world lies, rustic and laid-back, right on the sandy beach. La Huella is an experience and the place to see and be seen in. It also happens to be designed by one of our best Argentine friends, architect Martín Gómez (a fact we learnt after falling in love with it anyway!). A few days in Punta del Este will go a long way to complete the understanding of how the well-heeled Argentines (and Brazilians) live (or, rather, play).

*Best of the rest:*

In the vineyards of **Mendoza**, there is a trip called Ruta del Vino (wine route). The city of Mendoza has its charms but it is no Stellenbosch and the area is dry and arid. The closer you get to the Andes, the more beautiful the views (Uco Valley, in particular). We only discovered the charms of Mendoza when we hired a private guide and, together with our Argentine friends, went wine tasting and explored some of the magnificent restaurants and very sophisticated wineries Mendoza offers. Time and the love of driving permitting, consider taking Route 40 down from Mendoza to Junín de los Andes, through fly-fishing valleys. The Springbok rugby team was here in August 2012 for their inaugural international test in the new four nations championship against the Pumas.

In the north, **Salta** and **Jujuy** provinces will take your breath away with their magnificent vistas. It is a trip we missed and hope to do one day. But we visited the lovely historic town of Salta, where you can view mummies of Inca children sacrificed over 500 years ago in the Bolivian-bordering mountains, perfectly preserved in the cold, dry, desert climate. Salta also offers great *pena* evenings with folklore dancing and singing into the wee hours, and, some say, the best *empanadas* in Argentina. The trip around these provinces takes you into the winemaking area of Cafayate.

**Córdoba's** beautiful, ancient Jesuit centre is worth a visit, and the hills and sleepy villages around the town are popular with holidaymakers. Córdoba also boasts a huge university, the first in the country and the second in South America (after Lima) in the great Spanish Empire of the past.

# ACKNOWLEDGEMENTS

My entire ambassadorship and indeed the writing and completion of this book would have been impossible and inconceivable without the dedicated support and collaboration of my wife, Michal, my essential partner in all weathers and in all countries. In this adventure, as in my life over the past sixteen years, she is the pillar on which it all rests.

The period and events described in this book were greatly assisted by the close collaboration and friendship of many South Americans and South Africans. In singling out the following people on both continents I do not intend, to adapt a famous phrase of Argentine President Juan Domingo Peron, 'to define by exclusion'. Many others also enriched my life abroad and helped weave the threads described in this book. But certain people central to my 'accidental ambassadorship' stand out.

## IN SOUTH AFRICA

**Department of International Relations and Co-operation:** Bob Cloete; Ben Joubert; Janet Kotze; André Lizamore; Dr Ayanda Ntsaluba; Jonge Rabe; Nicolette Schreiber; and Monita Weenink.
**The Presidency:** President Jacob Zuma and Lakela Kaunda.
**Sport and culture:** Nikki Froneman; Tanya Harvey; Jurie Roux; Joost van der Westhuizen; Gavin Varejes; and Dr Sibusiso Xaba.
**Stellenbosch Institute for Advanced Studies (STIAS):** I would like to acknowledge STIAS, where I enjoyed a fellowship in January and February

2013 in an environment that was both invigorating and relaxed. A truly 'creative space for the mind', its facilities and the interaction with its scholars (my fellow-fellows) allowed me to elaborate on the last chapter of this book and write a more detailed answer to the vexed question, 'where in the world is South Africa?', which I presented in seminar form at the Wallenberg Research Centre in February 2013. A copy of the paper can be sourced from my website (www.tonyleon.com). Particular thanks for the generosity of support provided by STIAS director, Professor Hendrik B. Geyer, Professor Peter C.J. Vale, and to the support staff, especially Maria Mouton, Nel-Mari van der Merwe and Goldie van Heerden.
**SA Tourism:** Dinky Malikane and Evelyn Mahlaba.

IN SOUTH AMERICA

**South African Embassy in Buenos Aires:** Florencia Achcar; Honorary Consul Angel Auad (Asunción); Raul Benitez; Horacio Cajiga; Marian Ceccardi; Deborah Connon; Claudio del Medico; Maria Isabel di Liscia; Michael Dunlop; Jorge Giordano; Angela Gonzales; Graciela Hidalgo; Chargé d'affaires David Jacobs (Montevideo); Lesley Johnson; Mziwanele Langa; Lorato Legotlo; Florencia Lopez; Clara Miri; Mbulelo Mtilwa; Tilly Naiker; Mardi Pather; Aide Rodriguez; Lizzie Schiele; Luisa Taconni; Juan Carlos Tomic; Sonica van Rooyen; Alicia Vera; Juan Mariano Vieyra; Nadia Volonte; Zelda Vrolick; and Laura Wilson. And their long-suffering families, of course!
**Argentine Foreign Ministry:** Ambassadors Bibiana Jones; Silvia Merega; Norma Nascimbene; and Carlos Sersale.
**Foreign diplomats:** Ambassadors Mario Boyd (Panama); Naela Chohan (Pakistan); Francisco del Rio (Mexico); Soha Elfar (Egypt); Hicham Hadman (Lebanon); Empire Kanu (Nigeria); Gunther Kneiss (Germany); Vilma Martínez (USA); James McIntyre (Ireland); Shan Morgan (UK); Guillermo Pomi (Uruguay); John Richardson (Australia); Hüsrev Ünler (Turkey); and Vish Viswanathan (India).
**In Buenos Aires and beyond:** Sofia Aldao and Horacio Areco; Wency Luigi Arias; Patrick Carmody and Verena Schobinger; Alan Clutterbuck and Paula Montoya; Nick Damico; Nelson de Oliveria (São Paulo);

Marcello Dupont; Ximena and Charles Elizalde; Eduardo Elzstain; Patrick and Siobhan Esnouf (Santiago); Martin Gomez and Daniela Coll; Gustavo Grobocopatel; Oscar Hansen; Bobby and Erna Herzfeld; Victor Honore; Gabriela Josephson; Professors Gladys Lechini and Marisa Pinaur; Jorge and Martha Mandelbaum; Dr Alfredo May; Ambassador Luis Mendiola; Guido Minerbi; Luis Otero Monsegur; Julian Obiglio; José Papo; Stephen Park; Ferdinand Porak; Hugo Porta; Michael Rattagan and Marie-Jo Cardinal; Joanna Richardson and Luciano di Tella; Johan and Irina Roets; Frans and Brigitta Siegenthaler; Jorge Sigal; Hugo Sigman; Michael Soltys; Federico Sturzenegger; Adrian Werthein and Fabiana Ricagno; Darío Werthein; Norma Werthein; and Jude Webber.

PAN MACMILLAN SOUTH AFRICA

From the conception of this book to its execution, it has been a professional joy and a personal pleasure to work with the enthusiastic and excellent support of my publishers, Pan Macmillan South Africa. From start to finish, I have been hugely assisted, well directed and always encouraged by this great team. In particular, special thanks are due to Terry Morris (MD); Andrea Nattrass (publisher); Sally Hines (editor); and Laura Hammond (publicity).

Irritatingly, all the errors and mistakes in this book remain my own but, wherever possible, source material is acknowledged in the notes.

# NOTES

1. Boris Johnson, *The Weekly Telegraph*, 5–11 July 2006.
2. Charlayne Hunter-Gault, 'The Third Man', *The New Yorker*, 5 July 2010.
3. David Remnick, *The Bridge: The Life and Rise of Barack Obama* (New York: Knopf, 2010), p.561.
4. Abba Eban, *Diplomacy for the Next Century* (New Haven, CT: Yale University Press, 1989), p.89.
5. John Kenneth Galbraith, *A Life In Our Times* (Boston, MA: Houghton & Mifflin, 1981), pp.391–92.
6. Matthew Parris and Andrew Bryson, *Parting Shots* (London: Viking, 2010), p.147.
7. Parris and Bryson, *Parting Shots*, p.149.
8. *New York Times*, 16 August 2006.
9. Parris and Bryson, *Parting Shots*, p.150.
10. Miranda France, *Bad Times in Buenos Aires* (London: Weidenfeld & Nicolson, 1998), p.54.
11. *¡Hola Buenos Aires: A Practical Guide for Newcomers* (Buenos Aires: Argentina University Women's Club, 1995, third edition), pp.9–10. The new edition, edited by Michal Leon, is available in ebook from http://www.amazon.com.
12. David Landes, *The Wealth and Poverty of Nations* (New York: Little, Brown and Company, 1998), p.320.
13. Felix Luna, *A Short History of the Argentinians* (Buenos Aires: Booklet Publishers, 2000), p.16.
14. Paul Theroux, *The Old Patagonian Express* (New York: Mariner Books, 1979), pp.369–70.
15. Luna, *A Short History*, p.232.
16. Luna, *A Short History*, p.39.
17. Luna, *A Short History*, p.16.
18. Luna, *A Short History*, p.165.
19. Luna, *A Short History*, p.102.
20. France, *Bad Times*, p.55.
21. Jason Wilson, *Buenos Aires: A Cultural and Literary History* (Oxford: Signal Books, 2007), p.224.
22. Wilson, *Buenos Aires*, p.222.
23. Andrew Graham-Yooll, *The Forgotten Colony* (Buenos Aires: Lola Publishers, 1999).
24. Graham-Yooll, *The Forgotten Colony*, p.247.
25. Parris and Bryson, *Parting Shots*, p.56.

26. Geoffrey Wheatcroft, 'Can They Ever Make a Deal?', *New York Review of Books*, Volume LIX, Number 6, 5–25 April 2012, p.42.
27. Jill Hedges, *Argentina: A Modern History* (London: I.B. Tauris, 2011), p.10.
28. Ian Buruma, 'Tony Judt: The Right Questions', *New York Review of Books*, Volume LIX, Number 6, 5–25 April 2012, p.28.
29. Wilson, *Buenos Aires*, p.116.
30. *Financial Times*, 24 August 2011.
31. Alma Guillermoprieto, 'Drugs: The Rebellion in Cartagena', *New York Review of Books*, Volume LIX, Number 10, 7–20 June 2012, p.39.
32. 'Liberation Theology', http://www.bbc.co.uk/religions/christianity/beliefs/liberationtheology.shtml.
33. *The Economist*, 24 October 2009.
34. Hedges, *Argentina*, p.209.
35. Dr Lyal White, 'Dreaming of Brics: Understanding the Realities of SA's Invitation to Join the Big League', Centre for Dynamic Markets, Gordon Institute of Business Science, Johannesburg, (undated), p.14.
36. I am indebted to the excellent *Rough Guide to Argentina* (New York: Rough Guides, 2005, second edition), pp.40–41 for this list.
37. The best recent account of the 'travelgate' scandal and the convictions and sentences of the accused appears in Gareth van Onselen, 'Seven Crooked Comrades', Politicsweb, 27 June 2012, http://politicsweb.co.za/politicsweb/view/politcsweb/en/page71619?oid=308599&sn=Detail&pid=71616.
38. Gideon Rachman, *Zero-Sum World: Politics, Power and Prosperity after the Crash* (London: Atlantic, 2010), p.72.
39. Michael Reid, *Forgotten Continent: The Battle for Latin America's Soul* (New Haven: Yale University Press, 2009), p.1.
40. http://www.ustr.gov/countries-regions/americas/argentina20111123. The US Trade Representative website provides data on US trade metrics and a host of trade and policy matters. The South African bilateral and multilateral trade figures can be most easily accessed from the website of the Department of Trade and Industry (http://www.thedti.gov.za).
41. Galbraith, *A Life In Our Times*, p.392.
42. Ralph Selby, British ambassador to Norway, quoted in Parris and Bryson, *Parting Shots*, p.308.
43. Sir Alan Campbell, British ambassador to Italy, quoted in Parris and Bryson, *Parting Shots*, p.8.
44. James Neilson, 'How Not to Make Friends: For CFK's Government Being Nasty is a Matter of Policy'. *Buenos Aires Herald*, 5 April 2011.
45. Neilson, 'How Not to Make Friends'.
46. Quoted by V.S. Naipaul, *The Return of Eva Peron* (New York: Knopf, 1974), p.166.
47. Naipaul, *The Return of Eva Peron*, pp.166–67.
48. Tim du Plessis, 'South Africa and Argentina', *Beeld*, 16 April 2010.
49. Greg Mills, 'Argentina: Perpetually Snatching Defeat from the Jaws of Victory', Brenthurst Foundation, July 2011.
50. 'Fernandez Looks Set for Poll Victory', *Financial Times*, 23 June 2011.
51. Mills, 'Argentina'.
52. 'Queen Cristina', *Financial Times*, 21 October 2011.
53. 'The Privatisation of Power', *Financial Times*, 15 June 2012.
54. 'Politics in Argentina: Knock, Knock', *The Economist*, 21 July 2012.
55. 'Politics in Argentina'.

56. Max Chafkin, 'A Constant Feeling of Crisis', *Inc.com Magazine*, 14 June 2011, p.3.
57. 'Blood on the Tracks', *Buenos Aires Herald*, 25 February 2012.
58. Hedges, *Argentina*, p.109.
59. Hedges, *Argentina*, p.102.
60. Hedges, *Argentina*, p.131.
61. Hedges, *Argentina*, p.141.
62. Mills, 'Argentina'.
63. Peron is not normally linked to Darth Vader, but he certainly fits the mould. Former US Vice President Dick Cheney famously was – a comparison well developed by Barton Gellman in *Angler: The Cheney Vice Presidency* (New York: Penguin Press, 2008), pp.160–61.
64. Philip Kerr, *A Quiet Flame* (New York: Penguin, 2009), pp.387–88.
65. Uki Goni, *The Real Odessa: How Peron Brought the Nazi War Criminals to Argentina* (London: Granta Books, 2002).
66. Hedges, *Argentina*, pp.87–88.
67. The detail relating to the diplomatic posting of Chamorro and Astiz to Pretoria is recounted in Pieter Wolvaart, *A Diplomat's Story: Apartheid and Beyond, 1969–1998* (Johannesburg: Galago, 2005), pp.153–54.
68. 'Justice at Last for Argentina's Stolen Children', *New York Times*, 10 July 2012.
69. Francisco Goldman, 'Children of the Dirty War', *The New Yorker*, 19 March 2012, p.56.
70. France, *Bad Times in Buenos Aires*, p.13.
71. France, *Bad Times in Buenos Aires*, p.13.
72. Hilary Mantel, *Bring Up the Bodies* (London: Fourth Estate, 2012), p.61.
73. Hedges, *Argentina*, p.218.
74. Graham-Yooll, *The Forgotten Colony*, p.286.
75. 'Short Victorious War', *The Economist*, 31 March 2012.
76. Daniel Politi, 'Argentina's Big Mac Attack', http://latitude.blogs.nytimes.com/2011/11/24/argentinas-big-mac-attack/.
77. Jude Webber, 'Argentina's Rivals Bite into Global Beef Export Market', *Financial Times*, 6 October 2010.
78. 'Argentina's Inflation Problem: The Price of Cooking the Books', *The Economist*, 25 February 2012.
79. 'Argentines Feel Trapped by Currency Controls', *Buenos Aires Herald*, 2 September 2012.
80. Many sources can be found on the Argentine 2001 economic crisis. Among the better and more accessible works (in English) I consulted are: Paul Blustein, *And the Money Kept Rolling In (and Out): Wall Street, the IMF, and Bankrupting of Argentina* (New York: Public Affairs, 2005); Hedges, *Argentina*, pp.254–87; and Mario Blejer and Guillermo Ortiz, 'Latin Lessons', *The Economist*, 18 February 2012.
81. Blejer and Ortiz, 'Latin Lessons'.
82. Hedges, *Argentina*, p.275.
83. 'Protectionism in Argentina: Keep Out', *The Economist*, 24 September 2011.
84. 'Foreign Investment Dispute: Come and Get Me', *The Economist*, 18 February 2012.
85. Hilary Burke, 'Argentine Dream of Strong Industrial Sector Faces Tough Test', *Buenos Aires Herald*, 18 October 2011.
86. 'Argentina's State-owned Firms: So Far, Not So Good', *The Economist*, 12 May 2012.
87. 'Argentina's State-owned Firms'.
88. Professor Francisco Monaldi, quoted by John Gapper in 'But This Raid Can Only End Badly', *Financial Times*, 19 April 2012.

89. 'Oil Seizure Catches Eskenazi Family in Debt Bind', *Financial Times*, 20 April 2012.
90. 'Stepping Outside the Bounds of Logic', *Financial Times*, 18 April 2012.
91. 'Hue and Cry for Argentina', *Financial Times*, 21 April 2012.
92. Bruce Chatwin, *In Patagonia* (London: Jonathan Cape, 1977).
93. Richard Davies's excellent and detailed article entitled 'End of an Era for Argentina's Afrikaners' appeared in the *Mail & Guardian*, 1 December 2009, and was featured in several other South African newspapers. I am indebted to Richard for the detail and reportage in this piece, which forms the basis of my own account here. Several other South African journalists followed in Richard's footsteps during my term of office. Ricky Hunt of the *Mail & Guardian*, for example, also researched and wrote a fine piece on his visit to the Boer community (see Ricky Hunt, 'The Last Boers of Patagonia', *Mail & Guardian*, 4–10 February 2011).
94. The most useful current guide I have read is *Fodor's Patagonia* (New York: Fodor's Travel Publications, 2009, first edition).
95. I am grateful to Mark Sandham, a librarian at the University of the Witwatersrand, Johannesburg, for sending me his fascinating and very well-annotated account of the early Boer settlers in Patagonia based on the memoir of one of the founding members of the community: Petronella Elizabeth Niemann (edited and translated by Mark Sandham), *Bethulie and Chubut: Domestic Memoirs of the Boer War and Argentina* (Johannesburg: Piglet Press, 2011).
96. See, for example, Wikipedia, en.wikipedia.org/wiki/Camillo_Ricchiardi.
97. Niemann (ed. and tr. Sandham), *Bethulie and Chubut*, pp.37–39.
98. Niemann (ed. and tr. Sandham), *Bethulie and Chubut*, p.55.
99. *Fodor's Patagonia*, p.145.
100. John Carlin and Carlos Pierini, 'Maradona as a Metaphor for Argentina', *La Nacíon*, 5 October 2010.
101. I wrote a chapter in a book, in which some of this material first appeared, entitled 'The Argentine Affair' in Angus Powers (ed.), *Rugby in Our Blood* (Cape Town: Tafelberg, 2011), pp.229–36.
102. Mzukisi Qobo, 'South Africa's Foreign Policy Stuck in the Doldrums', *Mail & Guardian*, 1 September 2011.
103. Greg Mills, 'SA's Bit of This, Bit of That Foreign Policy', *Sunday Times*, 29 November 2011.
104. 'South Africa's Foreign Policy: All Over the Place', *The Economist*, 24 March 2011.
105. 'South Africa's Foreign Policy'.
106. See, for example, 'South Africa and Libya: Huff and Puff', *The Economist*, 3 September 2011.
107. Media statement, 'South Africa is Concerned about the Situation in Syria', Department of International Relations and Co-operation, Pretoria, 1 August 2011.
108. 'South Africa's Textbook Saga Shows Need to Tackle the Basics', *Financial Times*, 2 July 2012.
109. 'Minister's Refusal to have Handbag Scanned Cost R235 000', http://www.timeslive.co.za/local/2011/08/16.
110. Donwald Pressly and Michelle Pietersen, 'Cracks Show as DA Leadership Battle Heats Up', http://www.iol.co.za/news/politics/cracks-show-as-da-leadership-battle-heats-up-1.11579.
111. The Presidency of South Africa, 'Diagnostic Overview: National Planning Commission', http://www.npconline.co.za, p.29.

# INDEX

# ABOUT THE AUTHOR

Tony Leon was appointed in August 2009 by President Jacob Zuma as South African Ambassador Extraordinary and Plenipotentiary to Argentina, Uruguay and Paraguay. He returned from this post in late 2012.

Prior to his diplomatic mission, he was the leader of the opposition in the parliament of South Africa (1999–2007) and for thirteen years led the Democratic Alliance (DA) and Democratic Party (DP). He is the longest serving leader of the opposition since the advent of democracy in the country. For nearly twenty years (1989–2009) he served as a member of parliament, and played a leading role in the constitutional negotiations that marked the transition from apartheid to democratic governance in South Africa. His political career commenced as a city councillor in Johannesburg.

Leon is a qualified attorney and has previously lectured in Constitutional Law at the University of the Witwatersrand, his alma mater, which he attended after completing his schooling at Kearsney College in KwaZulu-Natal.

After stepping down from frontline politics, he was awarded fellowships to the Institute of Politics, John F. Kennedy School of Government, Harvard University (2007); the Cato Institute, Washington, D.C. (2008); and the University of Stellenbosch Institute for Advanced Studies (STIAS) (2013).

Leon is the author of *Hope and Fear: Reflections of a Democrat* (1998) and *On The Contrary: Leading the Opposition in a Democratic South Africa* (2008). The latter received the Recht Malan Prize for the best non-fiction work in South Africa in 2009.

Leon lives in Cape Town with his wife Michal, and writes a weekly column for *Business Day*. He advises local and overseas businesses and is involved in the lecture circuit in South Africa and abroad.

Visit www.tonyleon.com.